LOVE
DESPITE HATE

LOVE DESPITE HATE

Child Survivors of the Holocaust
and Their Adult Lives

SARAH MOSKOVITZ

SCHOCKEN BOOKS · NEW YORK

First published by Schocken Books 1983
10 9 8 7 6 5 4 3 2 1   83 84 85 86
Copyright © 1983 by Schocken Books Inc.

Library of Congress Cataloging in Publication Data
Moskovitz, Sarah.
Love despite hate.
Includes bibliographical references.
1. Holocaust survivors—Biography. I. Title.
D810.J4M598   940.53′13′03924   81–84112
AACR2

Designed by Nancy Dale Muldoon
Manufactured in the United States
ISBN 0–8052–3801–8

To those who have taught us to learn with our hearts
and remember:
Mordechai and Esther Nussbaum, the parents of Bianca Gordon,
and my own parents,
Yitzhok and Clara Traister.
May the time come when all children are our children,
when humanity is one.

Who is wise? He that learns from every man,
as it is said: From all my teachers I got understanding.
Shimon Ben Zoma in Pirke Avot
Sayings of the Fathers

Slowly I was coming to understand what was
indestructible in the human world.
Meyer Levin

Contents

Illustrations

Acknowledgments

Bianca Gordon suggested I do this book, and both she and David Gordon encouraged me. Generously they opened home and hearts to me whenever I needed to work in London. Their own refugee experiences made me aware of important issues. I am particularly indebted to David for the discussions in which, with his keen mind, he illuminated early adjustment difficulties and later restitution problems of survivors. With Bianca I mourn his untimely death.

Throughout the four years of writing the encouragement of colleagues and friends was vital. Particularly I thank Ruth Forer, Annette Dahlman, Joyce Huggins, Rie Mitchell, Docia Zavitkovsky, Betty Brady, Mike Auer, Dick Thiel, Jack Byrom, Libby Schorrow, Joan White, Susan Bredhoff, Anita and Edward Dimendberg, the Levines, Brynens Mehlmans, Varons, Rosenbergs, Barrs, Rabiroffs, Katzmans, Dwoskins, Katzes, Tibers, and Himmelsons.

Irv White and Marianne Marschak were especially helpful through their critical readings of various drafts; Livia Rotkirchen of the last one. Marianne Marschak, Marianne Wollman, and Hanne Favelukes contributed invaluable help with German translations.

Lucy and Les Fine cheered me on through difficult periods and through their generous gift made it possible for me to go to Australia.

The wise counsel of Norman Tabachnik and Norman Blumenthal was also important. I am grateful for all of the above support.

I thank all my family here and in Israel for their help; David, Ella, and all the Tspimans, Sarah Treister, Beryl and Raisa Treister, Rivka and Meir Steinmetz, Shula and Arye Caspi, Arik and Ossie Ben-Shachar, Yael and Yonatan Chervinski, and Chaya and Geri Shani. They contributed headquarters complete with chicken soup in Tel Aviv, Jerusalem, and Haifa.

In Paris my understanding of persecution was deepened by the experiences of my uncle Michel and Aunt Freyda Trajster whose son,

Claude Sjainman, was placed in hiding. I thank them for all they shared with me.

I am indebted to the following people for their valuable help with the research: Livia Rotkirchen, Hadassah Modlinger, Clara Guini, and Itzik Lev at Yad Vashem Archives in Jerusalem; Gita Johnson and Janet Langmaid at the Wiener Library in London; Messieurs Meraun and Husserl at the Centre de Documentation Juive Contemporaine in Paris; Chava Ben Zvi at Jewish Community Library, Adaire Klein and Margo Ramos at Simon Wiesenthal Library, and Shimon Briskin at UCLA Graduate Research Library, all in Los Angeles; Kathleen Potter at Caltech Humanities Library in Pasadena. Dina Abromovitz at the YIVO Library in New York was particularly helpful.

For her patience and intelligence I thank Donna Lathrop, who typed every draft.

Ardently involved in the creation of everything of importance in my life, my husband Itzik has been the mainstay of this work too. He sustained me with understanding, humor, and love, and made facing the facts of murder and the feelings of loss less lonely. I am grateful to him, my son David, my daughter Ruth and son-in-law Misha Askren, daughter Debbie and son-in-law Richard Miller, and grandchildren Rebecca, Miriam, Aaron, and Hannah for restoring me to present joys and cares when the past threatened to engulf me.

There could have been no book if Alice Goldberger and each of the courageous survivors who shared their lives with me, enriching my own beyond measure, had not been willing to open themselves to remembrances. I am grateful to each one. Each one's story could have been a book. Their rich and massive material was, especially in the beginning of the writing, overwhelming. Therefore the editorial direction and encouragement given by Chava Glaser from beginning to end was crucially significant. I acknowledge her guidance and thank her for her faith in me.

Pacific Palisades
August 20, 1981

═══ PROLOGUE ═══
London 1977

In the hospitable library of the Hampstead clinic, a group of American psychologists stood about conversing quietly, sipping wine as they met British colleagues for the first time. Bianca Gordon, my friend and a London psychoanalyst, came up to me.

"There's someone over there I want you to meet. She has done very important work." The passionate conviction in her voice impressed me as I followed her toward the fringes of the gathering, where an older woman patiently looked on at the reception. Grandmotherly and plain, she sat, firmly rooted, knees comfortably apart under the dark print dress. Her sturdy black oxfords added to the impression of a firm base that denied the frailty of age. Though there was something vulnerable in the slump of her narrow shoulders, she seemed like the single strand of pearls around her neck, enduring beyond fashion. As we approached, her back straightened to attention, and her large face turned upward. In repose resigned and impassive, it now came to life with a glow of interest.

"This is Alice Goldberger," Bianca said. Miss Goldberger extended a small sturdy hand and smiled warmly as she greeted me in English that was heavily accented with German. "Miss Goldberger cared for the children who came from concentration camps at the end of World War II. She was in charge of Lingfield House."

Something jolted loose and rolled its spiney edges across the pit of my stomach. The feeling was as old as my childhood, familiar as the muffled whispers of my parents in the dark sharing their fears for the lives of the family in Europe.

"I'd like to know more about you and your work," I managed to say. Why did I feel a sense of overwhelming, irrational gratitude to this woman? "Can we meet again?" I asked. That evening Bianca arranged for her to speak to our group.

When the day came, a group of about fifteen of us awaited her.

Alice came toward us dressed in a heavy dark coat, listing to the right from the weight of a shopping bag. That day, when Bianca introduced her, she looked even more like a grandmother than like a lay analyst from Anna Freud's Hampstead Clinic.

From the shopping bag, she retrieved picture albums of the people who had once been children in her care. The intense pride and passion with which she described them made us draw close.

"Here is my Fritz, who is now in Israel," she said, adding an anecdote to show us how clever he had been as a child. "And here you see our Sylvia. This is Sam and his lovely family in America."

And then she handed us several pictures showing the children when they arrived in England. Sullen young faces confronted us with the shocking reality of children who had been hunted and hurt. Through tears, I saw that all of us were struck with the enormity of the task that this woman had undertaken: "not to teach for several hours a day, not to treat for several hours a week, but," as Bianca pointed out, "to live day-in and day-out with children who had experienced the most profound losses and terror." What had created such unyielding commitment in her? How had binding ties been welded with children who had every reason not to trust? And what, in fact, were these people like today who had once been in her care?

It was at Bianca's suggestion that I began to work with Alice Goldberger on this book. At our first meeting in her apartment, I did not know that I was embarking on a 115,000-mile journey that would send me in search of people around the globe.

The cozy apartment smelled of fresh baked strudel made by Sophie Wutsch. Sophie, who lives with Alice, is the gentle Catholic woman whose title at Lingfield, "Cook," did not begin to describe her real importance. The small place was still alive with the people who were once Alice's children. Mementos of each child filled boxes, drawers, and closets. The desk in her comfortable bedroom-study was crammed with letters from the ones who lived abroad. Celebrations, phone calls, and visits with others who lived nearby were the pleasure of her days.

After several hours of listening to anecdotes and looking at photographs, I finally asked Alice: "How was it that you came to take on this job?"

"Oh, well, we were *all* eager to help right after the war," she said.

"But you, unlike others, stayed with it for so many years. . . ." I pressed.

A little nervously she began opening a brown cardboard box from which she extracted an album of photographs. "Look here, Sarah," she distracted me with pictures of children at Lingfield. "This was the party where they played the Haydn *Toy Symphony*. It was marvelous. See, here is Tania and Mirjam, and this is . . ." She went on and on, each picture reminding her of an event, of something special about a child. It grew late. I was about to leave when she went to her desk and picked up the small silver-framed family portrait I had noticed there.

"This was my brother, his wife and child." There was a pause. "The Nazis killed them." The usual soft, patient look was gone; her face was hard and set in anger. "The Nazis did not even let them die together. They took Max first to what they said was a labor camp, but it was Auschwitz. Then three days later his wife and little girl were told they could join him." Her narrow shoulders raised while she inhaled deeply, as if bracing herself. Her voice rose. "Couldn't they at least have let them die *together*?" She searched my eyes. "I failed them," she continued softly. "I was supposed to have sent for them after I got to England. But I couldn't. Being a German citizen, I was interned as an enemy alien. . . . I couldn't . . . I failed them."

Finally, my urge to console overcame my shame at the inadequacy of words. "But surely you did what you could. How could you have done differently if you were interned?" The words opened a chasm between us, and seemed to confirm for her only my inability to understand.

PART ONE

= 1 =

The Arrival: 1945

Spring 1945: As the shocking eyewitness accounts out of liberated concentration camps began to appear in the British newspapers, it became clear that there would be a number of child survivors, children whose entire families and communities had been destroyed. Responding to the compelling necessity for adult guardianship, two prominent British Jews, Lola Hahn Warburg and Leonard Montefiore, went to the British Home Office as representatives of the Jewish community. In exchange for a promise to be completely responsible for the children, they obtained permission for the entry of a thousand child survivors. Immediately appeals began to appear in the Jewish press for funds with which to begin caring for the children due to arrive in England in May. An outpouring of generosity greeted these first appeals—mainly from people who understood how fortunate they themselves had been to be spared. But who was actually to care for the children?

The search for people with the experience, the commitment, and the sheer nerve to undertake the extraordinary job of working with children who had endured massive trauma led to Oskar Friedmann and Alice Goldberger, both refugees from Germany. Friedmann had been the director of a Berlin orphanage, while Goldberger had worked in German child-care centers entrusted with the care of children from families in crisis. At Anna Freud's request, Goldberger had been released from an internment camp for aliens on the Isle of Man to serve as superintendent of Anna Freud's War Nurseries (established to care for the children of British working mothers shortly after Anna Freud had arrived from Vienna). In addition to their high professional qualifications, both had the commitment of people who had escaped Germany in time and felt a profound responsibility toward those who had not. Together, Friedmann and Goldberger assembled a staff of approximately thirty-five people, who began preparing to receive the first children who would arrive in England.

By August of 1945, the reception camp at Windermere, in the English Lake District, had been scrubbed and rescrubbed as the staff worked off the disappointment of repeated delays. First the children had been scheduled to arrive in May, then in July. Many were too weak to travel; the ravages of malnutrition, typhoid, and dysentery made it necessary to feed and strengthen them in Terezin and in Prague before the journey. The delay also gave Red Cross and United Nations Relief and Rehabilitation Administration workers a chance to determine that those who would fly to England had, in fact, no adult relatives who could care for them.

When it was certain that the arrival would take place on August 15, the camp was electrified by a mixture of excitement and anxiety. Crisp white sheets were placed on beds. Flowers were freshly picked to brighten the setting: the immaculately clean camp that would temporarily house the children had been a wartime barracks for members of the British Royal Air Force. Alice herself arranged little bowls of sweets on the night tables adjoining the beds to let the children know that now there were people to take care of them who truly wanted to give them pleasure. Expecting that most of the new arrivals would be young children, the staff placed dolls and teddy bears on the beds.

Late in the morning of August 15, Alice and key members of the staff set out for the Carlisle airport to welcome the children. Questions abounded. What languages would they speak? How old would they be? And, more hauntingly, what would they be like after the almost unimaginable horror of the experiences they had endured? The terrifying images that composed the first photos of concentration camp survivors crowded the mind: human beings with eyes pleading or glazed over dully, the cadavers heaped as refuse, with human beings still breathing among them. Just what had these children seen? What were the circumstances of each one's loss?

The airstrip at Carlisle adjoined a field dotted with haystacks, where people lounged as they waited for incoming planes. The day wore on, producing rumors of bad weather over the Channel. The crowd that had gathered to welcome the children included social service, medical, and immigration workers, as well as Leonard Montefiore and other pillars of the Central British Fund, the Jewish organization that had pledged financial responsibility for the project.

As shadows lengthened that afternoon, the planes still had not arrived. Now worry over the fate of the flight began to overlap Alice's worry about what the children had experienced, and what they would be like. Wondering about them stirred a memory of the children she had left behind in Berlin. She saw their faces clearly. Their eyes, looking out to the playground forbidden to Jews, haunted her. Self-reproach filled her and abated only with the pledge to care for these child survivors with all her heart. This time she would not leave. As she heard the distant roar of the first plane, the welcoming crowd began to shout with excitement. She realized for the first time that today, August 15, was her birthday. She was forty-eight.

The hope had been for one thousand children to constitute the first airlift, but the actual number assembled to fly to England was only three hundred. Of these, only seventeen were under the age of eight. It was difficult to find child survivors. They were rare, those little ones who had been strong enough to survive disease, separation from parents, the traumatic conditions of ghettoization, and the death camps themselves. Almost all the children assembled in the Square in Prague waiting to be taken to the planes were the sole surviving members of families that had once formed vital, thriving Jewish communities of Europe.

Edith Lauer, a former inmate of Terezin Concentration Camp, who had been allowed to function as a social worker in the children's quarters there, agreed to come on condition that her husband, George, who was recuperating from tuberculosis, be allowed to come with her. She remembers that, after the long, chaotic train ride to Prague, about fifty people were packed into each R.A.F. Stirling Bomber. The seats were hard wooden benches, and most sat on the floor.[1] Prague to Carlisle Airfield was a fourteen-hour flight in 1945.

The first plane arrived at the Carlisle airport at four o'clock. The excitement had hushed, and it was a quiet welcome. Leonard Montefiore walked among the children, shaking their hands. A woman of the Rothschild family handed out apples, the first many of the children had ever seen. The Carlisle Women's Voluntary Services people served refreshments. The *Carlisle Journal* wrote: "Nobody present could fail to be affected by the sight of the orphaned toddlers sitting by themselves on the grass and quietly sipping milk. They quickly became the favourites of the RAF officers."[2]

In her notes, Alice later wrote:

Plane after plane of youths arrived, mostly boys, very few girls. They had a gray-aged look which made it difficult to tell how old they were. We were relieved by their happiness on arrival. They joked, they laughed, they asked us whether they would be able to go to school. . . . We welcomed each and when asked their age, most said they were between thirteen and fifteen, but it was hard to tell. (Later, we realized that even those who were over sixteen would not admit to it because they would have not been allowed to enter the country as part of this special children's airlift if they were older.) We began to worry after so many planes of youths arrived that there would be no small children. I thought about the dolls and bears in each of the beds and what a joke that would be to these adolescents when they go to their beds in Windermere. Finally, the last two planes arrived with less than twenty young children in them. It was late by then and dark. We drove back to Windermere and some slept. But as we came into Windermere the townspeople had come out with torches and stood on the streets shouting their welcome to the children. This terrified the younger ones. We got them ready for bed and decided that the adults, Edith Lauer, other staff, and myself who put them to bed should sleep in their quarters. I did not want them to see strange faces in the morning, faces different from those who had put them to bed.[3]

The general anxiety over what the children would be like and the relief experienced at the first sight of them is described by Margot Hicklin, a social worker who awaited them back in Windermere. "We were extremely frightened and tense, without exception. The task, we felt, might be beyond us. And then the first busload arrived. They were singing and waving to us. We waved from our respective houses and shouted 'Shalom,' a Hebrew greeting. And one glance at them assured us that they were human."[4]

The importance of food and clothing to the children became apparent at once. Alice recalls:

The first morning after they arrived, I had food put out on the tables in the same way I had in Miss Freud's nurseries, where children could help themselves freely. But now this was a mistake because it was too much at once for them to cope with after not having enough. Some children would take so much in each hand they could not eat for fear of putting it down, they would hoard it near themselves and be too involved watching it to eat. Or they would stuff their mouths with so much they couldn't eat. From this first breakfast I learned to serve only one thing at a time: bread, then cereal, etc.[5]

Bread, according to Hicklin, had special meaning:

Bread stood in a category of its own, and especially the supply of white bread in ample quantities, in contrast to the dark bread of all their war-time years, played a large part in their daily contentment. During the first weeks, a tendency to grab and hoard, to clamour for more while supplies were still on the table, and to quarrel with one's neighbours, simply showed the automatic repetition of camp behaviour. In time, however, the habit to offer the plate to others, to see that the long tables were evenly supplied, and to eat no more than needed, began to grow. Along with it, there were outbursts of waste and of playing with bread and even throwing it about at each other. Such actions must be understood as part of the testing out of the adults, as well as showing a reaction from the immense value that the smallest crumb of stale or mouldy black bread used to possess, often . . . making the difference between life and death.[6]

Alice knew that to clothe each child well was of paramount importance. "These children who had come to us in rags had to be fitted properly with clothing that fit them, that they liked, and in which they felt good about themselves. But," she recalls, "it was a very hard job. Some were not easy to please. In Prague, they had been promised new clothes when they came to England. But England was not a rich country after the war. It wasn't possible. I think I was like a saleslady then, standing in front of a mirror with some customers and telling them how nice this and that looked on them."

The difficulties with clothing were understood by Hicklin in this way:

Clothing turned out to play a very vital part in the lives of the children at Windermere. Many of them had, in their early years, belonged to small-town Jewish communities where hand-tailoring was one of the chief crafts, and the pride in their fathers' good work made them apply their home standards to the new surroundings. It was unfortunate but inevitable that the clothing sent to us by helpful organisations did not correspond in any way to those standards, and that the youngsters felt hurt and offended at being offered inferior goods. This led to the most remarkable scenes, reminiscent, no doubt, of life in the concentration camps.[7]

It soon became clear to Alice and to Oskar Friedmann that the stay in Windermere Reception Camp ought to be kept brief. The children, especially the youngest ones, could benefit most by being moved as soon as possible into group homes. Immediate adoption for the youngest group of three-year-olds was discussed but rejected. It was thought that the acquisition of the English language would ease the transition to adoption. Lady Clark, the wife of a member of Parliament, donated her cottage in Bulldogs Bank when she learned from Anna Freud that a small, quiet place was needed for the six three-year-olds.

Like all the children, they were small for their age and looked even younger, but they were precocious in their unusually strong attachment to each other. They helped each other in innumerable ways, were upset when separated, and stood up together against the adults who cared for them. Most sucked their thumbs. All were noisy, bit, spit, hit, and were easily upset. Two of the three little girls had vision problems. On October 15, after more than two years in Terezin Concentration Camp, a month of waiting in Prague, and two months in the Windermere Reception Camp, five of the six children moved to Bulldogs Bank—the third uprooting into totally new surroundings. To help ease the transition, Alice personally accompanied the children to their new home with the sisters Sophie and Gertrud Dann, two German Jewish refugees who had also worked with Anna Freud in the War Nurseries.

Alice remembers these three-year-olds as:

(GADI) GODFREY JACOBSEN—a red-haired, imaginative child who was curious and enjoyed pretending

BELLA ROSENTHAL—a placid, self-possessed little girl, also with red hair

(BERLI) BERL BARUCH—a little boy who became anxious when any child of his group was out of sight, and who had trouble walking because of malnutrition

JUDITH AUERBACH—an affectionate, blonde child with impaired vision due to a vitamin deficiency

JACK JONAH SPIEGEL—a sensitive little boy with dark, curly hair, who was alert and very observant

LEAH ROVELSKI—fair-haired and hungry for attention, she was kept for an additonal six weeks at Windermere because of a ringworm infection. Severe strabismus of her eyes would necessitate surgery

These six toddlers are the ones described by Anna Freud and Sophie Dann in "An Experiment in Group Upbringing." [8]

With the youngest children settled in Bulldogs Bank, the four- to nine-year-olds still needed a home. At this point, Sir Benjamin Drage stepped forward to donate Weir Courteney, his beautiful country estate in Lingfield, Surrey. Moving himself, his wife, and his daughter into a small part of the house, he arranged to share it with the children. Alice was to bring them as soon as the place could be readied.

It had been years since any of the children had been inside a home. Some had been driven from their own homes within the first few days of life. Most striking when they arrived was their apathy and lack of emotion. But while they were at Windermere, getting good nourishment, their personalities had begun to emerge. Now, eight long months since their liberation, they would have a home with Alice, who remembers them as:

DENNY MUENCH—four, with curly red hair; anxious, fearful

TANIA MUENCH—five, fair and placid

SAMUEL SCHWARTZ—four, blue-eyed, sandy-haired; eager to please

SYLVIA GRUENER—five, very nearsighted; affectionate to all

ZDENKA HUSSERL—five, with dark, curly hair; vivacious, and particularly attached to Edith Lauer

MARTA VINDFOGEL—eleven, a fair, clinging child given to sudden outbursts

It was not known until years later that Denny and Tania, who bore the same surname but no resemblance, were related as half brother and sister. Records were nonexistent or chaotic for all the children who had been incarcerated in Terezin. What had that been like for a child?

2

Terezin

The small garrison town of Terezin was built between two rivers as a fortress in the 1400s. In 1942 the Germans evacuated its population to make Terezin a concentration camp for Jews, crowding seventy-four thousand people into the space previously occupied by three thousand. During September and October of 1942, twenty thousand people were added. During this time thirty-five thousand people fell ill with dysentery, and thousands died.

At the beginning of the Final Solution, Terezin was intended as a holding place for the aged and for some Jewish elite, a show-camp that could be used to assure suspicious international committees that the Jews, uprooted from their normal lives, were living in a resort town while their possible ransoming or other fate was decided. It was promoted by the Germans as an ideal place for old people, "Theresienbad," where, in exchange for all their property, the aged could live out the rest of their years in pleasant surroundings. German Jews were heartened by the formal contracts given them in exchange for their possessions. They stepped off the trains, some of them still calling *"Träger"* (porter), believing they had bought safety.[1] Sometimes it was not until they were crowded into their quarters that they realized they were prisoners, and that the slim possibility of staying in Terezin and alive depended on their ability to withstand disease, hunger, or slave labor in exchange for rations. In addition, it took luck or influence not to be called up for what the Germans called a transport "for resettlement to the East," which meant slave labor or death.

Births were forbidden, and women discovered by the German authorities to have given birth were subject to immediate expulsion to the East. Yet 207 children were born in Theresienstadt, 25 of whom survived. Births were disguised by registering the newborn in place of a child that had died. The children who managed to survive experienced the worst conditions just before the end of the war. Transports to the East were increased, which meant more partings. Then in April

10

1945, groups of children that had been liberated from Bergen-Belsen and Dachau, among other camps, arrived. Within a three-week period, starting in the third week in April, approximately 300 children arrived. They came as skin and bones, carrying typhus, the kind transmitted by lice. Many of them died. Beneš, the Czechoslovakian president, sent his personal physician to help.[2]

Despite these conditions, there were attempts at caring, and, when permitted to do so, the Jewish leadership of the camp designated the best housing for the children and the best rations. Those inmates who had functioned as child-care workers, nurses, and teachers were insofar as possible designated to care for them. But as workers who were themselves inmates whose lives were in danger, who suffered separations from loved ones, crowding, hunger, and overwork, they were limited in what they could do.

Educating children was strictly forbidden by the SS and subject to severe punishment, but teaching took place nevertheless. In the groups where the older children lived, there was an attempt to teach the ideals of communal Zionist life, to enact plays, to learn Hebrew, to celebrate the festivals, and to help the aged. The older children were warned to pretend to be working at camp tasks if an SS inspection group came. But most of the time, hanging a sign on the door announcing "Typhus" was enough to keep the SS away.[3]

In December 1942 there were close to 5,000 children in Terezin: 3,367 under the age of sixteen, 1,398 staying in their mother's living quarters, and 1,969 in group care. The following winter only 800 children under the age of fifteen remained in Terezin. The rest had been sent to death in Auschwitz.

One hundred fifty thousand people passed through Terezin, and were funneled east to death camps, mostly Auschwitz, starting in 1942. Of these, fifteen thousand were children. "Shall I keep my child with me in the adult quarters? Or shall I put the child into the nursery run by inmates, freeing myself for labor, consequent rations, and survival? And when my name appears on a transport list, shall I take him with me if his name does not appear?" These were the life-and-death questions with which parents wrestled.[4]

"Some mothers," Edith Lauer reports, "kept their infants with them in the chaos of the crowded adult quarters. Mothers there struggled and fought for a turn at the one stove, clinging to the privilege of preparing a bit of gruel for their own child. But keeping your child with you was extremely dangerous, because if the mother was called up for a transport, that meant the child went too. We tried to tell the mothers if the child lived in the children's houses we were better able to protect them." But Edith's own sister kept her child with her, and Edith could not protect her own little niece, Evanicka, whose last words to her aunt were, "Don't cry, you'll see, we'll be back for Christmas." In order to be together until the last moment, Edith had volunteered for work in "The Lock," the holding area for those called up for transport. This was the most dreaded duty because from there few returned; even those whose names were not on the roll call for transit could be taken there in a moment at the whim of the SS.[5]

Some children arrived in Terezin without parents, packed into trains manned by Reichsbahn (national railroad) civil servants, who processed children as readily as freight. The SS with whom they contracted this work was charged only half-fare for children, and those under two went free of charge, as usual.[6]

Here is how an eyewitness described the arrival of a large children's transport:

> Transports of children from many different countries came to Theresienstadt. So on August 24, 1943, 1260 children. They were frightened and speechless, many barefoot, all in a sorry state and half starved. Insofar as any had possessions, they clutched their small suitcases or prayerbooks. They were not received into the main camp but were immediately separated from the other prisoners. They were taken to the West barracks surrounded by barbed wire. Police patrolled this children's quarters so as not to permit anyone near. From the main camp a group of caretakers and a doctor were appointed who from then on were not to have anything more to do with the main camp. These children had come from Bialystok and had seen everything that Jews could suffer. They were taken immediately in groups to a disinfection bath where they made terrible scenes. These children knew of gas chambers and would not set foot in the bath area. They screamed desperately "no, no, not gas!" They would not obey the SS men. Consequently they were pushed in by force. They cried and clung to each other. We who saw this were beside ourselves but we had been forbidden to speak to them under threat of death. . . . Before their departure from Bialystok they were lined up in a place and divided into three groups: men, women and children up to age 14. Fathers, mothers and older brothers and sisters were then shot before their eyes.[7]

The fate of this same transport of children is reported by Kraus and Kulka, survivors of Auschwitz.

> After several weeks in Terezin the 1260 children who had arrived from Bialystok in August, 1943, could be heard singing in the West Barracks of the Terezin camp. Then a rumor began to spread that they were being got ready for an exchange with children from abroad. Sure enough after six

weeks, orders came that they were to leave. By now they were thoroughly fit. Fifty-three men and women were selected to accompany them, all of them being required to give a written statement that they would not spread any propaganda hostile to the Nazis when they were abroad.

The inmates of Terezin saw them off with every good wish for the future. They were convinced the children would soon be at liberty.

The convoy left Terezin October 5, 1943. It went to Auschwitz, where all the children and all the adults ended up in the gas chamber.[8]

Martha Wenger, who cared for babies and toddlers, reported:

In Terezin everybody tried to work as little as possible to make up for the lack of proper nourishment. In the ward of motherless children there was always too much work, too few people to help me. Besides looking after the children we had to see to their clothes, etc. . . . which took time. We looked after the bodily welfare of the children as well as possible, kept them free of vermin for three years, and we fed them as well as possible under the circumstances. But it was not possible to attend to their other needs. Actually, we did not have the time to play with them.[9]

But in a letter written to Alice six months after her liberation from a displaced persons camp in Deggendorf, Germany, Martha Wenger revealed the depth of her attachment to the youngest children, inquiring after each by name and begging Alice to take particular care of Judith Auerbach, who had suffered pneumonia after each childhood illness. "I tried to replace [her] . . . mother," she wrote. "She loved me with all her little heart."[10]

A special attachment also sprang up between Zdenka Husserl and Edith and George Lauer, who dreamed at Terezin of adopting Zdenka if they all survived. Other children formed strong attachments to each other. Some clung to any passing adult. Some became attached to no one. A few became attached to their only possession in Terezin, their spoon.

Fifty-eight thousand people died in Terezin. Fifteen thousand children had passed through the Terezin death funnel. Twelve of the one hundred who survived were on their way to Lingfield.[11]

=== 3 ===
At Lingfield

The mansion called Weir Courteney stood on a gentle rise surrounded by acres of fields, woods, orchards. The three-story brick
structure had twenty rooms and was framed by colorful gardens
which led back from the country road. Smaller houses for servants
were nearby, as were the greenhouses where Sir Benjamin tended his
prized carnations.

When she first saw Weir Courteney, Alice felt it was like a dream. "It
couldn't have been more beautiful. I felt it would be a gift to the
children—so different from their camp surroundings. I hoped so
much that the beauty of it would in some way make up to them for
what they'd been through."[1]

The children arrived at night. It was the first night of Chanukah,
the Festival of Rededication commemorating the ancient victory of
the Jews over the power of Hellenism. The house was filled with
guests waiting to welcome the children, including people from the
West London Synagogue who had undertaken their financial support.

"The children's faces as they came in," Alice remembers, "are
unforgettable to me—eyes so wide; most where shy at first. But it did
not take long and they were at ease discovering the place, running
upstairs to see the rooms where they would sleep, calling to each
other to show things. Then we got them together, helped them to
light the first Chanukah candle while Rabbi Reinhart sang the
blessing. To see these children singing and happy was so gratifying to
us."

In this idyllic setting, some of the children for the first time met
adults with enough energy and resources to attend to them. There
was the creative attention of staff people such as Etta Pickhart, who
was to teach them English by putting on plays with them. Etta also
helped some to relax with massage. Sir Benjamin Drage himself liked
to take the children for walks, and to share his treasures in the
greenhouses. There were also several teenage girls—Asta Berlowitz,

14

Dora Teichner, Judith Stern, Renata Strauss, and Traute Lossau —who had been sent to Lingfield to rest and recuperate from their concentration camp experiences before embarking on schooling or training with their own age groups in hostels elsewhere.

Sophie Wutsch had left her native Austria when Hitler came to power. A devout Catholic, she had become a cook in Anna Freud's War Nurseries, where she and Alice first became a team. Sophie could cook for twenty or two hundred with equal ease and enjoyed the company of children. Her kosher kitchen became a place where one could go for time out and special treats. Sophie's creativity with available ingredients triumphed over the austerity of postwar conditions, and she and the children were overjoyed with the arrival of the relatively luxurious ingredients sent in Foster Parents Plan care packages.

There was an atmosphere of peace and plenty at Lingfield, and it drew as weekend visitors some of the older teenage boys who were settled in hostels in town—Wolf Blomfeld, Ben Helfgot, (Yezhek) Jerzy Herszberg, Hugo Gryn, and Henry Green. Alice called them "Our Boys," and they provided welcome older male companionship to the young children.

But the pastoral setting could not obliterate the privation and chaos of the children's pasts. The serenity of the estate was a dramatic contrast to the inner turmoil of painful memories, anger, and fear. "Will the house be here tomorrow?" some children asked at first, touching the walls. The emotional residue of death, destruction, and loss stormed within as the children struggled to find—or to avoid —new attachments, to explore the limits of freedom and find a sense of self with new people in a new place.

From the moment of landing at Carlisle, four-year-old Samuel Schwartz had begun urgently asking, "*Bist du mein?*" of every adult he encountered. He had come to Terezin without a parent, not yet two and suffering an ear infection, when the entire Berlin Jewish Hospital was evacuated to a concentration camp. His question persisted, at first in German, and then, "Are you mine?" The earnest, hopeful way in which the handsome little boy approached people reflected his consuming search for a person whose name he could not remember but whose persistent imprint filled him with yearning to be bound in that special relationship again. Sammy was essentially a shy child whose slow smile, beneath downcast eyes, was cautious. His usual reserve made his sudden approaches to adults with the question, "Are you mine?" all the more urgent. Although Sammy expressed his yearning with keen directness, the other children who shared this same void behaved in a variety of different ways.

Sylvia Gruener, despite her poor eyesight, was at age six so finely coordinated physically that she could move beautifully and juggle balls. She searched for adult attention by juggling, and by organizing the other little girls in songs and dances. Periodically, she would come out in front of the others and bow for applause. She had survived not only three years in Terezin, but had lived in an orphanage after her foster mother was deported. Eagerly she would approach visitors to Lingfield and ask boldly if they had brought a present for her. To gain the affection of other children, she periodically gave away all her possessions, only to suffer regret later. Though she coveted the attention of adults, she never went into an adult's room without the protection of another child. Once, in Etta Pickhart's room, she spotted a photo of some other children. She looked at it intensely and asked, "Are they dead?"

"No, they are not dead," Etta answered. "They are children from another place."

"Then why aren't you with them?" she scolded. "You must never leave your children. Always you must stay with them."

As she began to learn English, Sylvia became fascinated with rhyming and went about repeating rhymes like "My dear, bist du here?"

Zdenka Husserl's yearning for someone to take care of her like a mother had been fulfilled in her relationship with Edith Lauer. Zdenka had been sent to Terezin at age two with her mother Helene, in November 1942. Her father Pavel was deported elsewhere. Two years later, in October, Helene disappeared. The pain of losing her mother had been quieted by her growing affection for the Lauers, who were looking forward to adopting Zdenka and starting a new life in America. In Lingfield Zdenka followed Edith Lauer everywhere, not letting her out of her sight.

Some children, like Denny Muench, found satisfaction in play-acting endless victory over Hitler. Red-haired, freckle-faced, he walked hunched over and withdrawn. "Did you know my parents were shot?" he would ask. Over and over again, with toys and blocks, he played at killing Germans. He woke frequently at night, wet and screaming in terror, and ran to Alice's bedroom. One day, angered by something a staff member said, Denny ran into the kitchen, grabbed a large knife, and came out gritting his teeth and muttering menacingly, "I'm going to kill her."

At times he could be seen taking excessively large steps, creating an exaggerated version of a grown-up. Once he told Alice, "Some children have parents. I don't have parents, so I have to be a big man."

Tania was placid, watching and following along in an acquiescent way that did not risk causing trouble. But her longing for close connections was clear in her eagerness to comply with adults and in her excessive gratitude for a piece of candy. Alone on a walk with Alice, Tania bloomed, only to retreat again when back with the others. On one of these walks, Tania burst into tears. With remarkable clarity for a five-year-old, she cried, "I can't forgive my mother. She came into the room, gave me a piece of bread and said she would come back soon, but she never came."

For children like Denny and Tania, whose birthdays were not known, Alice invented birth dates. Denny, afraid of dying, asked endless questions about birthdays and about death and God.

Marta Vindfogel, too troubled to sustain play, saw adults as hostile and unreliable. But angry as she would become with Alice, she still clung to her, following her about and accusing Alice of making dogs come to terrify her.

Not surprisingly, the security of the children was easily jarred despite the constancy of Alice's involvement and the efforts of the rest of the staff. Alice recalls one such incident:

> I had taken the children for a walk in the woods, and I was walking along, holding some by the hand, singing, when suddenly I was knocked down to the ground and the children were climbing on me, screaming in panic, tearing at my clothes. They had heard a dog barking. They were frightened to death of dogs because the Nazis used dogs to frighten the captives. Every dog was a threat. This fear persisted for some children for a long time, even when we began to have pets ourselves.

Whether battling daytime panics or nighttime fears, Alice had a reliable device, the harmonica, which she regularly took out in order to soothe the children with a familiar melody.

By February all the children who were five or older had started school except for Marta, who was still unable to refrain from outbursts or to be away from Alice. School in the village would involve new adjustments and challenges. Mr. Faud, the principal, was sympathetic.

Despite some night fears, and occasional flareups at meals, most children now settled down in a secure routine—so much so that to the casual visitor to Lingfield who saw them skipping around the old oak tree, playing with dolls in the sitting room, and dipping lollipops into their glasses of milk to enjoy sucking milk off the sweet candy, it appeared that this was "a group of the happiest children simply abandoning themselves to the joy of living."[2]

=4=

The Second Group Arrives:
From Auschwitz

Routine was shaken on the morning of May 8, 1946, by a phone call from Oskar Friedmann, who had been collecting stray children still arriving from the European continent. He asked Alice, "How many empty beds do you have?" Alice thought she had two but could arrange to put up two more.

"Four," she answered. There was a long pause at the other end.

"I've just put eleven children on the train to Lingfield," he said.

"Oh." She gulped. There was another long pause as her mind began racing for ways to make places for them. "Where have they come from?"

He cleared his throat. "From everywhere." Then he paused. "There are some little ones from Auschwitz."

The ordeal of survival in Auschwitz began on the trains carrying the human cargo, packed in, starved and thirsting, living in excrement, with the odor of sickness and death stifling the air. The transport from Trieste in June 1944 held its people locked into the cars from 6 A.M. to 9 P.M. before the train got under way. Crusts of bread were distributed only after forty-eight hours. The journey took eight days.[1]

In Auschwitz the smoking chimneys, the electrified barbed wire, the unrelenting selections for death left those who passed through it abandoned to despair, isolated in a world without mercy. To remain alive for longer than it took to be processed for immediate death required the strength to withstand starvation, slavery, and disease. Extraordinary stamina was required to stand immobile for interminable hours in bitter cold while roll calls were taken and selections for death were made. The tenacity to endure the oppressive power of death made hope an act of defiance, when throwing oneself against

19

the electrified wire or volunteering in a selection for gassing was a constant temptation. But stamina was not as great a factor in survival as sheer chance.

Here as in most of the other death camps (unlike Terezin), it was rarely possible for the community to act as a whole in the care and protection of the young. A singular person, the charismatic educator Freddie Hirsch, who could not believe that the Nazis would gas children, continued in Auschwitz as he had in Terezin to try to teach the young and to sustain their hopes. But his profound faith in humanity could not prevent the end: when the truck in which he was being transported with children turned, not toward the village of Auschwitz, but toward the crematoria, Hirsch took cynaide, saying, "I cannot bear to see my children massacred."[2]

A child in Terezin might still sense the protection of adults powerful enough to secretly defy the injunction against educating children. But the process of community destruction begun in the cities, and escalated in the ghettos, the concentration camps, and finally the death camps, rendered adults powerless to protect the young in Auschwitz. Protection now existed only in the isolated acts of a few people conspiring together to hide a sick child from the ruthless selection of the weak for death, or of an inmate warning mothers on the arrival platforms to say a ten-year-old was fourteen (thus making the child a candidate for slave labor rather than for immediate death).

One survivor, Esther Wajs, reports that women on the arrival platforms in August 1944 were warned, "Vilt ihr lebn bleibn—varft avek die kinder" (If you want to remain alive—throw the children away.)[3]

In this milieu of total powerlessness, each day of survival was a miracle. And yet children played. Hanna Hoffman-Fischel, who had been a teacher before she was sent to Auschwitz, reports:

> We had great difficulties with the youngest children. We tried to tell the children stories about life as we wished it to be. But when we couldn't take care of them they played out life the way they lived it. They played "Block Leader" and "Concentration Camp Chief," and "Roll-Call." They played "The Sick" who fainted during roll call and were beaten for it, or "Doctor" who took away your food ration and refused help if you would not give it to him. Once they also played "Gas Chamber." They made a big hole into which they shoved stones one after the other. These were supposed to be the people who came to the crematorium, and they imitated their screams. I was asked to show them how to erect a chimney.[4]

The situation of children in Auschwitz is discussed in an exchange between Prosecutor Smirnov and Witness S. Smaglewská, before the International Military Tribunal at Nuremberg in 1946.

SMIRNOV: Did you yourself see the children being sent to the gas chambers?

WITNESS: I used to work very close to the railway lines leading to the crematorium. I used often to stand near the lavatory in the early morning; from here I could watch what happened to the convoys without being noticed. I saw lots of children with the Jewish people who were brought to the camp. Some families had several children. The Court is aware, no doubt, that a selection was made before the people were sent to the crematorium.

SMIRNOV: The selection was made by doctors?

WITNESS: Not always; sometimes it was done by SS men.

SMIRNOV: But there were doctors there too?

WITNESS: Yes. At the time when these selections were made, only a few of the young and healthy Jewish were admitted to the camp. Women carrying children were sent with them to the crematorium. The children were then torn from the parents outside the crematorium and sent to the gas chambers separately. When the extermination of the Jews in the gas chambers was at its height, orders were issued that children were to be thrown straight into the crematorium furnaces, or into a pit near the crematorium, without being gassed first.

SMIRNOV: How am I to understand this? Did they throw them into the fire alive, or did they kill them first?

WITNESS: They threw them in alive. Their screams could be heard at the camp. It is difficult to say how many children were destroyed in this way.

SMIRNOV: Why did they do this?

WITNESS: It's difficult to say. We don't know whether they wanted to economize on gas, or if it was because there was not enough room in the gas chambers. I should like to add that it is impossible to say exactly how many of these people—Jewish people, for instance—were sent straight to the crematoria. They were not registered or tattooed, and often they were not even counted. Those of us prisoners who tried to keep a check on the number of children gassed had no means of judging except by the number of prams brought into the store-room. Sometimes there were a hundred, sometimes even as many as a thousand.[5]

Some of the children who miraculously survived Auschwitz were described by the pediatrician Poltawska:

All the children were rachitic at the moment of liberation, and some were so skinny and starved that the bones were the only part of their bodies that weighed anything, other children were swollen from starvation, the age of all the children was defined more or less accurately by the physician who examined them and as it turned out later due to the fact that they were so emaciated the age was usually defined lower than in reality. All the children suffered from changes in their eyes. In some cases it was known that they suffered from suppurative inflammation of the conjunctiva as well as the cornea. Some of the [adoptive] mothers maintained that something had been done to their eyes in the camp.

In addition to furunculosis [severe skin infections] which was very widespread among the children at the time of liberation, they had traces, bruises on their body. . . . Some had TB of the glands, others bone TB.

In Auschwitz at the beginning the children were scattered all over the camp, sometimes purposefully, by adult women who hid them in various blocks, some of them in the "Revier" [hospital block], and finally due to the efforts made by Dr. J. Kosciusko, they were placed in a special children's block set up at the end of 1943 and the beginning of 1944. Not many children managed to live longer than one year in Auschwitz. To each one of us the physician signified salvation, the mother—security, but that is not so in the case of these children. The white gown means death, and adult means starvation, a uniform means pain, mother is doomed to die, a new dress signifies selection to the gas.[6]

It is difficult to establish the number of children who were killed in Auschwitz. At the Nuremberg Trials, witnesses gave approximate numbers. According to Poltawska, some based their estimates on the number of prams left in front of the crematoria.[7] Kraus and Kulka estimated that a million children under sixteen were killed.[8] Kulka reported also that blood was taken from children recovering from typhoid to provide immunization for the Reich army.[9]

On November 26, 1944, Himmler, foreseeing defeat and concerned for his own survival, gave the order to shut down the crematoria.[10] Frantic efforts to destroy evidence ensued, to dismantle the machinery of death. Potential witnesses, including children, were shot or taken away on death marches. The skies were red as the camp warehouses burned for days. Bursts of gunfire could be heard drawing closer with the approach of the Russian front. On January 27, 1945, the day the camp was liberated by the Russian soldiers, approximately three hundred children were found, barely alive. Among these survivors were four little girls and a boy. All had blue numbers tattooed on their arms. The little girls did not know how old they were, but knew they were pairs of sisters. They were nursed and fed by the Russians, and two months after their liberation they were on the train to Lingfield.

As Alice described them on their arrival, the children were:

SHANA TRAUBOVA, six, #8106, and ESTHER TRAUBOVA, four, #8107, speaking Yiddish
LILLIANA BUCCI, six, #776 484, and ALESSANDRA (ANDRA) BUCCI, five, #776 843, speaking Italian
JULIUS HAMBURGER, nine, #B4141, speaking Slovak and German

All their ages were approximate, for there were no papers.

The day of the new group's arrival was extraordinarily beautiful. Spring flowers were in bloom. The new arrivals, their heads shaven to deter lice infestation, were small, and their ages could not be established until later through examination of bone structure. The smallest child, Esther Traubova, turned out to be about four. Esther's soft cherubic face was framed by little bits of what one could see would be curls. Esther enjoyed cuddling with her sister, Shana, who managed her younger sister well, and provided her with some security, especially at night, when they clung together and spoke a secret language, a soft baby talk. For a time, both little girls appeared pale and puffy and bore lingering skin infections; nevertheless, they behaved with surprising cheerfulness and showed great interest in new activities, sometimes shrieking with delight over a new toy. Visitors soon remarked on their outgoing, affectionate behavior.

Of the second pair of sisters, Lilliana, the dark-haired one, was the older. She treated Andra with motherly, patient direction. Andra, blonde and more frail, looked up to her sister adoringly. In the beginning Andra frequently daydreamed and stared off into space. The more outgoing Lilliana was quickly involved with the other children. Both especially liked playing with dolls, tending and comforting them for long periods. Alice thought that this play was based on memories of their own mother's attention to them.

When it was time for the children to start school, Andra cried and had difficulty leaving Alice. Touched by this, their teacher, Mrs. Faud, called Alice and invited Andra and Lilliana to spend a night with her. Alice was invited to bring them before supper, leave, and return to say goodnight. When Alice came to say good night, she found the children bathed, wrapped in blankets, sitting contentedly with the Fauds before a warm fire. The next day Andra went to school readily, and from then on all the other children asked, "When can we go to the Fauds?"

Julius was looked up to by all four little girls. He was blonde, blue-eyed, and well coordinated. Soon after his arrival Alice learned from adult survivors that he had protected the little girls in Auschwitz, where he had given them crusts of bread and instructed them to hide under the beds during one of the final shooting massacres before the Germans left the camp.

═ 5 ═
From Orphanages

The second group Oskar Friedmann sent to Lingfield on May 8 included a family group of three children. It was hard to tell the age of Magda, the oldest girl, because, although her body was still childlike, her face carried the sad strain of an adult woman. She behaved like a strict mother toward the younger two, Hedi and Fritz, keeping them constantly within sight, shouting at them in Hungarian. Gradually Alice learned that after a brief stay in a Hungarian prison camp, they had been separated from their parents and sent from one orphanage to another.

Unlike any of the other younger children, these three knew their ages and place of origin. Although she appeared so much older, Magda was not yet twelve. Hedi was eight and carried her little brother, Fritz, six, on her back, for polio in infancy had made walking painful for him.

All three had been in orphanages during the Hitler era.

Since biblical times orphaned children have been regarded in civilized societies as highly vulnerable and deserving of special protection. The concept of a legal guardian, *in loco parentis,* derives from this understanding that orphans need adults to protect them. During the Nazi regime, however, this time-honored assumption was abandoned, not only by the German government, but by other governments as well. When Slovakia was occupied, Jews escaped across the border to unoccupied Hungary. But when the Germans advanced into Hungary, the Hungarian-German government began to pressure Slovakia to relinquish its claim to protect these refugee Slovaks. In response, the Slovak government replied that they were "interested in the repatriation of a few Jews, but not interested in the fate of refugees, particularly the orphans and children who had recently crossed the Hungarian border illegally."[1]

There was a pattern for the destruction of Jewish orphanages, and the first step was usually relocation into an already crowded and deprived ghetto. The exodus of children and teachers was often terrifying. Yitzhak Hertz, the head of the Dinslaken Orphanage, gave this account:

> Facing the back of the building, we were able to watch how everything in the house was being systematically destroyed under the supervision of the men of law and order—the police. At short intervals we could hear the crunching of glass or the hammering against wood as windows and doors were broken. Books, chairs, beds, tables, linen, chests, parts of a piano, a radiogram, and maps were thrown through apertures in the wall which a short while ago had been windows or doors.
>
> In the meantime the mob standing around the building had grown to several hundred. Among these people I recognized some familiar faces, suppliers of the orphanage or tradespeople, who only a day or week earlier had been happy to deal with us as customers. This time they were passive, watching the destruction without much emotion.[2]

The reports filed routinely concerning these operations by German officers are remarkable for the way in which both humans and property are accounted for with no distinction made between them.

> In the early morning of April 6, 1944, in Izieu Ain [France] Security Police forced their way into the [Jewish] Children's Home and moved out with 51 persons including 5 women and 41 children between the ages of 3 and 13. Cash or other valuables according to the report could not be secured.
>
> [Signed] Obersturmführer Barbie[3]

Once expulsion and relocation had taken place, the second step was to reduce rations and deny medications, encouraging starvation and disease. In many instances, the respected heads of these institutions were reduced, as was Janusz Korczak in Warsaw, to demoralizing daily rounds of begging food from other hungry ghetto inhabitants. In Warsaw in 1942, before the first mass roundups, there were thirty orphanages housing or feeding four thousand children.[4] The orphanage at 39 Dzielna Street in the Warsaw Ghetto was one. Korczak, who served as its doctor, dubbed it a "pre-funeral home," and described it this way: "This orphanage was turned into a kind of children's rescue station: sick, abandoned children were collected in the streets and brought there. The number of deaths gives an idea of the conditions and the situation: ten to fifteen deaths daily."[5] For children surviving in such places, a depressed, self-protective apathy often muted feelings. "They moon about. Only outer appearances are normal. Underneath lurks weariness, discouragement, anger, mutiny, mistrust, resentment, longing."[6]

In some institutions, when the staff grasped the unthinkable—that orphanages would be primary targets—they decided to turn the children loose on the streets to try to survive on their own.[7]

In all the hard-pressed ghettos, stray orphaned children were a problem. Emmanuel Ringelblum noted in his diary:

Mid-November, 1941. The first frosts have already appeared, and the populace is trembling at the prospect of cold weather. The most fearful sight is that of freezing children. Little children with bare feet, bare knees, and torn clothing, stand trembling in the street weeping. Tonight, the 14th [of November], I heard a tot of three or four yammering. The child will probably be found frozen to death tomorrow morning, a few hours off. October, when the first snows fell, some twenty children were found frozen to death on the steps of houses. Frozen children are becoming a general phenomenon. The police are supposed to open a special institution for street children at 20 Nowolipie Street; meanwhile, children's bodies and crying serve as a persistent background for the Ghetto. People cover the dead bodies of frozen children with the handsome posters designed for Children's Month, bearing the legend, "Our Children Must Live—A Child Is the Holiest Thing."[8]

The third step in the general pattern of the destruction of orphanages was the removal of staff and children to death camps. Whether it was the German shout of *"Raus! Raus!"* (Out! Out!) or its equivalent in another language, it signaled the final deportation. These shouts, often accented with a few gunshots, sent the children and the staff streaming into the courtyards. There, assembled at gunpoint, they waited while police searched the orphanage for stragglers. Then, herded by armed guards, the children—sometimes walking in long rows, two by two, holding hands—were marched to waiting cattle trucks or trains that took them to death camps. Hundreds of devoted adults—like Korczak and his nine teachers—voluntarily went with them.

There came a time when even the most protective adults were powerless to shield the children from fear and the realization that they would die. Hilberg, quoting an eyewitness account (by Solomon Bloom), recognized that "in the end, even the children knew the purpose of the deportations. When during the summer of 1944 in the Lodge Ghetto [Poland], the children of an orphanage were piled on trucks, they cried, 'Mir viln nit shtarben! Mir viln nit shtarben!' [We don't want to die!]"[9]

A rare instance occurred in which a small group of children was released. In late June 1944, when the fate of concentration camp victims could no longer be denied, the Red Cross negotiated the release of a small number of children from the Hungarian prison camp at Kistarsca, just days before their parents were deported to Auschwitz. The children were taken to Red Cross–sponsored Jewish children's homes; the Red Cross flag hung in front of these homes in order to protect them. Then, on Christmas Eve, the Red Cross children's homes were stormed by the pro-Nazi Hungarian Arrow Cross.

While bombs and mines exploded all over the city, the Nyilas drove the children across the Buda into the Radatsky barracks. Here workers in labor companies, clad in Nyilas uniforms, turned them back with forged orders. Tragically, the children were placed in homes where caretakers denounced them to the Nyilas members. Some of the children were shot; some were thrown in the Danube; a few managed to escape.[10]

Among those who escaped were eleven-year-old Magda Liberman, her two nieces, both named Hedi, then aged eight and five, and her little nephew, Fritz, aged six. Of the four, only three arrived at Lingfield on May 8, 1946, all suffering from malnutrition, and the younger two from skin rashes. They explored the grounds together, apart from the other children. Fritz was lively and crawled freely about; when he appeared to be going off limits, Hedi, on cue from Magda, would retrieve him, carrying him on her back.

At the dinner table, where all the new children behaved badly, snatching food and stuffing their pockets, Hedi and Fritz followed suit. But Magda, old enough to remember a decent meal at home, was unable to tolerate the sight of Fritz and Hedi stuffing themselves and grabbing more food than they could eat. She lashed out with a burst of slaps at the greedy hands and faces of her children, and immediately started to cry with them. Their wailing brought Alice on the run. Magda spoke little German, Alice no Hungarian, but Alice's comforting voice telling Magda that the children would learn gradually reassured her.

Clearly, Magda was to be respected in any plans for Hedi and Fritz. The next day, Alice explained to Magda that the little ones' rashes were contagious and asked her to help settle the two in a separate room. When Alice came in with books and sweets, she found Hedi sitting up in bed playing at stringing beads. But Fritz panicked at her approach and scampered up the drapery, where he stayed, hissing at her and dangling his lame leg. Alice placed sweets beside his bed and then played with Hedi until he tired and came down.

At first Magda watched Alice carefully, as she did all adults. Finally, one afternoon, with more trust in Alice and more English mastered, Magda told Alice how she had been sworn to three oaths by her mother when they parted for the last time in Kistarsca prison camp: to take good care of the children; to see that they said the *Shema* prayer before going to bed; and to take the children to Palestine if their parents did not survive. With bitter tears, Magda cried that she had not been able to fulfill this last oath. Quietly, Alice promised to help her do it in the future. In the meantime, she wanted Magda to enjoy being a child, to ease the burden of the awesome responsibilities she had carried so long.

In time, Fritz, taking his cue from Magda and Hedi, became friendlier toward Alice. Several corrective operations would be necessary in the next four years. But Fritz, though brooding at times, began to adjust, secure in Magda's and Hedi's special protection. Early on, he approached visitors to Lingfield to ask, "Do you have children?" If they answered "No," he would tell them, "Oh, you must—you should have lots of children. You should have a big family."

Hedi communicated with smiles before she learned English. At first her eyes showed incalculable sadness, but in time she, like Fritz, showed sparkle and wit. Taller and larger-framed than the others of her age, she often won the part of Queen in dramatic plays—which she adored.

Hedi's special place as Magda's helper with Fritz gave her a sense of security and importance. She would swoop down to defend him against anyone, ready to hit them if necessary. Eventually she could be depended on to look out for all the younger children at school. When Zdenka did a cartwheel that broke a bedroom window, it was Hedi who gave her first aid.

The bonds between Hedi, Fritz, and Magda remained a source of comfort and strength, yet old longings persisted. About a year after they had come to Lingfield, when Etta Pickhart was putting Hedi to bed one night, Hedi asked, "When we go to Israel, will you come? Then you can be my mother." Then she murmured something in Hungarian and smiled. It meant "Sugarmother."

= 6 =

From Hiding

Among the second group that arrived in Lingfield on May 8, 1946, were two children who had been in hiding. In a bold stroke of courage, Ervin Bogner's mother had dressed him in a little Nazi youth uniform. Blonde, blue-eyed, and thus disguised, Ervin was protected as he and his mother foraged the Czechoslovakian countryside, moving with caution in an effort to survive.

Mirjam Stern, age eight, arrived with her sister Judith, fifteen. They had gone into hiding together, but Judith, at thirteen, was discovered and sent to Belsen. Mirjam then spent two years confined alone in the tiny upstairs bedroom of a Czech peasant family. Reunited now, their parents dead, they were sent to Lingfield to help them regain strength and balance.

About a year later, two more children who had been in hiding arrived. Eva Folkmann, eight, was brought to Alice by an aunt who could not care for her full time. Around her neck, Eva still wore the cross which had, for three years, protected her as she lived in hiding in a convent.

Charles Kessler, nine, had been placed in hiding in Belgium. After the war, he was taken to an orphanage in Belgium, and then brought to Lingfield.

The essential facts about the children who hid from Nazi persecution are not fully known. In Germany, Poland, Lithuania, and the Ukraine, Jewish communities were in surroundings so hostile that no large-scale attempts at hiding were possible. A few children were hidden by non-Jewish families, schools, and convents. Totally severed from their communities, they remained alive through the bitter success of their disappearances from their families, and by their continuing concealment from Nazi authority, by dissemblance as non-Jews. This very disappearance and concealment account in part for the lack of information about how many were hidden; how many survived and continued to maintain their false identity; how many were placed so young that they did not know their true identity; how many ever returned to identity as Jews. The parents, the relatives, the communities who might have retained or passed on such knowledge were destroyed.

The situation in western Europe was relatively more fortunate. In Holland, eleven hundred children were successfully hidden by the efforts of organized students; in Belgium the number was thirty-three hundred. According to R. Lowrie, six thousand children remained hidden in France until the American troops stormed up the Rhone Valley.[1] Meyer Levin's estimate is eight thousand.[2] These figures only underscore the tragedy of almost total indifference elsewhere.

Still, even in France, Belgium, and Holland, it was rare that children went into hiding with their families as Anne Frank did. Such arrangements, while preferable psychologically to being hidden alone, were very difficult to secure, costly, and hazardous.

Where there was sufficient prior warning of a roundup, the decision to place a child in hiding could be a planned maneuver in which parents, realizing that they could not save themselves but desperate to save their children, proposed the idea of hiding to non-Jewish friends or neighbors. But often the decision to hide one's child had to be made in an instant, during a Nazi roundup.

It is hard to imagine any act more difficult for a parent than making a split-second decision to send a child into hiding totally on his own, without even the security of knowing that some advance arrangement has been made. Mrs. Soral's decision, described by Levy and Tillard in their account of the roundup of Parisian Jews on July 16 and 17, 1941, is rare documentation of what was an all too common event:

> As soon as she saw the other prisoners, Mrs. Soral realized that something terrible was going to happen. This was not just a matter of checking identity papers.
>
> She wished she had taken advantage of the inspector's kindness when he let her go and do some shopping even though she knew that with her two youngest children it would have been impossible to find somewhere to hide. The eldest, Jean, was ten years old. Standing in the confusion of the collecting center, she came to a hard decision. Taking the boy aside, she explained to him what she wanted him to do, and then, as a group of new prisoners crowded into the door, she pushed him into the general muddle and watched him work his way out onto the steps in front of the police station. No one noticed him as he hurried off down the Rue Soufflot.[3]

Had Jean Soral's mother not made that decision to send him off to hide, he would have been confined for days in Vel D'Hiv, a stifling, enclosed sports stadium described as a "bird cage," and sent to the sorting pens of the Rivesaltes concentration camp. Four thousand fifty-one children were sent from Rivesaltes to Auschwitz and death.

Those children who escaped death through being hidden in France and Belgium owe their lives to courageous individuals willing to risk death themselves. According to Lowrie,

> The whole operation was a joint effort by Jewish and Christian organizations, mostly OSE [Organization pour Sanitée et Education] and ORT [Organization for Rehabilitation and Training] and, on the Christian side, CIMADE [Comitée d'Inter-Mouvement auprès des Evacuées] and the Catholic institutions. Protestants did not have many places that could be used for storage of a whole group of children at a time, as the Catholics did. For instance, a group of young Protestant conspirators in Grenoble planned to "kidnap" forty Jewish children from the fortress where they were being held, scheduled for deportation eastward the following day. With the aid of some French authorities they arrived at the fortress gates one midnight with two trucks and forged papers authorizing them to move the children to another prison. The Vichy police never could trace those two truckloads of children, who went directly into a convent school in the city. A few days later our committee looked them over and, one by one, they were taken into private homes.[4]

Among the most daring rescues was the one executed by the Jewish convert to Catholicism L'Abbé Glasberg. Slipping into the Rivesaltes barracks at midnight, he moved with two assistants from bed to bed asking "Do you have children? We've come to save them." They implored parents to wake a child from sleep for a separation that might be forever and succeeded in spiriting one hundred children out of the concentration camp.[5]

These children were dispersed, one or two at a time, throughout the farming country west of Lyon. It was not possible under such circumstances to learn the names of each of the younger children, so new names were given to them. Thus it was that some children went into hiding, never to learn their true identities. All those adults who could have claimed them after the war went with the transport of French Jews from Venessieux to Auschwitz.

Wherever they were isolated from their own families, it was common for children in hiding to begin to identify with their Christian benefactors. They learned not only to hide their Jewish origins from suspicious outsiders, but also to reject these origins themselves. Many began to see Christians as their only protectors, as

did a nine-year-old girl hidden in a devout Catholic family: "The
Jewish God killed my parents. He burned my home. Jesus Christ
saved me."[6]

During their period of hiding, many children had become "impreg-
nated with the feeling of the certainty of destruction awaiting Jews."[7]
For these children, the end of the war brought severe new shocks and
adjustments. Where a parent had survived and came to claim the
child, it was not uncommon for the child to refuse to go with the
person whom he saw as having abandoned him. One survivor said,
"I did not want to go with my mother because I liked sleeping
under a big feather quilt in the same bed with Granny. I was by then
very attached to her."[8] To leave that environment meant losing the
only feeling of security he had. Heartbreaking scenes were common.
"Many children reacted with bitter tears, hunger strikes, running
away and threats of suicide when faced with leaving their rescuers and
being returned to Jewish surroundings."[9] Some spat at the mothers
who had come to claim them.[10]

The ordeal of years in hiding with him had left Ervin's mother
exhausted. By the end of the war, she no longer felt capable of caring
for him.

At Lingfield, Ervin was a child who seemed confused and fearful.
Often, when other children cried or were frightened, he would laugh
inexplicably. Having been deprived of the company of other children
while in hiding with his mother, he behaved as if he were a much
younger child, teasing or pushing to gain attention. His habit of
playing tricks on others earned him the ambivalent nickname of "Mr.
Jokes."

Like many of the others, Ervin feared for a long time that SS men
would come and kill them in their beds.

Thunderstorms, too, were a cause of panic, reactivating fears near
the surface, and, for the fortunate few who could remember, memories of home a long time ago. One stormy night, frail, blonde Mirjam
was frightened and called out for someone to come. Upset that no one
arrived quickly enough, she demanded of Alice, "Didn't your mother
come to comfort you in a thunderstorm?"

Mirjam appeared very delicate, hanging back as if perpetually
afraid. Her large brown eyes seemed too big for her pale face, and she
was preoccupied with observing and appraising everything intensely.
In time, her passive stance gave way to claims for attention and to
whining and dissatisfaction. She slept poorly, waking in fear of being
sent back to Czechoslovakia. In the chaos of mealtimes she seemed

lost and without appetite, but later she would go to Manna, her favorite worker, to ask for a spoon of malt to lick. After years of hiding, longing—but fearing—to trust again, she began slowly to relate to adults. Then for a time she would hug Manna, facing her and standing on Manna's feet so that she would be carried along when Manna walked. Here, in Lingfield, she discovered she loved to draw and that it was safe to assert her will and tease and test the people she liked.

Unlike other heads of Jewish children's homes, Alice did not insist that eight-year-old Eva take off the cross she had worn while hiding in the convent near her home.[11] Alice felt Eva would take it off when she was ready, and did not wish to deprive her of the security it gave her in the meantime.

Eva, a sturdy child, was poised with adults and confident with the other children. She enjoyed showing guests around the house and engaged in conversation readily. Her aunt in England, to whom she was first sent from hiding, was unable to care for her and brought her to Lingfield. Eva visited her on some weekends, which gave her special status with some of the other children.

The last child to arrive in Lingfield was handsome, sandy-haired Charles Kessler, ten years old. He lashed out immediately, letting Alice know that he hated the food and did not like the clothes given him. But after settling in he revealed an essentially cheerful outlook, and his intelligence and athletic prowess made him popular with the other children. He spoke only Flemish and French, but quickly became a leader, often coming to the rescue of anyone he thought was being unfairly teased. Charles had been in hiding in Belgium for most of the war. His mother was working as a chambermaid in England, and he had not seen her since 1941. Although she had arranged for him to come to England, she was unable to provide a home for him. He visited her on some weekends in the hotel where she worked.

=== 7 ===

The Lingfield Milieu

The arrival of the latest group brought the number of young children in Alice's care to twenty-four. There were also six girls between the ages of thirteen and sixteen whose concentration camp experiences had been so devastating as to require a period of recuperation before attempting school or work. Mirjam's sister, Judith, was in this group.

Withdrawn, tired, haunted by the past, Judith like many other children wondered if this English countryside fairyland was a Nazi trick. Would she wake up one morning to find it gone? Eventually she was able to tell Alice about the time in Belsen when she didn't want to live anymore. She had stopped eating and washing. Washing meant going into a dark room where the one faucet was and where dead bodies lay in heaps, with rats feasting on them. At fourteen she had given up—death was preferable. Then her mother's voice came to her in a dream. "Take care of your little sister, Mirjam," it said. The next day, Judith washed.[1]

Alice began meeting weekly with the older girls, encouraging each of them to take responsibility for one younger child. For Judith, it was Mirjam; the sisters had to get reacquainted after two years apart. Some, like Dora Teichner, whose entire family of ten younger brothers and sisters had been wiped out, were particularly gratified by attending to the little ones. But more staff was needed. Manna Weindling was interviewed by Anna Freud and sent to work in Lingfield just a few days after the second group arrived. She became important to many of the children, and for three years she served as Alice's assistant.

For Manna, the desire to work at Lingfield was spurred by the painful memory of the Friday evening in 1938 when she saw her parents, two older brothers, and her ten-year-old twin brothers on the other side of a locked metal gate in the Cologne central train station. "Those little pale faces of my brothers, saying, 'Manna komm mit uns' (Manna, come with us)—I shall never forget that."

"Coming to Lingfield that spring morning was a stirring moment in my life . . . a salvation," Manna recalls. "Here was a way of starting anew. Every one of these children represented the twins I had left." On her arrival, the doors opened to a scene of children, some with shaved heads and numbers on their arms, dancing and singing a Hebrew children's song. "I was so moved, I couldn't stop crying. I put my suitcase and violin case down and watched with tears streaming. When I recovered I just joined in and started dancing the hora, laughing and crying at the same time."[2]

Manna taught singing and dance, Etta Pickhart organized dramatic presentations, and "Our Boys"[3] led games. Later, Susie Tietser, an artist, joined the staff. Alice employed all their talents to create Friday night celebrations and special parties. Weeks of planning, making costumes, decorations, and props for skits went into such parties, with Sophie baking for days.

Members of the Committee, those responsible for raising the money to support Lingfield, often attended these parties, sometimes bringing their own children. They arrived in elegant attire, creating waves of excitement as they drove up in their large cars. Alice would greet each one with polite caution; she felt nervous around such aristocracy.

Every month Alice, striving to look especially proper, put on her hat and gloves and, armed with the accounts, went to London to face the Committee, and explain the necessity of expenses such as music lessons, a carpentry teacher, amenities that would help each child develop confidence and the ability to express individuality.

The Committee was constantly scrambling for income to meet the ever-expanding needs of growing children through fund-raising events and appeals in synagogue publications. In the *Lingfield Bulletin*, its annual report, Sir Benjamin Drage wrote:

> We are dealing with children who have been frightened and starved, whose nerves have been shattered by seeing their parents and brothers and sisters taken to death. They want special medical, psychological, and nursing care and we cannot begrudge money in such a cause.
>
> My readers have been most generous but our expenses have been much heavier than anticipated and we need much more money. We would warmly welcome another hundred subscribers.[4]

Through Anna Freud's connection with the American Foster Parents Plan, an annual grant was obtained covering between one-quarter and one-half of Lingfield's expenses. But as the children grew older, the Lingfield Committee carried on alone, and it was to that committee that Alice was responsible.[5]

Over the years, Lingfield became a place whose unique function and enlighted practices attracted such visitors as Margaret Mead and Rabbi Leo Baeck. It became known, Alice recalls, as "the hostel without punishment," where children were treated with understanding. When a child's behavior troubled her particularly, she would write to Anna Freud and receive a prompt, thoughtful reply filled with encouragement and helpful observations. If a child seemed persistently troubled, Alice sought counsel with Freud about whether psychoanalysis was advisable. Occasionally Freud herself saw a child and then took pains to find a suitable therapist.[6]

Within six months of their arrival, the suspicion that had armored the children's expressions began to melt, revealing their soft, individually appealing childish faces. Visitors to Lingfield could not believe that these were the same children they had seen only months before. Although Sammy still wanted only Alice to stroke his head before he would go to sleep, at mealtimes he went back and forth from Alice's lap to Manna's. He had not found an answer to "Are you mine?" yet, but at least he seemed comforted. And Tania, on coming out of the bath, wanted Manna to kiss her "and nobody else!"

In time, as new routines and the security they produced became better established, the whining, clinging, and tearful upsets lessened. But the peaceful scenes of the children playing freely could be destroyed in a moment. One afternoon in a field adjacent to Lingfield, the appearance of some German prisoners of war, wearing their striped uniforms and shouting to each other in German, sent all the children running and screaming. The panic lasted for days, and Alice had to face the fact that the sense of security she had worked so hard to achieve was fragile indeed. As always, each child reacted in his or her particular way. Andra was more indignant than afraid:

"It's not fair," she said. "They have shoes and can smoke and work in the sun; we Jews didn't have that!"

In the evening Mirjam was especially distraught. Alice said, "My room is opposite yours, and I will let no one harm you." Alice remembers the child's touching answer: "We are near to each other not only outside but inside too." Long into that night, Alice went from bed to bed, passing sweets, playing lullabies on the harmonica. The lights were left burning until dawn.

Panic broke out again several months later, when England was swept by the rumor that Hitler was still alive. On the day they heard it, the children ran home from school, frantically shouting, "Hitler is not dead!" Then they ran wildly around the house, repeating it over and over.

By August 1947, as the peaceful days began to outnumber the chaotic ones, Alice decided it was time to take the children to see London. A one-day train trip was planned. The children would see Buckingham Palace and begin to get a feel for their new country. The staff carefully prepared them for the trip. But when the morning of the great day came, breakfast began with unusual quiet and then, with squabbling, built quickly to sobbing and havoc. Mirjam hung onto Manna every time she went to the kitchen. Esther was glued to Shana, almost the way they had been when they first came. Julius and Ervin wildly imitated Fritz, crawling after him, and Berli joined in.

Getting everyone out to the waiting bus was impossible. Even after a year at Lingfield, some of the children saw the bus as a transport to death. Some children cried and refused to go, some were suddenly "sick"; pandemonium prevailed. Finally the older girls helped to calm the children, and it was their decision to go that convinced the little ones. The snacks that were passed around later on the train helped, but Tania cried forlornly when she realized that her seating position meant that she would be among the last to get food.

The trip was a turning point, for it proved to the children that they could leave as a group and still come back. And Denny returned with a fascination for British toy soldiers. Now he lined them up carefully in front of his door every night: he had discovered a new source of protection against his bedtime fears.

There were many events that Alice could not control, and that rekindled disturbance and anxiety. During the first year, Alice and others who worked with the children received the news that their relatives or friends had been killed. The hope that no news of one's loved ones meant they still were alive was finally shattered. Each time such news arrived, those children who still did not know whether their own parents were alive, or those who refused to believe that they were dead, relived the agony of their losses.

There were some disturbing leavetakings as well. George Lauer, now well enough to travel, had been offered an engineering job in America. Edith learned that some of the Committee thought survivors of concentration camps should not work with the children, that the children should not be reminded of the past by their presence. The Lauers wanted to take Zdenka with them to America, but there was as yet no official notification of her parents' death.[7] Without it, she could not be adopted, and the wait for clearance could be a year. They promised Zdenka to return for her and that meanwhile they would write. Zdenka was beside herself, unable to understand or accept what was happening. She was six. On the day the Lauers left, she had to be physically torn from Edith's arms. Zdenka cried hysterically and was inconsolable for days, shivering and complaining of cold in the heat of summer. She insisted on wearing a wool jacket at all times and refused to take it off at school, where she buried her face in its sleeve. Eventually, the Lauers' first letter came for Zdenka, but she showed little interest in it. The Lauers continued to write, and they kept their promise: they came back for Zdenka a year later. By then, Zdenka was afraid to leave Lingfield and all she knew to go to America. She was now attached to Alice and Sophie.

Edith Lauer might have fought harder to adopt her, but an uneasy feeling stopped her, the same one that could intimidate natural parents as well as prospective adoptive ones. For the life at Lingfield looked so beautiful, with its advantages of space, beauty, luxury, and psychological and medical help, that many ordinary people, especially refugees like the Lauers, felt humbled by their own modest resources. This time there was no struggle, and Zdenka did not cry when they parted.

In the fall of 1946, Alice received a letter from Italy enclosing a photograph of a couple named Mira and Giovanni Bucci. She called Lilliana and Andra into her room and asked them if they knew who the people in the picture were. The girls recognized their parents immediately and radiated smiles of excitement. They agreed to part with a photograph of themselves together, so that it could be sent to Italy.

Once their identities were confirmed, the Jewish Refugees Committee arranged for their return to Italy. The girls were ecstatic to be going home to their parents, but their excitement deeply troubled the other children. Their chorus of questions mounted to a crescendo: "When will my mother come?" "Where is my mother?" "Why don't you find her?" Alice could only reassure them that everything would be done to find out if their parents were alive.

Sophie had made Lilliana and Andra beautiful coats and hats for their journey home. Their hair had grown shiny, and their eyes were sparkling. The children gathered at the door to wave and shout good-bye as the girls were driven away, but their departure left a wake of sadness that hung in the air for days.

The six toddlers who had come from Terezin and gone first to Bulldogs Bank rejoined the older children in Lingfield eleven months later. The plan was for the little ones to live in Lingfield while every effort was made to arrange for their adoption. Gertrud Dann came along to ease the transition, and stayed with them in Lingfield for a few weeks.

Most of them seemed to fit in well with the older children. Jack and Berli enjoyed tagging after the older boys. The sight of Berli in a sailor suit prompted Julius to cry, remembering his own brother. Following Julius around comforted Berli, who still could not tolerate being by himself. If he was alone for even a moment, he would shout or cry. He did not like starting school and had no patience for stories. Nevertheless, he was a jolly, lively child.

In the beginning, Jack spoke sadly about Bulldogs Bank, calling it "Our Bulldogs Bank." But gradually he began to assert himself, expressing his lively curiosity with such questions as "Where did I come from?"

Independent in her new Lingfield surroundings from the first, not waiting for an adult to help her find her way back from one part of the big house to another, Bella led other children in play and scolded them as well as adults if they did not perform according to her expectations.

Adults found Gadi charming and affectionate. He liked to pretend that they were his babies, and he made up clever explanations for things. One day, when not allowed to accompany some adults on a walk, he warned: "You'll see, it will rain!"

Judith was especially fond of Alice, whom she remembered from Windermere and from Alice's visits to Bulldogs Bank, so leaving for Lingfield was not a sad occasion for her. Smiling broadly, she played with dolls and followed Alice around, whenever possible holding onto her hand or her skirt.

Shortly after arriving at Lingfield, Leah had been sent away for eye surgery, and she returned unhappy and depressed. Excitable, sensitive, and easily frustrated, she had difficulty in play and took to aggressive outbursts to vent her misery.

After all the youngest children had started school or been adopted, Alice realized that Leah would not be able to function in the local school's classrooms. Alice chose a special boarding school for her that was within easy visiting distance of Lingfield. Soon a childless couple appeared who wanted to adopt her. The prospective mother, a teacher of young children, had come from Vienna before the war and was eager to teach Leah.

Marta, too, required special schooling. She was placed in a Rudolf Steiner School, which was spiritually committed to the loving treatment of children with special problems. She stayed there until 1951, when her mother was located in Germany.

Some problems persisted. There were children unable to control bed-wetting, who had to be quickly bathed every morning before school. Denny was so consumed with games of war and killing that on the advice of Anna Freud, Alice began taking him aside for play therapy. She continued this for about a year and a half. Gradually, the mock killing stopped.

For a year, soup on the table continued to be cause for revolt. It was a reminder of the only food outside of a crust of bread, or found greens, that had been available to most of the children. Food remained an extremely important part of security, and the arrival of a food package from the American Foster Parents Plan continued to be a great event.

Conversations about dead relatives persisted for a long time in play and were not discouraged. Alice recalls doll play with children discussing their dead relatives. "Part of the family is dead," one said. "Grandpa was shot too, but it doesn't matter. We can manage without them. We are the lucky ones—we're alive."

All the children were struggling with English. For some, like Fritz and Hedi, the difficulties with language were shortlived. But residual anxiety, compounded by school competition and demands, overwhelmed others. Julius, so confident and charismatic on the playground, became more defeated at school day by day. One day, enraged, he climbed the old oak tree, stripped naked, and threw all his clothes to the ground.

The emotional turmoil the children had brought with them from the time of persecution was further fueled by any inadequacy and confusion at school. Berli and Ervin had difficulty keeping up with the local English children. And despite Mirjam's fine drawing skill and her powers of observation, she had great difficulty learning to write and was easily discouraged.

Watching other children win praise for their work at school while they—no matter how hard they struggled—remained behind was a new crushing form of persecution for many of the children; it devastated any kernel of confidence and self-respect they had left, for they felt themselves to blame. Although Alice remained in close contact with the schools, she was unable to alter what, for some, would be a new course of defeat.

Within the next two years, all of the Bulldogs Bank group of youngest children were adopted—all, that is, but Berli, the very youngest. He was a lively, friendly child who could go up to a stranger on a train and say "I like you. Give me thruppence, please." But each of the two times adoption was tried, it failed. Berli simply could not bear the separation from Alice and from the other children. The second time, he stayed for three weeks before the family called to say that he had been crying the entire time, and to ask Alice to come and take him out of his misery.

The "Big Girls" (Judith, Magda, Traute, Renata, Asta, and Dora) left Lingfield within three years of their arrival, and Julius and Ervin left for Israel within two to three years of theirs.

The ones who grew up in Lingfield, cared for by Alice, were Denny, Sammy, Sylvia, Tania, and Zdenka, all of whom had come from Terezin; Shana and Esther, who had come from Auschwitz; Charlie, Eva, and Mirjam, who had come from hiding; and Fritz and Hedi, who had come from orphanages. They had many changes to face. A new boy, Peter Wagner, came to live at Lingfield for a time and left for Australia with his mother. Manna Weindling, whose vitality and directness, had so endeared her to the children, left for Israel, a deep loss for many. Gertrud Dann, who had been with the youngest group at Bulldogs Bank, came to take Manna's place; she was a small, middle-aged, energetic woman who could be relied on totally to keep things running smoothly and efficiently. She could also say "No" more readily than Alice, and the fact that she had parents to whom she routinely went home gave her added status in the eyes of some of the children.

In 1950, after Alice had scouted for almost a year, there was a major move—from Lingfield to Isleworth, to a large house closer to town. The move was made to help the children grow up in an environment that was more ordinary, less isolated from the actual world, and nearer to schools and eventual workplaces. Isleworth was also closer to the West London Synagogue, where they attended Sunday School and where they sat as a group during the High Holidays. For those who were receiving therapy, the trip to town was shorter. Out of nostalgia for the old home, the new house in Isleworth was named "Lingfield."

Here the children all had pets. Zdenka took exquisite care of chickens, watching over them, feeding them faithfully, nursing them when they were sick, and when any died, burying them. Denny kept a turtle. Sam had rabbits, Mirjam had her dog Teddy, and Berli had guinea pigs.

The children were growing up. Some were bar mitzvahed or confirmed, in the West London Synagogue. Hedi dreamed of becoming a nurse, Fritz a doctor, and both of going to Israel to join Magda. Sam had fantasies of airplanes and mechanics and of visiting a favorite "auntie" in America. Denny won a competition and hoped to become a concert pianist. Still fascinated with rhymes, Sylvia dreamed of writing songs. Tania talked about being glamorous, while Charles dreamed of the Air Force and faraway places. Mirjam wanted to be an artist. Eva's ambition was to be a hotel manager, and Shana's to be a teacher. Esther wanted to be a mother and Zdenka wanted to go to America and become a florist. Berli dreamed of being a policeman.

Then Sam got the exciting letter that his mother was in America, and that she wanted him. Zdenka received the first official word of her mother's death. The shock sent her screaming through the house. Later the word of her father's death came shrouded in doubt; there *was* a Pavel Husserl who had been deported to Poland's Lodge Ghetto and died there, but it was not certain that this was the same Pavel Husserl who was her father.

Alice tried to steady the children in the crises that growing up brought. Hers was the task of counsel and comfort in plans for each day and in plans for each life. She was there to be rejected in the struggle for the growing child's independence, to be the ever-present guardian, constant and constantly accessible. She had help from Sophie, who fed the children so well, made few demands on them, and whose kitchen was a haven. She had help from Gertrud Dann, and support from the Committee. And there was Anna Freud, who could be consulted. But Alice had the sole daily responsibility for raising the children whose lives had thus far been so painful.

What became of these extraordinary children? What do they remember of Lingfield and of the bitter time before? How do they view Alice and their upbringing? And what do they have to teach us? To answer these questions I set out to find as many of them as I could. Four years of travel, one hundred and fifteen thousand miles, and more than one hundred reels of tape later, the twenty-four interviews that follow speak for themselves. Their voices stir us to expand our understanding of human resourcefulness. These child survivors speak to us of the indestructibility of the yearning for love, of the tenacity of hope, and above all—through their inspiring strength and humanity—of human resilience.

Alice Goldberger at fifty, 1947 (*courtesy of ERICA, 12 Forty Close, Wembley Park, Middlesex, England*).

Right: Appeal for funds, May 1945
(Jewish Chronicle, *London*).

Left: Gadi Jacobsen handed out of R.A.F. bomber, August 15, 1945 (*courtesy* Journal of the '45 Aid Society, Thirtieth Anniversary of our Liberation, *London, May 1945*).

The older boys arrive, August 15, 1945 (*courtesy* Journal of the '45 Aid Society, Thirtieth Anniversary of our Liberation, *London, May 1945*).

Above: The toddlers from Terezin Concentration Camp in the Windermere Reception Camp, September 1945. *Left to right:* Jack Spiegel, Gadi Jacobsen, Bella Rosenthal, Berli Baruch, Leah Rovelski, teacher, unknown child, Judith Auerbach *(courtesy* Pictorial Press, *London).*

Below: The toddlers in Bulldogs Bank, December 1945. *Left to right:* Bella Rosenthal, Gadi Jacobsen, Judith Auerbach, Jack Spiegel, Berli Baruch, Leah Rovelski *(courtesy of Godfrey Jacobsen).*

Above: The toddlers in Bulldogs Bank, 1946. *Clockwise from left:* Judith Auerbach, Bella Rosenthal, Jack Spiegel, Berli Baruch, Gadi Jacobsen *(courtesy of Godfrey Jacobsen)*.

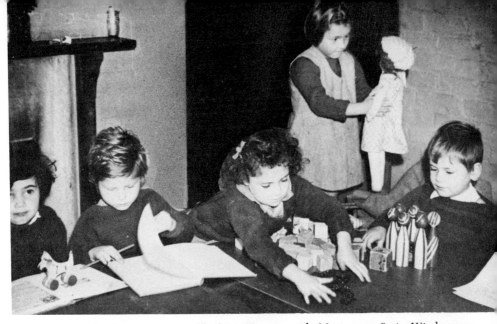

The four-to-six-year-olds from Terezin with Marta, age 9, in Windermere Reception Camp. *Left to right:* Sylvia Gruener, Tania Muench, Zdenka Husserl, Marta Vindfogel, Sammy Schwartz (*photo given to Alice Goldberger by photographer for HEUTE, American Armed Services Information Services Branch, U. S. Army*).

The children with the big girls in Lingfield. *Left to right:* Sammy Schwartz, Denny Muench, Esther Traubova, Fritz Friedman, Asta Berlowitz, Sylvia Gruener, Tania Muench, Traute Lossau, Judith Stern, Shana Traubova, Hedi Friedman, Magda Liberman, Eva Folkmann, Renata Strauss, Judith Singer,

Weir Courteney, Sir Benjamin Drage's estate in Lingfield, Surrey *(courtesy of Alice Goldberger)*.

Marta Vindfogel, Lilliana Bucci, unknown, Andra Bucci, Milly Schwacht, and Mirjam Stern *(H. Connold, photographer; courtesy of Malcolm Powell, E. Grinstead, England)*.

Esther Traubova is given a birthday, April 1, 1946. Alice in front of window, Esther, Hedi Friedman, Fritz Friedman, *(courtesy of ERICA, 12 Party Close, Wembley Park, Middlesex, England).*

Right: Esther Traubova *(courtesy of ERICA, 12 Party Close, Wembley Park, Middlesex, England).*

Above: First summer in England, 1946. *Front, left to right:* Fritz Friedman, Tania Muench, Sylvia Gruener, Mirjam Stern, Andra Bucci, Zdenka Husserl, Lilliana Bucci, Hedi Friedman, Judith Singer, and Esther Traubova. *Back, left to right:* Berli Baruch, Shana Traubova, and Sammy Schwartz. *(H. Connold, photographer; courtesy of Malcolm Powell, E. Grinstead, England).*

Left below: Gertrud Dann and Berli Baruch at Lingfield (*courtesy of ERICA, 12 Forty Close, Wembley Park, Middlesex, England*).

Below: Manna Friedman teaches Israeli dancing. *Left to right:* Shana Traubova, Manna, Sylvia Gruener, helper, Julius Hamburger, Hedi Friedman, Berli Baruch (*courtesy of ERICA, 12 Forty Close, Wembley Park, Middlesex, England*).

They Came in Agony from Belsen . . . to Forget

THIS story is all about children . . . anybody's children . . . most of them nobody's children. Sixteen of them came to Britain from the Belsen horror camp, some nameless, all speaking strange languages, all afraid of the world.

In a lovely Surrey village they are learning to live again, learning to live our way in freedom. These pictures by Malcolm McNeill tell a story of which all of us can feel proud.

Free!

THEY have lost everything—their parents, their homes, their little brothers and sisters, but in Britain they have won back something they thought they had lost for good. Freedom of spirit is theirs again—and this picture of the little waifs running out of school breathes this spirit that all of us hold dear. They will soon be ready to take their places again with all the lively youngsters of the world to whom the future belongs.

FROM FEAR . . . TO SMILES

THE battle against the memory of the past in a child's mind is a difficult one. Terrors cannot be forgotten as easily as broken toys.

With eleven-year-old Maria success is coming slowly. It took two visits before she would face our camera unafraid.

Sir Benjamin Drage had a dog all the children learned to play with—except Maria. She shrunk away. The Nazis used dogs to track down her parents.

Report in the *London Sunday Pictorial* in which it was assumed that all the children came from Belsen (London Sunday Pictorial, *February 24, 1946*).

Fritz Friedman, Magda Liberman, and Hedi Friedman on arrival (*courtesy of Alice Goldberger*).

Fritz Friedman, Magda Liberman, and Hedi Friedman one year after arrival (*courtesy of Alice Goldberger*).

Sammy Schwartz, Mirjam Stern, Charles Kessler, Shana Traubova, and Sylvia Gruener watch Berli Baruch fight *(photo by Howard Byrne from "They Learn to be Children Again,"* John Bull *[London] October 9, 1948).*

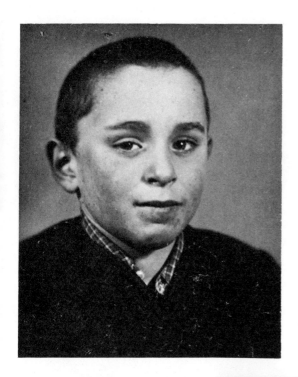

Above: Ervin Bogner on arrival (*from The Illustrated, "Four Years after the Belsen Story," September 10, 1949*).

Right: Ervin Bogner four years after arrival (*from The Illustrated "Four Years after the Belsen Story," September 10, 1949*).

Opening care packages from the American Foster Parents' Plan. *Front, clockwise from left:* Sammy Schwartz, Hedi Friedman, Fritz Friedman, Esther Traubova, Tania Muench, Zdenka Husserl, Mirjam Stern, Julius Hamburger, Denny Muench. *Back, left to right:* unknown, Shana Traubova, Sylvia Gruener, Berli Baruch *(courtesy of Alice Goldberger).*

PART TWO

The following chapters are based on verbatim tapescripts. It is understood that when adults recall events and persons from their childhood, the truth is necessarily subjective. The author cannot, of course, attest to the accuracy of all recollections, but she does attest to their importance in the portraits of these survivors.

From Terezin to Bulldogs Bank
to Lingfield: The Toddlers

(GADI) GODFREY JACOBSEN

Green Harbor, New York June 1979

I waited for him in the dim dining room of the airport motel, its red and black vinyl and Formica intended to look like a medieval inn. I was reminded of the authentically medieval appearance of Terezin —the barren concentration camp nursery in which the man I was about to meet, now thirty-six, had spent the first three years of his life. The tiny child in the photograph being handed out of the RAF bomber on arrival in England had been Gadi.

The late afternoon sunlight silhouetted his small form as he entered the dark room. He saw me wave, and as he walked over, details emerged from shadow: reddish hair, pale, freckled skin, a high forehead and small nose, anxious, dark brown eyes, strangely without eyebrows. His handshake was cautious.

He consented only to tea; Christel had already served dinner, he said. He had a special diet, now, and turned in early these days. Sitting far back in his chair, as if to place maximum distance between us, he was alert and seemed ready to leave at any moment. We talked about teaching school for a while, gaining surer footing with each other. Finally, he lit a cigarette and took off his jacket.

"Are you a psychoanalyst?" he asked.

"No, I'm not."

"I don't like psychoanalysts," he stated flatly. "They ask too many question."

"Sounds like you've had experience with that?"

"My aunt was a psychoanalyst. She was always prying, prodding and trying to get in. I hated it." Still, it turned out that he had nursed this aunt the previous year when she had been dying. He had her flown

47

up in a hospital plane from New York, and he and Christel took care
of her until the end, he said, just as they had done six months before
that with his father.

"Is Christel your wife?"

"Oh, no. She was my father's nurse for seventeen years. Worked for
him in his office, then when he got a stroke she moved in to help me
take care of him."

"It seems you're a loyal kind of person," I said. "First you cared for
your father, then your aunt."

"I suppose," he considered it. "I don't make a lot of changes. I've
been teaching in the high school eleven years. Other teachers are
looking for greener pastures, but I' like it where I am. Been in this
town since I came here as a child."

He offered to show me around while it was still light.

His black Mercedes was immaculate. He put on driving gloves and
soon we were quietly cruising between velvet green lawns. He pointed
out his first school and the house he had first come to when he was
four and lived in for the next thirty years. It housed his late father's
medical offices and their living quarters. He would have gone on
living there, but when his father got sick it was too hard for Christel to
run up and down the stairs all the time.

"So one afternoon I went out and did it. Bought a new ranch-style
house. Came home and said, 'Christel, I did it.' It was much easier for
her." He smiled a little.

"Were you close with your father?"

"I was much closer to my mother than I was to my father until I
finished high school. My father was very busy. He wanted me to
become a doctor. He gave me an old doctor's bag, and I had to go on
all the house calls with him, and I suppose it was that, sitting in the
cold car . . . Well, I didn't like that and there was a lot of work
involved . . . so I didn't want to, *never* wanted to become a doctor but
he always wanted me to." He sounded wistful. "You see, his attitude
had always been, unless you were a doctor you were a nobody. But
then when I became a teacher," he laughed quietly, "then he thought,
well, teachers are pretty good too. I think he was very proud of that.
After my mother died and after I came out of college, I became very
much closer to my father. I went to private school all my life, which I
don't think was such a great idea." He paused and then added, as if to
justify something, "Well, when they sent me away was when my
mother had cancer; that was what my mother's big concern was."

"How old were you then?"

"Fourteen to fifteen. She knew she had terminal cancer and," he gulped, "they didn't want me to witness that. It was lung cancer and she'd already had one leg, I think, amputated. So I went to a Quaker boarding school. I never liked it."

"What didn't you like?"

"I didn't like being away. . . . And it was a different group of kids. I didn't have that much in common with them. They were more New York City kids, and I was upstate New York."

"What's the difference?"

"Different things were important to them. Society was much more important, and that never interested me."

I asked him what his first memory was. It was of getting lost in Shannon airport when he was on his way, alone with his teddy bear, from England to America to be adopted. "The stewardesses finding me. There's a picture of me published in the local paper when I arrived. Do you care to see it?" He spun the car around responsively and drove to a newer part of town.

Christel, fiftyish, and warmly attractive, greeted me in her German accent.

"They'll get sane eventually," he promised paternally at the yapping puppies. "Right now they only chew and bark. Down, Katinka!" He tried to sound stern.

The living room in which we sat contained fine oriental vases and works of art. Books lined the shelves.

"My aunt arranged my adoption. Somehow Anna Freud had written an article ["An Experiment in Group Upbringing"] about the effects [of life in the concentration camps] on the children—which, by the way, my aunt gave me to read when I was older."

"What was your reaction?"

"Oh, I knew immediately which one I was."

"By the birth date?"

"No, I figured I was the bright one!" he laughed rakishly. "Well, Anna Freud and my aunt were very close, and that's how they got me chosen. In fact, downstairs somewhere I've got pictures which they sent of the children and myself before I arrived. I even have my original alien card. I always carry it. I don't know why." He smiled sheepishly as he dug it out of his wallet. "It's an immigration card, and I always carry it." He handed me the card, which bore the picture of him as a little boy.

"My mother came to meet me when I arrived in New York."

"Had you ever seen her before?"

"No."

"And you were how old?"

"Four and a half, and then my mother took me here by train, . . . must have been an eight- or nine-hour train ride. Don't remember much of that. My mother told me that at the beginning of the train ride I was at one end of the car and she was at the other, and she worked her way closer to me." He chuckled.

"Yeah, and then she was sitting next to me. When I saw my room I said, 'Is this all mine?' and my father said, 'Yes.' The room had cowboy curtains. And I still have my original dresser which I had when I first came. And my toy chest, still have that. I still use my dresser. They brought the kids down the street to be friends, to introduce me. And," he paused to think. "Probably I was too young, uh . . . I had a lot of trouble adjusting, to school. I threw temper tantrums. I locked myself in the bathroom from time to time. Got into trouble. Once," he sighed, "I was told I ended up going to the bathroom, locking myself in and they couldn't get me out. They had to send for my father." Silently, he pondered something out of reach.

Christel brought tea. "I heard the story," she said, "of how he came here. How he behaved in the beginning, trying to escape."

"Yeah," he chuckled. "I tried to walk back to England."

"He packed his suitcase to go back. Mrs. Jacobsen was smart enough to let him go. He went to the corner and had second thoughts, then came home again. He was the best son in the world. His father came first and then everything else, his schoolwork, college."

"How far did you go in college, and what do you teach?" I asked.

"I have a master's degree in education, and I teach history. Political history is actually my main interest, but I teach what is known as world culture in the ninth grade."

"What do you cover there?"

"It's a whole program. You ask questions like: what is the origin of man? You talk about the divine theory, the evolutionary theory—even get into some things like the outer space theory. Then we talk about values: what are they, first of all? How do people develop values? How do values change?"

"What are your predominant values?"

"Privacy. Individualism. Education. Creature comforts. Art. I enjoy that, I've grown up with it. I guess human rights is a great one. I suppose the Kennedy years influenced me a great deal. Idealism. I was still a liberal in the sixties.

"But now, of course, I've regressed as I've gotten older." He laughed. "I suspect maybe riots have influenced me, and I think civil rights are fine, but maybe people on an individual basis deserve individual rights. I find a lot of people now, especially kids, demand that they get grades, and I always remember an incident: a young man came to me and he said to me in class 'You gave me a D because I'm black, and I said to him, 'You're probably right,' I said. 'If you'd been white I'd probably have failed you.' I always remember that.

"I've seen a lot of overanalyzing of things in school, where you psychoanalyze the kids, why they're misbehaving and all that. That might explain why, but it still doesn't bring about acceptable behavior. One has to face life as it is, and you still have to belong to society. That's very important."

"That's a fascinating point of view for somebody who grew up in a home with a psychoanalyst close by," I commented.

"My mother and my aunt didn't get along. My aunt had no family and wanted to be involved in every decision about me. I'm not in favor of psychoanalysis. I think we overanalyze too much. Like in the papers you see a person who for murder pleads temporary insanity. Of course, someone who kills is slightly off. Antisocial. But it doesn't excuse it, whatever the action was."

"Was there any religious orientation in your home?"

"I never saw any Jewish holiday. My father never celebrated it, and I now celebrate Thanksgiving, Christmas, and New Year's. That's about it. And birthdays. Once when I was very young my mother took me to a Saturday class in a synagogue, I think. I must have been about ten, and I didn't like it. In one class the teacher said, 'Now we will talk about how people have been prejudiced to Jews and how you've experienced it,' and I objected to that. It may be true. But I cannot believe that here in Green Harbor they've experienced it at that age! So I said 'that's nonsense,' and I wished not to go back again. My parents respected that.

"I think the only time I've been in a temple was to watch someone have a bar mitzvah. Two bar mitzvahs I saw, and a memorial service for a friend, and that was it." He appeared to be struggling with something. "I reject certain things about the Jewish religion that cause certain problems for themselves."

"Such as?"

"Racial identity. Judaism is not a race, it's a religion which has its beliefs. But you're isolating yourself, marrying within the Jewish religion, living within the Jewish community. I find that that sets people up to have what you had in Germany. Generally whenever you are different—make a point of being *different* to the entire group —you let yourself in for being abused. That's why I reject it. I reject it because of what happened in Germany. Especially around here in this area, Jews are very self-conscious of their Judaism. My father never went to temple. Never. He knew the Bible as a scholarly piece of work. He went out of his way not to be a Jew, and I suspect that carried over to me. And I suspect that having to leave Germany and the war made him very much more sensitive to what people were saying about him, so he went out of his way to become more acceptable, and I suppose that's what I've done too. Any time a group of people separate themselves, you know, a Holocaust type of thing could easily occur."

"How do you regard yourself?"

"I regard myself as an American who has . . . I haven't really figured out my religion yet, what I believe in. I suspect that maybe later in life I will. But I certainly won't make that the dominant factor of everything. Well, it can get to the point of ridiculousness: having the wife walk ten paces behind the husband. Very Orthodox Jews do this."

"I think you have this mixed up with old Japan," I laughed.

"No, no, no. It's true!"

"Really?"

"No, no! It's a fact! It's the *true* Orthodox way. I still remember one of my father's patients. His wife walked behind him that way. My father asked why, and he said that's what women are expected to do. That's their position. I don't reject it for others. But I warn people, be careful of that."

"Of what?"

"Of isolating yourself. It's always a danger. What was it in Illinois, the Nazis—I forget the name of that town."

"Skokie?"

"Yeah, the Nazis chose to march through the Jewish section of the city. Well, to me it's too bad there *was* a Jewish section. Isolation breeds lack of understanding. Lack of understanding leads to prejudice. America is a great place for breaking that cycle: so many different people from so many different backgrounds. I think most people here consider themselves American, and then they pick out their own individual differences. One of them might be religion. But it shouldn't be such a dominant thing. . . . I certainly am not a Zionist. I think Israel's a great place for people who've experienced a sense of insecurity, who are looking for a sense of security. Many people here, I suspect, feel that what happened in Spain, what happened in Germany, might happen in the United States. I suspect it *might* as long as people isolate themselves. When I teach the Holocaust I always give them a run-down on my own experience."

"What do you tell them?"

"I tell them I was a victim of the Holocaust. That when I was three weeks old I was left on a park bench, picked up by a nun, taken to a convent, and then picked up by the Nazis and put in a concentration camp, Theresienstadt, till I was about three. That area was liberated by the Soviet Union, and a group of children was there, the British made some kind of deal to take them. Then I was there in an orphanage in England till I was adopted when I was four and a half. After that I show them the movie *Night and Fog*. It's not a good movie. I've only watched it once. I don't need that. It's a little bit too descriptive. Kids find it very shocking. I suppose that if you've shaken them, you have taught the Holocaust."

"Is that a sardonic smile?"

"No, it gets the point across, and then you don't have to say anything."

"Have you ever been back to Europe?"

"Yes, 1966. I had just graduated from college. My father was in Switzerland. And I went to Berlin, where Christel's aunt is. Took a trip to East Berlin. It was very nice. I enjoyed it. I don't speak German, so it makes it very difficult to ask questions."

"Did your natural parents come from East Berlin originally?"

"Yes, what is now East Berlin, as much as I understand. They may have come from somewhere else, been in transit. I think my father was nineteen or twenty, from the information that I've gotten on my original parents. His name was Heinrich and hers was Ingrid. Ingrid Froma Zettlin Joseph. The last name is not a German name. Scandinavian name, I think. That's as much as I know."

"What did you do in East Berlin?"

"Just looked around. I was curious. The street is still there, typical East German. Not much. I don't remember it anymore. Just went to satisfy my curiosity."

"Was it upsetting?"

"No, no, no. I wasn't upset. Someday I may do something through the German Embassy. . . . I might want to go back to Berlin. There may be some living relatives there. But right now I'm tied up with my illness, chemotherapy treatment. I get tired easily. Luckily, the surgeon is convinced he got it all, so the chemotherapy is preventive. I'll know in about nine months. Basically I don't like to talk about it because it gets me tense. People at school think they're being kind. . . . I'd just as soon not talk about it. Christel helps a lot. Gives me my medication. Takes care of me."

"You're due for some better years," I wished. "What would you like to do if you could?"

"Travel. Europe, around this country, Grand Canyon, maybe Canada. . . ."

Back in the car, on the way back to the motel, he asked, "Can you imagine what it must have been like for Christel in Germany during the war? Two brothers in the army, one got killed on the Russian front. She was terrified of the Russian army: afraid of being raped, looted, overrun. She says she didn't know anything about what was going on." He looked at me directly, challenging me.

As we said goodnight, I asked what the inscription was on the gold chain around his neck.

"Jake," he said. "Christel gave it to me. That's what they all call me at school." So the Jacobsohn of Germany, Nordicized in the new world by his father to Jacobsen, was still "Jake." He fingered it as he spoke, then looked down at it, pleased.

The note from Christel a year later was brief:

"I regret to inform you that Godfrey Jacobsen passed away on Sunday, August 10, 1980. He had a third cancer operation in June which was unsuccessful and the end came very quickly."

BELLA ROSENTHAL

London, June 1979

She smiled broadly as she pulled up in her red sedan. Radiating vitality from her shining auburn ringlets to her brisk stride, she opened the car door for me. As we drove she told me of her husband's recent serious surgery. He was home now, convalescing. "He knows all about my past," she said matter-of-factly, "but my children don't, and I don't want them to, so please don't say anything to them." Then she asked, "Can I introduce you as 'just a friend' from America?" Her smile was irresistible. "Actually, I have some good memories of my past, from before I was adopted."

"But you can't tell your children?"

"See, my main reluctance to tell my children is that my parents have been reluctant to admit I'm adopted. They like to keep up this front. And as a child I wanted to rebel very much against this, because I wanted to be adopted for myself and not sort of pretend." She paused, and then burst out laughing.

"I must have been a terrible child to bring up! I'm sure I was! I don't want to spoil the illusion for my children, because they [her adoptive parents] *are* the grandparents, and if the children feel they're not, then a certain affection might be lost. And that would be unfair," she said thoughtfully, "because I haven't been a very good daughter."

She turned off the main road to a short private drive and pulled up in front of a country house just as its door was flung wide to sounds of welcome. Two children and a dog stood in the doorway. Bella's husband stood behind them, his arms around them in a sheltering gesture.

We sat in the comfortable library. After a brief conversation about school, Bella dispatched the children to do homework, while her husband David and I talked. The son of a religious family, at one time he had wanted to be a rabbi. Now his middle-management job was in jeopardy because of his health. "Still, I thank God I'm coming along so well. I assume my wife told you about the surgery. She's been the Rock of Gibraltar through it all. She's taken full-time work, and it hasn't been easy, I needn't tell you." His dark eyes are eloquent.

"What hasn't been easy?" Bella asked, returning.

"The surgery and all that followed," he said.

"Mmm, that's true," she said soberly as she sat beside him on the couch. "But," she brightened, "it hasn't been all that bad. We've managed." She turned to me and said gravely, "I think we can come through anything together. Absolutely." David's voice was kind as he rose a few minutes later. "I'll see that you're not disturbed; I'm sure you have much to talk about."

"What makes you think you were such a bad daughter?" I asked when he'd gone.

"Once I realized they weren't my real parents, I rejected them. I was a very determined child, matured very young emotionally, and I had a lot of problems and I admit it. I'm sure most of them were from my end. Now I'd like to see them get some pleasure out of their grandchildren that they probably didn't get out of me. . . . I don't want the children to feel at a greater distance from their grandparents. I want there to be a certain loyalty."

"Do you think blood matters that much to children?"

"It made a difference to me!" She bristled. "That's all I can say. I was never particularly close to them, though I accepted them quite naturally as parents. But as soon as I found out that they really weren't, then they had no real authority over me.

"I went to live with them when I was five or so, I don't remember much about Lingfield House." Her body tensed, and her voice began to sound strained. "I think I was about three when I came over from

Germany, so I must have been about a year at Bulldogs Bank and a year at Lingfield. So I don't remember much: the house and Alice, a little bit—not a lot because I was very much the little one." She laughed nervously. "I was always excluded from the lessons, I just had to play about—kill time. Alice was much involved with the older girls, I remember. It may not have been so, but this is the impression that one had. In fact, later on in years, when I met her, I hardly recognized her."

"Do you remember any one person responsible for you?"

"No. There was just a group of us. The younger ones. I don't remember any one person." Her voice grew tighter. "We were in a house, it was like one big family, really. They would help us. I seem to remember I'd spend a lot of time in the kitchen." Then she winked at me, laughing. "I remember Sophie in the kitchen at Lingfield," she said. "We all had a little patch of garden which we cultivated ourselves. Mine never seemed to grow anything, and everybody else's looked fantastic. I suppose being the youngest I did everything wrong, nothing grew.

"From time to time, one or two of us were obviously adopted, though one wasn't too aware of what was happening." She seemed strained again, but she went on. "One day they were there and the next day they were gone.

"I remember we were always on the first floor, within shouting distance of Sophie. Most of my memories were very happy, I can't remember very many incidences that were unhappy. I think I was a rather naughty little girl, got into all sorts of mischief.

"When we were brought over, I suppose we were undernourished and we were getting this malt, which is sweet and supposed to fatten you, build you up. It's all sticky, like honey. Of course I loved it, but you were only allowed a spoonful a day. So I found out where it was kept, and one night with an accomplice, I think Berli, maybe Denny, we raided it.

"I remember being very frightened of dogs at that time, and the people in the next house had a very yappy terrier. One day in the garden, I remember having to hide under the table. I probably upset the whole picnic!" Again, she laughed.

"Whom did you run to in a situation like that?"

"I don't think I ever did run to anybody. See, I think my way was to hide under the table. No, I think I was very self-sufficient even in those days. I seem to remember being a leader, I think it just happened that way. I used to be able to commandeer another child to lift me up to something I couldn't reach. I don't remember ever running to anybody.

"I remember a bit of Bulldogs Bank. One of the women there was always using a very old-fashioned sewing machine. I was fascinated. And there was a wooden horse in the garden which I was much too tiny to jump on.

"There was a younger boy who came, and who I thought was very inferior because he still wet his bed. Jack was his name. He must have been a year younger than I—very inferior," she said, with mock haughtiness. "We didn't wet or have bottles or nappies or anything like that.

"Berli was there. Funny, I don't recall any of the girls.

"We were all given red suits one year, woolen all-in-ones that zipped up and of course, with my red hair I was the only one who had a green one, and of course, I wanted a red one." She laughed nervously. "Funny how you remember all the little things." She paused and said gravely, "It was a very hard winter."

"I have a memory of going to spend a week or a weekend with a woman. It wasn't my adopted mother. It was somebody else. I can't place where that would have been. Probably it was here in England, but I'm not sure."

"The name Bulldogs Bank, is this something you've remembered, or been told?"

"Yes, I remembered; well it's such a lovely name, isn't it? I think I possibly remember the journey there, getting on a bus. But nothing before, just a vague impression of oppression and heat and being crammed in a tight place and hating the noise. I didn't know at that stage that it was a plane, but obviously that's what it was.

"I remember my last birthday party at Lingfield House. I think everybody knew I was going. I had a big birthday cake with five candles on it, and we danced around. Of course I hadn't realized that it was my last party there." She sounded wistful. "Then it was all cut. Oh, Denny came occasionally, because my mother was his 'aunt.' But that was quit. I felt he was a bit resentful that I'd been adopted and he'd been left. It was all a bit awkward. In fact, later on they usually invited him when I wasn't around. So really, the connections were cut.

"Incidentally, they changed my name. They didn't want any reference made to my past. That always annoyed them. I remember deciding what my name was going to be in the car when they drove me away from Lingfield. They said, 'Now we're going to choose a name for you,' and we discussed it in the car. After that, I remem-

bered changing it, but I never remembered what I was called before.
I never remembered it being used."

"Do you know now what it was?"

"Bella Rosenthal, that's what they told me."

She sighed deeply. "It's pretty strange, isn't it? All during childhood and adolescence I wanted to know a lot about my background.
My parents were very reluctant to tell me anything or to allow me any
contact with family that was living, which I gather I have. And up to
the age of about twelve, I was very anxious to find out, and it caused a
lot of friction. My only real thing was to get away to boarding school
because I wasn't getting any answers. So from that time on, really, I'd
virtually left home because by the time I finished boarding school, I
went to Paris for a year. Then I got a job, took a flat, became
completely independent. Eventually I got married and all these
problems don't matter so much anymore. And I feel that my
[natural] family really could have gotten in touch with me if they'd
really wanted to. There was a letter once to my adoptive parents. I'm
sure they know where I went. I know they did; any compensation
money went to that family; I think it went to my mother's sister who
lives in Germany. I'm sure they could have gotten in touch with me if
they'd wanted to.

"I've made a new life for myself here with my husband and family.
No, it doesn't matter so much to know now. Perhaps when my
adoptive parents die I might take it up. I suppose I do feel rather
guilty. I did give them a rough fight as a child. I'm sure they thought
they were being model parents: I never wanted for anything. I'm sure
they couldn't understand why I behaved so badly. They gave me all
they could. They wanted a docile child to do this and that, and I
didn't behave suitably.

"I remember there was one incident that must have been shortly
after I went there. I think I took two sweets instead of one, and from
then on I felt they thought I was a liar and deceitful.

"I felt I was struggling for the right to be myself all of the way. I
remember even at sixteen, reminding my mother, 'I'm grown up, you
can't tell me what to do anymore.' I think I must have been like a hot
potato to them. They didn't know what to do with me.

"It confused me that they wanted me to make a success, make a
good marriage, yet when I graduated boarding school, they didn't
introduce me to the sort of society they would wish me to enter."

"Why do you suppose that was?"

"I suppose they always felt a bit ashamed of me. I'd put on a lot of
weight, and I was awkward as far as social graces were concerned. I

was far too direct. There were times when I wished they would have sent me to finishing school to help me overcome some of these things, even to learn to put on makeup. The maid showed me how to put on makeup eventually. I went through all those teenage problems on my own, learning the hard way, painfully, as one always does as a teenager.

"Still, I know they tried to raise me as best they could. That is why I feel I owe my adoptive parents the friendship of my children that they didn't have from me—for what they've done for me. I want it to be as perfect as they can make it between them.

"The other reason I don't wish my children to know I'm adopted is that they'd find out what happened in Germany. I suppose there are two schools of thought on this. One is that Germany should never be forgotten, there is a lesson to be learned—which I feel strongly, obviously, in my circumstances, but I also feel that in the main there should not be too much bitterness because the new German generations cannot be held responsible for the faults of their parents and grandparents. Though I think it should obviously be remembered in history.

"I don't want to give it too personal a touch, because hate is such a terrible thing, and to bring one's children up in hate—I don't want to do that. When they're grown up and their characters are formed and feelings formed, then, well, I don't think they'll bat an eyelid about it, and then I'll tell them why I didn't tell them earlier.

"I don't live day-to-day with the knowledge I'm adopted. About ninety percent of the time I don't even think of it anymore, so it's not a cloud hovering over my head that I'm not telling my children. None of my friends know. My family brushes it under the carpet. It's not a question of hiding it, it's just that it doesn't come up."

"There is a bit of humor in saying your family brushes it under the carpet, but it's not hidden. I have a feeling you're helping them brush."

"I am now, yes, because when I was young I took every opportunity to reveal it. But now I feel I don't want to fight it anymore. What am I fighting? It's a nebulous idea. I'm just myself and what I've made myself." She looked at me.

"You've done a terrific job."

She laughed. "It's been a lot of hard work. But I've learned a lot from my experiences, and I learn all the time."

"What are some of the things you've learned?"

"Well, I suppose basically that the only person you can rely on is yourself. Never to borrow money from anybody—the quickest way to lose a friend. That if you love people enough, they'll love you. That other people matter. And the great wealth of information and interest that people of all kinds have, whether it's the milkman knocking on his rounds or the stray."

"What do you mean by 'stray'?" I interrupted.

"Strays in society. The people who haven't always treaded the straight and narrow path that's expected of them. They're far more interesting than people who live in the same house, on the same street all their lives. Some say, how can you associate with so-and-so? I find they're just fascinating, because they don't follow the normal pattern, and I think you learn to have a look at life that other people don't have. Quite a different view. You see life in 3-D effect. I think that having gone through all this I can sympathize and understand other people better. I can actually put myself in someone else's position, because I've had such varied experiences, and felt so deeply about things. I always feel like I experience things for other people. A lot of people who've been in trouble come to me, and I can spend hours listening."

"Can you also tell others what troubles you?"

"My husband. We have so much in common, and he understands so well I don't really need to talk to anybody else. I always solved things myself.

"Sometimes I think I've missed my calling, I could have been a psychoanalyst. I've done a lot of different things. For a while I did temporary secretarial work, and things were slow. Then one day the agency asked me if I could cook. I said yes. 'There's a canteen that needs a manageress, could you try?' I said yes. They said it's for a hundred people every day. So I took it. Why not? I did it for about three months. I didn't have anything to lose. I'd cooked for large parties at home. I figured the kitchen there must be very well equipped, the saucepans would be enormous, so I figured I'd just put in five times the amount of stuff I'd do at home. There was staff there to wash up. It was largely a matter of organizing people to do things. I think it was a tremendous experience."

"What sort of work are you doing now?"

"I run the financial side of an art gallery. I have a good business sense. I'm learning quite a lot about painting. Also, several times a month I'm called in to do some arbitration work. I've been asked to do some cases having to do with adoption, but I've refused. I think I might be too biased, having seen families where the adoptive parents don't understand the needs of the child. I would then hate to send a child for adoption. If children come from good [group] homes, where they have the companionship of other children, I think sometimes they're better off [there] than being isolated individually into families that don't really know how to cope with them."

"What do you think the alternative problems would be in a children's home?"

"I think in a well-run home, I don't see any problems to it because in a group, you're all in the same boat."

"Do you raise your children any particular way? How do you regard yourself?"

"Well, very Jewish in thought, extremely so. I had a very strong religious feeling at about eighteen. I think that's quite normal. That's how I met my husband. I was training to be a Sunday class teacher. I was very interested in the history from biblical times right through. I feel that having Jewish identity is learning about the history of Judaism and the Jewish people. That way one had a continuity, and I suppose in a way that substituted for my lack of family: the whole Jewish history and race was my family. But one must be careful not to raise one's children too Jewish, because that breeds intolerance and separateness. One has to be friends with everybody. All religions, races, colors—that doesn't matter: it's what they are that matters. I have friends of all kinds."

Before David joined us again, I asked her what name to use for her in this book. She thought for a long time, and then said, "I would not want to hurt my parents by revealing my adoption: use Bella, please."

(BERLI) BERL BARUCH

Newport, New Jersey, July 1979

It was drizzling when my bus pulled into the station. There he sat, looking vulnerable, staring off into space with his hands in his jacket pockets, making no effort to find me.

"Are you Berl?"

He stood up. "Yah, Mum," he said, snapping politely to attention, and offering to carry my briefcase. As he led me to the car, he moved with a sudden swagger. His accent was still English, but there was something else; was it the way he ran words together that made his speech difficult to understand? His voice was deep, with an assertive, staccato quality.

"So you want to know about life in a children's home?" He stared straight ahead at the road.

"Well, okay. I was raised fifteen years there. Right?" He turned to me to check. "Came out of Germany when I was three years old. I went to school in England. You get your breakfast. You get your lunch. You get your dinner. Most times I went to school about eight o'clock. Went on a bicycle. Didn't start school over there till I was seven: first coupla years when I got over there I had a lot of problems. They had me in a hospital over there for a year and a half right away. Polio."

"You must mean Bulldogs Bank?" I recalled his difficulty walking due to malnutrition.

"Yeah."

"Do you remember anything before you came to England?"

"No. Only thing I remember vaguely is about flying on the plane. Crying for about three days. That's all. Miss Goldberger trying to calm me down and I'm mostly upset, you know."

When he said "free" for "three," I realized that all the teeth of his upper jaw were gone. Now I could interpret his speech more easily.

"I didn't know all what's goin' on. It's shortly after the war, and here comes a woman who I didn't know very well then but who I know very well now, and she raises us up the best she could through the Jewish Refugee Fund, or whatever it was. But . . . you know, you cannot give everybody the attention they actually would need, that a real mother would give me. And that's the whole disappointment about being in a children's home myself."

"That's the whole disappointment," I reflected.

"Look, you can have a lot of social problems, or something else like that. You can discuss it with her, but she's never been a mother herself. She might read books and like that, but books are not going to tell you everything you gotta know. Well, anyway, if you live in a children's home most of what you do is learn for yourself. You have to get out in the world, you know. I worked in a farm—well, she sent me to a farm because I was kind of a bad boy for a while."

"When?"

"I was fifteen till I was eighteen."

"What do you think you did that was bad?"

"Well, she said I was uncontrollable." He said this with sadness, looking to me as if to verify whether I, too, believed this was the truth.

"And what do you think?"

"Well, I don't know why. Really, I've seen people a whole lot worse than me. I was a mischievous kind of guy. But I'm a lot different than I was then. You know, when you're a kid you're a kid. But she sent me there for correction, more or less. It was a farm training school, like they have in the States here, you know."

We were pulling up to a suburban ranch house. A large German shepherd dog barked ferociously behind a chain fence as a rotund, dark-haired man in his sixties, Berl's uncle Adolph, pleaded with it in German to be quiet. He shook hands with me; his eyes were arresting in their sadness, accentuated by heavy, down-sloping lids and brows. He took me to the immaculate kitchen where his wife, Ruth, stood at the sink, cutting up a chicken. She avoided eye contact and appeared too absorbed to engage in conversation. She was balding slightly, and something about the tightly drawn quality of her face made me wonder if long malnutrition had distorted an earlier beauty. I remembered that Berli had been crippled by malnutrition when he first arrived at Bulldogs Bank. Was Ruth, too, a concentration camp survivor?

"You'll have dinner with us in about an hour," she said in a heavy German accent.

Berl showed me to his room, where CB equipment predominated. We resumed speaking about his life in England.

"It was a very big place, twenty-seven rooms. Miss Goldberger was the head of the place there. She had Sophie and another woman, I forget her name."

"Gertrud?"

"Yeah, Gertrud. I remember an old car that she had there. She had a 1947, I think it was, Citroën . . . stick shift, an old one. One day I got in, drive right through the garage doors, and I don't think she appreciated it."

"How old were you?"

"About nine or ten. I pulled the throttle, shifted gears. Took it right through the garage doors." There was a kind of pride in his voice.

"You were very mechanically inclined?"

"Yes, and to this day I am. Alice said I had to help pay for the garage doors. I was more or less a mischievous little guy when I was young. Well, I was curious as well, you know what I mean? Well . . . Gertrud locked me into the bathroom and said I couldn't come down for dinner and I got mad, put my fist through the window. She was a bossy woman. . . . Her and I never saw eye to eye. . . . I remember one good time when there was this old tree stump sticking out of the ground, and I stuck my tongue out at her and I started running. I stubbed my toe on it and she tripped over the old tree stump. Today I look at it different. I should of never done it; she coulda gotten hurt."

"Do you remember why she was running after you?"

"No. Oh yeah, it was with the car, when I took the car through the garage door. . . . Like I say I was mischievous. But all kids get into mischief," he continued. "In the house where we used to live, four guys lived in the same room. So us guys go out in the back yard and make bows and arrows and take them up to our room at nighttime, see, screw it to a bird. . . . They were all older than me, Fritz, Sammy, I forget the other one. I must have been the youngest in the whole place, you know? And I was mischievous and I don't know why. . . . But when I got about twelve, thirteen, fourteen, I started calming down quite a bit. Took me awhile." He looked away.

"I used to raise rabbits in the back yard. Rabbits and me. I had a big old one called Butch. So the guy across the street from me said, 'You want to sell me a rabbit?' So I say, 'Yeah.' He told me he was going to keep it as a pet. Next day I came home from school and I say, 'Where's the rabbit?' He says, 'I took it down to the butcher shop.' 'What! wait a minute!' I had the rabbit for about two years already. So I got my bicycle, and I rode down to the butcher shop. And I say 'Did a guy come over here and sell you a rabbit?' 'Yeah,' he says. So I pay the guy and took my rabbit back home. Then I say to the guy, 'Why did you take my rabbit to the butcher shop?' 'Well, I didn't want him,' he says. *'If you didn't want him, then why did you take him?'* " His outcry came from the depths.

"I had white mice as well. That's when Miss Goldberger had a fit. I started off with two, and then there were about a hundred fifty of them. I didn't realize that the two I had was a male and a female. In a year they can breed six thousand. Next thing we know, they're all over the place. So she got a coupla cats. And a dog as well. Dog chased the cat. Cat chased the mice. Finally I let the cat get both of them, so they couldn't breed no more. Hang them up in the air and drop them down to the ground. The mouse still bit me, but the cat got him. The young ones somehow didn't make it."

But *you* did, I thought. I saw his need to participate in a repetitive litany of successive disasters of which he alone was master.

"I must have been the most rowdy one they ever had in their whole life over there. She'll probably tell you what a terror I am. I have no remorse for what I did, really. But I do appreciate what she's done for me. But with eighteen people that woman did one heck of a job, believe me. You can't give her no discredit for that. She tried the best she could, she definitely accomplished something, the way we came out of it.

"Even in school I got disciplined a lot of times. I was in school about eight years, and I must have been caned eight, nine times. I got out of school when I was about fifteen, and then I went to training school. More or less, I think she called it a reform school. But I didn't."

"Who called it a reform school?"

"Miss Goldberger. She told me I was getting pretty uncontrollable. She said I always did like farming, right? So she figured maybe I'd be getting good training in farming, maybe getting a little bit of education and getting out of some of my mischievous ways. So I was forced to go, you know. She used to come down about twice a month, and I'd come home for maybe the summer. I think that farm school definitely did me a lot of good. I learned more about the country and ways of life."

"Did she call it a reform school?"

"Well, she called it a training school where young guys who don't have the capability of doing ordinarily get a little bit more training for themselves in the social life."

"How many boys were there?"

"Four hundred fifty. I used to be over in the guy's house cleaning floors and everything else like that. You get your regular meals there. Sit down and they give you a cup of coffee or tea. Nighttime you go back to your own bungalow, on the weekends you go wherever you want to go. There were no guards there to hold you back. You could run away and they couldn't do nothin' to you.

"I learned a lot about machinery. About tractors. I mean I can drive anything that comes along now. Even with me being in National Guard now, I can drive any heavy vehicle they got.

"I always liked to take things apart and see how they worked. Miss Goldberger had a vacuum cleaner that worked, and I took the whole thing apart and when it came down to put it back together, I had no way to get it back together. It cost me for a new vacuum cleaner in the end.

"When I was nine I played around with electricity. Wasn't afraid of nothin'. Used to get a hold of 110. . . . What I used to do is get two wires in there. Put my finger on two wires and person come back and you go like that. They get a kick. You don't get nothin'."

"You wouldn't feel anything?"

"No." His face was blank.

There was silent formality around the table which amplified the sounds of plates being passed and of Adolph's sighing.

"How you know Miss Goldberger?" Adolph asked, appraising me with a cool look. He sat directly opposite me, sighing so frequently that it seemed part of his normal breathing. I noticed that he, too, had no upper front teeth. I explained my involvement.

"You are born here? American-born?" he asked with disbelief that anyone American-born could be so interested in all this.

"How did you learn that Berl was alive?" I asked.

"Through the *Wiedergutmachung.*"

"Restitution," Ruth translated. "I claimed for my parents and Berli claimed for his grandfather and grandmother. And *they were my parents!*" she cried out.

"The lawyer wrote a letter," Adolph sighed. "There's a boy living, from her sister."

"When I got the letter, six weeks later I flew to England," Ruth said. "Miss Goldberger wrote that Berl is a nice boy but I shouldn't expect an eighteen-year-old boy. So I thought whatever it is, it's my sister's boy. When I went to England, I saw he has a long, small hand."

"Yes, your father's hand! Oh my God, yes." Adolph sighed.

"My sister and my father had this hand. When I saw him I said, 'You *are* our boy, you *are* our boy!' And I took him in my heart right away. Look, we treat him as *our* boy! We are the parents! But when I was there, I couldn't get him—he has to go by quota. So I went to the American consul and I talk to them, and I explain them everything. And Berl was saying, 'Take me to America. Take me to America.' And I say, 'If I can, I'm going to take you.' 'Take me to America,' he says."

"Good land." Berl injected.

"But he got special quota; I was [there] in October and the consul promised Berl will be for Christmas here. He was eighteen years old then, and he looked like a boy nine or ten years."

"One day before Christmas, he comes." Adolph said. "He wants everything what is on this earth. And we bought it."

"Yes," Ruth said. "Toys. Any kind of toys. He built ships. Such ships! Autos, a bicycle and television in his room, a movie outfit! What didn't he have?" At each enumeration by Ruth, a contrapuntal sigh was heard from Adolph. "And then he wants to go bowling!" she continued.

"And there she was—his wife," Adolph recounted with disgust. I listened as Adolph and Ruth recounted Berl's long, troubled marriage and its ending, years later, in a bitter court battle. Berl was silent. After a particularly long, bitter sigh, Adolph said, "Sarah, we went through plenty. But I don't want to talk, I'm glad my boy is here."

"We are glad now he's here," Ruth confirmed. "And I will tell you, he's not *shuldish.*"

"He's not guilty!" Adolph translated.

"Zorgt nit. Ich farshteh altz. Mein tateh iz geven a yiddisher lehrer. Fun vanen kumt ihr?" I addressed Adolph.

He smiled, repeating my question. "Where I come from? Oh ho! Ich kum fun lagern. Dortn lang gezesn. [I come from concentration camps. Sat there a long time!]"

The gate of mistrust had been crushed, and Ruth rose. "Come on, Sarah, come on! You don't eat anything! Come!" She brought the platter of chicken to my plate, and motioned Berl to pass me the vegetable bowl.

Then Adolph urged, "It's from our own garden, Sarah, this lettuce. Take! Take! In *lagern* we only speak *mame loshn* [mother tongue]." He shared this bond with me.

"Wait! Wait a minute!" Ruth was shouting authoritatively. "First you let her eat, *then* we talk!"

"I was in Riga," Adolph began, but he was interrupted.

"Sarah," she said, "why do you go back this evening? It's too hard to make it in one day. We have place for you. You go back tomorrow, yes?"

"You're taking such good care of me," I said, smiling.

Her eyes narrowed, and her mouth tightened fiercely.

"You speak Yiddish very good." Then she began naming camps. "Riga, Salesbilds, Kaiserwald, Stutthof, Gottendorf . . ." These were the camps they had been in, Adolph and Ruth. Some they had been in together. In Stutthof, Ruth was alone and had seen the Germans pour gasoline all around, preparing to burn them all before the Russians arrived. "Forty-five persons of my family are gone! Forty-five!"

Adolph looked away, mourning with deep, moaning sighs. With trembling hands, Ruth began to clear the table.

When the drizzle ceased, they took me out to the back yard to show me the neat green rows of their vegetable garden.

"We had a garden in Berlin," Ruth said.

"It's so peaceful here," Adolph said. "Peaceful, *ja.*" He enjoyed the moment of contentment.

Their German shepherd, ever alert, barked menacingly at something in the neighbor's yard. Adolph seemed pleased. "I love her," he said passionately. "Good protection."

"Put in two years in the regular army," Berl told me over coffee. "I enlisted in the army in '68. I was a year in the States and a year over there, in Vietnam, from February 21, 1969, to February 1970. A year of it."

"When he came back, he weighted 132 pounds only. His wife didn't want to pick him up." Adolph spoke. "That's the kind she is. . . ."

"Yeah," Berl corroborated, "yeah, she said the best thing you coulda done for me is to get killed in Vietnam! Then she gets the life insurance money, see? . . . I'm a nice guy, and I came up through hard times, being raised the way I was being raised. Then I served my country. I didn't have nothin' to hide about serving my country. And I had to go through all this with my wife and everything else. Since I been here serving my country I was under tension all the time, being harassed and humiliated by my wife.

"Now he's going to college. He takes up law enforcement," Ruth said.

"And in the National Guard I've got a responsibility as well. I'm the head of communications in my barracks. I'm also the section chief and commo chief [commander, field telephones, wire, radios]. I'm a sergeant. I teach, too."

"What do you teach?"

"Oh, basic communications."

"And in Vietnam, what did you do?"

"Basically support for the artillery, ammo positions, convoy runs, make sure they get rations. Driving close to ten-ton trucks, fifty-sixty machine guns on top, which was kind of hazardous in Vietnam. But I never did get wounded once. . . .

"When I was in Vietnam I had a refrigerator, a fan, and a TV. Went down to the Tan Hep orphanage, rest of the kids who didn't have no mother or father. . . . I wrote to Mom and Pop, ya got any old clothes for these kids, send them to me. I figured I didn't have no mother and father to guide me, right? So I figure these kids could use some help, right? She sent me some packages when I was there." He nodded to Ruth. "I wrote to my mother, send me anything you can get like clothes, cookies, candies. Every week I was there I used to get a box from her.

"All the nuns were taking care of all the kids, more or less they were kids who didn't have anybody attached to them—didn't have nobody to come and see them. And the Father and I were very good friends, you know. . . . The kids—when you come through the gate, they would all be swarming around you. They grab hold of your hand, and—I was going to bring a child back from Vietnam, you know. I paid nine hundred dollars to bring a child back. But it couldn't get clear on the visa, and I never got back to Vietnam again, so—the child was seven years old, a beautiful little child. She used to walk around holding my hand. She used to sit up in the truck, she thought I was

comin' there to see *her,* you know? I mean that kid got really attached
to me. If I'd stayed there six more months I coulda gotten to bring her
back."

"Do you write to her?" I asked.

"No, I don't know where she's at now."

"What was the name of the orphanage?"

"Tan Hep. They had nobody. They had three to four nuns, a
Father. Some of those kids were in bad shape, needed medical
assistance. Lotta times I'd bring down medical advisors, they'd give
'em first aid and everything else. I even went down there when I
carried my weapons. I'd put myself in the same place they would be.
So me and a coupla guys, we'd go down there. We'd buy maybe a case
of soda or three or four cases, go down there and treat all the kids.
Once in a while you could take the kids out of the orphanage. Bring
'em down to Saigon, somewhere. Bring 'em back, you know? I mean
they look forward to that. See, they were kids, they were more or less
in the conflict. We wanted to show them we're not the enemy, that we
want to help them as much as we can. All they wanted was bubble
gum, bubble gum. So we get these big cases of bubble gum. We'd get
the truck half loaded with clothes, everything we could get. I mean
that thing was loaded. The nuns came out, open the gates up, all these
kids came flying out of there, about a hundred twenty of 'em. The
nuns came over and give us Coca-Cola or something like that. They
appreciated what we did. I really enjoyed it. It was more or less
therapy for me to go down there every week, it was. Even when I left,
the guys were still going down there. I started it."

"Did you tell these guys in Vietnam that you were raised in an
orphanage?"

"Naw, I didn't."

"Do you ever tell people about your experience?"

"No, not really. There's nothing, not a thing they can do about it,
really. Okay, if you're in a war-torn land at the time, what can you say?
Stop the war and rescue all these innocent people first? You can't do
it. Like in Vietnam. Started in 1960, that's when, and to this day how
many people know what they were fighting for?"

Berl continued. "My life was rough. A lot of people get it on a silver
platter. Me? I never had no silver platter. I never did believe in
charity. I believed in working. I worked two jobs, but my wife told me
I'm not good enough of a man. It got to a point where I take so much
and no more. Why stay there if nobody gives a damn about you?
'You're no man; you can't get in the service,' she told me. Then when I
got in the service, I was in Oklahoma, she took off with a guy for a

whole month. I came home and told her, you do that one more time, I'm all done with you. Then she did that again so I'm all done. It's all down the drain. Like Vietnam. A lot of people gettin' butchered, lotta fighting. Lotta getting killed. I see these young kids—nineteen, twenty years old—at Medi Vac hospital, get their legs amputated. One guy got his hands taken off. I say to myself, you're lucky to come out of there."

"So you had enlisted? Because you thought you'd be drafted?"

"No, no. I figured, me being here in the United States, I thought I had an obligation to serve my country. I'm not a coward, but anyone goes to Vietnam tells you they're not scared, they're a fool. I was scared there twenty-four hours a day, fifty-two weeks a year. I was always scared. I was shot at twice—missed both times. Whole jeep in front of us was totaled, none of us got hit really. A couple of nights after that, we were in a poker game, a 122 MIG rocket landed about two hundred feet away, blew the whole door in, got hit with shrapnel in my hand, not really bad though. They wanted to give me a Purple Heart for that. I told 'em I don't want it; I'm not even wounded."

"When you got out of the army in Vietnam, was there any counseling that was given to you?"

"Oh yeah," he said, without irony. "When I was in Vietnam, they wanted me to reenlist for six more months, and I told them no. I figured I was lucky over there, a whole year and didn't get killed. Who knows, maybe I get killed in six more months if I reenlist. They offered me another rank. I told them no."

We were in the car on the way to the station. Ruth and Adolph sat in the back seat, listening intently as Berl spoke.

"I'm thirty-seven now. I feel more secure now than I ever did in my whole life. Even when being raised with Gertrud and Alice, I never did actually feel the security at all. But since I got my own stability, I know what I want out of life, right? I know what I can do. I know what I can't do. I know I have two people here who really care about me. They have conscience about me. I have a security behind me. I know if something happens to me, if I need a personal advice I have somebody to turn to. When you're in a children's home, you don't have that. Every child needs love, attention, and affection, right? If you don't get that love, attention and affection, you don't have no security at all. In a children's home, if they want to, they can throw you out.

"Like I say, I was a mischievous kid and I made Miss Goldberger nervous. Don't forget she had eighteen kids to try and care for, which was a burden in itself for a start. I think that tension alone more or less got to her quite a bit. She over-burdened herself quite a bit. Come right down to it, she had to do all the things, parent-mother and parent-father, which everyone with any scientific knowledge knows that a woman can't do that. Anytime you've got a bunch of kids there you gotta have a woman guidance and a man guidance behind them. Even when you get older, like they teach now in the schools where they have sex programs and everything else. Now you being as a child, you supposed to ask a woman there, well, what about this? What's the difference between a woman and a guy? Well you couldn't go ask Miss Goldberger that, or you'd be putting her in a complicated business, see what I mean? You had to go find out your own way."

"Well, how did you find out?"

"Well, I was asking Fritz. I was asking Sammy and everybody. They were about three years older than I was at the time. I tell you one thing, it has been an experience. But I would never want to go through that experience again. Okay, like I say, you get your meals every day, right? You get a roof over your head, right? But you still don't get the security every young child needs. Me being the youngest, I was always in the way of the bigger kids. They were too busy for me. You can try and forget the past, you know. It can be beautiful, but it can be ugly as well. Me, I'd rather forget the past and all the past ever consisted of, really. I'd like to get hold of these other people, but I haven't had contact with them in nineteen years. . . . There should be a link to find out how people are doing, but the way it's going now, nobody gives two hoots about how or what or why is anybody doing. We were raised in the same environment. We should try to have a little contact."

Later I learned that a week after my visit, Berli called Zdenka and asked her to marry him. He also called Alice and asked if he could stay with her for a visit in London. They both said no.

JUDITH AUERBACH COHEN

London, July 1979
There was little time in which to see her. She had house guests, a group of Israeli women who had become widows in the Yom Kippur War of 1973. Over the phone she told me that this evening was the

final party of their visit, but that if I came at 4:30, she'd find an hour to see me.

I heard dogs barking as I stepped up to the double doors of the large suburban house. The tanned, good-looking man of about forty who greeted me was Judith's husband.

"I think your book is a great idea," he said as he took my coat. "What made you think of it?"

His candor took me by surprise. "You certainly know how to make a person feel welcome," I said.

"Oh, I have to," he smiled, flashing perfect teeth. "I'm a dentist."

He went to get his wife. I remembered the appealing toddler on the far right end of the Windermere photo, the one the Terezin baby nurse had tried so hard to mother.

Judith's home was full of people, warmth, and sunlight. The sounds of children at play drifted in from other rooms, and a child's voice in the kitchen was repeating French phrases after a young woman.

Judith entered in quick stride, with her husband. She looked petite and lovely in a crisp, white cotton dress. Her green eyes were direct, but her smile of greeting seemed uncertain. As we sat down, she crossed her tanned, bare legs, displaying modish, high-heeled sandals.

She told me that her adoptive parents were concerned about her seeing me. They felt she should not be reminded of the past.

"What do you think?" I asked.

"I don't really remember anything of the past before I was adopted," she said tensely. We talked for a while about her interest in young children, about her own son's bar mitzvah and about the group of their friends who had gotten together to help the Israeli war widows. "You see, I consider that I've been very fortunate," she said, with solemnity. "I was saved from the Nazis. Adopted by wonderful parents who've been good to me. I mean, I have so much, my parents, my husband, children, so much!"

Her husband went over to sit next to her, and put his arm around her.

"We've been to Israel several times," he said. "Our son was bar mitzvahed at the Wall. I think it would be wonderful to be there, even to live there,." There was passion in his voice.

Judith stiffened and pulled away from his embrace. She looked frightened.

"We've talked about this many times," he said dejectedly. "But Judith gets upset each time, so I don't bring it up anymore."

Slowly and deliberately, she drew herself up with the conscious effort of someone who is about to make a strong defense. "I can't consider the idea," she said.

"Why not?" I asked gently.

For a moment, she looked surprised. "Why, I cannot consider putting my children in such danger! I cannot consider making them vulnerable! I know how much it means to my husband, but I can't," her voice dropped to a whisper, "not after what I've been through."

He drew her close again, and she did not pull away.

"I know I told you I didn't remember anything before I was adopted, but I remember something somewhere, because one evening a few years ago we went to a dinner given by The Forty-fivers [the London organization of people who came out of the camps in 1945]. And I saw an older woman that I knew I had seen somewhere before. Finally I went up to her, and it came to me that her name was Alice. 'You're Alice,' I said, 'aren't you?' and we embraced. She remembered me." She smiled warmly.

The doorbell rang, and three Israeli women entered, carrying assorted packages. With them was Arye, one of their other sponsors, who spoke Hebrew. He had driven them to town for sightseeing and shopping. Amidst Hebrew-sounding English and English-sounding Hebrew, we were introduced and two of the women eagerly accepted Judith's suggestion that they go try on the dresses they had bought for the party. The third, a heavy woman in her mid-forties, said she had a headache and did not think she would go to the party.

At once Judith excused herself and went to get aspirin and a glass of water.

"Tell her to take these," she said to Arye. "We'll fix her a nice warm bath, then she'll feel better."

But the woman continued to look bleak, whereupon Judith excused herself, put her small slender arm around the larger woman, and guided her upstairs. Our interview was over.

JACK JONAH SPIEGEL

London, July 1979

For a while after he was adopted Alice kept contact with the family, until the parents asked her not to come. They wanted to excise the past and to be left in peace with their adopted son. They did not want Jack to know the pain of his concentration camp and orphanage past.

Please, let him start anew, they said, and be simply theirs, like any normal child.

He hadn't seen Alice in over thirty years when her face suddenly appeared on his television screen as an honoree of the program "This Is Your Life" in London in 1979.

"Immediately I say to my wife, 'I know this woman!'" His handsome, animated face was flushed with excitement as he leaned forward on the upholstered sofa in his living room. At thirty-seven, he was almost completely bald, but he looked young and fit.

"I'm a taxi driver, very flexible in my hours, and I was just getting ready to go out. So naturally I stay and try to recall where I've seen that face before, and who she is. And in a flash everything is revealed to me! I knew she'd been the matron in charge of me, and come to the flat of my adoptive parents, and that we'd seen her on the bus occasionally. And suddenly she's there on the TV. It was quite a shock. I left for work, but I went straight to the TV studio. The guard at the door did not want to allow me in. Then I told him I have to get in and see this woman, 'I belong here with the others,' I said, 'because I am one of those children!' He let me in."

Lita sat in a wing chair, nodding sympathetically at her husband's words. Her attractive, good-natured face radiated protective concern.

"Most of my recollection of the past has come in my dreams, believe it or not," Jack continued. "I've dreamed about Lingfield. I'd never been there besides in my dreams until—just as I got engaged, we went down there to try to find it, and on the way I described to Lita exactly how it was, although my only recollections outside my dreams were when I was about four or five."

"What did you remember?"

"Exactly what the place was like." The explosive precision of his diction echoed something locking into place. "A big roundabout in the front. A stately-looking place, and the main thing was that the garden backs onto a racetrack. For inexplicable reasons, in these dreams I'd go through this house and I'd be in the garden, and this is how I dreamed about it." He was triumphant that what he had remembered in the moldering dark of childhood dreams had been confirmed in bright daylight.

"Was this an uncomfortable dream?" I asked.

"No, not at all—you know, sometimes you think you are going bananas or something. But I wondered why do I dream these dreams? And see, for a long, long time I never knew I was adopted. And then it was explained to me."

"How?"

"It was pointed out to me in school by a young kid that I'd been adopted. How he got to know I don't know. So I went home, just like any kid would, and said, 'Some kid said I was adopted.' Well, my mother says, 'You don't know what you're talking about.' Anyway, the same evening they gave me the whole spiel."

"How old were you?"

"Can't remember, must have been ten, elevenish. They said they. had told me I was adopted when I was very young, but I couldn't remember. But they never told me about my *other* past. They said they loved me, and I said, I love you, *you're* the only parents I know." He grinned. "I'm quite satisfied, I'll take you, I told them!" He shrugged his shoulders, half jesting, half resigned, and became serious.

"I didn't know where I came from, my *other* past. That wasn't revealed to me then. . . . It was like coming up against a brick wall. And it's like everything not revealed to you eventually comes out in the worst way possible. One day I went round to my grandmother's, and she said, 'Jacky, you know you're not English.' 'Is that right?' I said, 'What am I then, an alien?' "

"A what?" I asked, not sure I heard correctly.

"An alien, from outer space," he joked. "And she said, 'Yes, you came from Austria.' 'Oh,' I said, 'that's very nice, all the best people came from Austria.' When I went home my father was in a rage that she revealed that to me.

"I felt from being English, I was suddenly a foreigner. That I was something different completely, with a different past, and I naturally wanted to know more about it. But there was this brick wall with my parents."

"He asked them whether he spoke German when he came. And they said, don't drive me mad," Lita said.

"After I met my wife, I was engaged at the time, I don't know where I got it to try to find Lingfield. I said to Lita, 'C'mon, I'm going to find out where I'm from.' I had the car. My father was a bookmaker, which is in the racetrack world. I knew there was only one racetrack in Lingfield, and in my dreams I saw this house backing on to it. I wanted to find it. So we went down there. I asked everybody around. I got no satisfaction. Then I said, 'Just tell me. Is there a house that backs onto the racetrack?' And someone said, 'Go down here, go down there, and you'll find it.' And I went down there, and I found it. I knocked on the door. 'Is this the house where many years ago many Jewish people brought children?' I said. 'Yes, come in,' they said. They showed us around, gave us a lovely time, made us very, very welcome. They showed us the clothes pegs where the little Jewish boys hung their clothes. The name Fritz was there. But mine was not. I was with the youngest. There was a group of us that started out in West Hoathly in—"

"Bulldogs Bank?"

"Yes. And that's another thing: also in my dreams, I dreamed of being very high up and that I could see for miles, and I never could work it out why I dreamed this. Well, you go to Bulldogs Bank and you see what I mean. It's very high up, and you can see for miles. . . .

"It had become a quest, you might say, of finding out about myself, and until I had to register to get married, I didn't know about my other past—because you need proof that you are Jewish. Your mother's birth certificate. It was a terrible hassle to get the papers back from the past—that I'm Austrian, and I'm Viennese, and . . . anything else?" He turned to Lita to help him retrieve the unthinkable.

"And that you came from a concentration camp," she said.

"Right, and again, another upheaval—I wasn't from a normal Austrian family, I had to be from . . ." His voice trailed off sadly. "It was unhappy times in Austria in 1941. So now it's revealed to me that I was in a concentration camp for two and a half years. So this is really something that shocks me as well. I'm thinking, how did I survive, and what was I doing there? And . . . anything else?" Turning to Lita, he asked the final question.

"You saw your mother's name, your real mother's name."

"Oh yes, Elsa Sanesh Spiegel." He spoke the name softly, and then sighed. "But there's no reference to my father. Absolutely none. . . . Anything else you want to remind me of?" he asked again.

"And your own name?"

"Yes, I saw my own name, Yona Jacob Spiegel, not Jacky. So, needless to say, I'm," he sighed, "I'm very thankful to be here at all after that. . . . So we get all the letters right, things pertaining that I am Jewish, and they give me a very hard time at this place, the Woburn House [the Jewish community service headquarters of the time], and they want to know if I speak German, and I say, 'What is this, an interrogation? I've been here for thirty-odd years, and I've given you the papers to prove I'm Jewish, so what is this?' I felt like tearing every paper up and saying to hell with the religion and everything! Anyway, we made it."

"He was so upset," Lita recalled, "I said, 'We'll get married anyway, it doesn't matter, if this is such an upset.' "

"You know sometimes you have to—" he said, "well, you bite your tongue, you wipe your eyes, and eventually you make it.

"But I was still up against this brick wall with my mother. I wanted to find out if I had spoken German when I came. All of a sudden, about four years ago I woke up one morning, I decided I had to go to Vienna. I had this feeling to go for a long time, even though I knew there's nobody sitting on the corner waiting for me. But I had two addresses I'd gotten shortly after we were married, when I made a claim against the Austrian government for restitution." He sighed, and after a long silence, during which he hunched over and stared at the carpet, he looked straight into my eyes. For the first time, he spoke with unadulterated bitterness.

"If you want to know what it costs to lose a mother, it costs you . . . You get six hundred pounds. That's all I got absolutely, for the whole family. The lot, that's it. I never got riches out of it—not that I wanted that!" His voice rose. "But I felt if somebody's going to pay, they should pay!

"It took me fifteen years to get up the nerve to go to Vienna," he continued, calmer now.

"You were afraid something might happen," Lita said softly.

"I felt something was saying no, don't go. I felt maybe I'll be in a crash. It was fear for my family, too. Then, one day I woke up and thought, I'm going to go. By myself. If anything is going to happen, it will only happen to me: they'll be all right." He nodded to Lita. "And that day, when I woke up and decided, that was the day I phoned up and went. That's how I am, it takes me time, but once I decide, I act."

"And how was that flight?"

"Actually it went very well, about three and a half hours. I had an interesting conversation with an Asian man, and the time went quickly. I do that in my cab too, try to find out about people, where they come from and so on, particularly if they have a foreign accent. While I'm living I've got a lot of seeing to do, for my parents who died live through me, and I've got to see for them as well." He looked away, and it was awhile before he resumed.

"I arrived in a snow- and thunderstorm in Vienna. It was December. The minute I landed there was a feeling of danger." He laughed nervously. "I said to myself, 'Well, Jack, you made it here, now what's going to happen to you?' I had visions of this avalanche or something, but there were no mountains." His humor and bravado had returned, and he laughed.

"By the time I got in, it was late. Vienna that time of year is a pretty deserted town. I got into a hotel and I couldn't sleep, I was in a terrible state. I'm used to going out at two or three in the morning because sometimes I work late at night. I think it must have been

about one in the morning when I went out. The few people in the
hotel lobby looked at me like I was mad, you know, 'Where's he
walking to?' I walk out and I have a look along the Gartnerstrasse, and
I walked around till about three in the morning. I didn't fear for my
life, but as a stranger, alone, that time of night I could have turned
any corner and anybody could have been waiting. . . . I kept on
walking. I stopped at a hot-dog stand."

"Open so late," I mused.

"Yes, well, I suppose they cater for the few nuts that walk around in
Vienna," he smiled, in full control again, "and then I decided I was
tired enough and I went back. I think I must have had about two
hours of sleep, and then I got up at six, as early as I could. I think I
was going to fill myself with coffee and I started out walking, looking
around. I was very close to the opera house, and I thought, that's
where the great Viennese opera was! Opera to me is something
wonderful, through my adoptive parents. My mother always liked
opera. It's something, you either have it or you don't. I love it. Well,
then I got a cab and say, take me to this address. It was all an
impossibility," he said in disgust. "First of all, I don't speak German,
I'm in a strange country, it's not my home. I go to these addresses and
I stand. . . . At one of these addresses, there was demolition, there
was nothing there. And I just stand there. . . . The other one was a
big block of flats with one big doorway, and I stand across the street
from it and I say to myself, I'm a sensible adult. This place is thirty
years hence. The people around here all speak German, and I speak
English. We're not going to get a long way in a long time, and I just
decided there's nobody going to be here, just nobody, so I looked. I
took photographs of the place. I had a chat with a Jewish person
who's got a deli around the corner from the place called The
Tempelgasse. The only idea I have about these two addresses is that
my mother, who I found out was deported to Minsk in Russia a few
weeks before I was, must have realized that she was going to be
deported so she got hold of me and took me around to her friend or
somebody to try and save me. So she got deported, and then a few
weeks later there was another address where I was. Or it could have
been another relative or somebody. That's the only way I see it. . . .

"In this deli, they started speaking Yiddish to me, and I cannot
understand a word of it. Ah, where's my mother? I thought. My
adopted mother can speak wonderful Yiddish. I cannot. So he said,
'Wait a minute. I'll bring someone back.' I must have waited an hour
and a half, and I said to myself, I'm too tired to wait any longer, so I
go. I'm sorry that I didn't wait, but where has he gone, the other side

of Vienna to get hold of this guy? So I never really got to the bottom of the thing. He's probably kicking himself that he's gone all over Vienna to get hold of a guy and," he giggled nervously, "this guy does a run-out."

"You came that far—and then lost patience?"

"I did, I really did. I went back to the hotel and then again that same night I couldn't sleep too well. I did more walking, saw more and tried to see as much as I can. . . . My money was going very fast, so I phoned Lita and told her that I'm coming home." His voice was burdened with defeat.

Nicole, fifteen, appeared in the doorway, carrying books. Her dark, curly hair was very much like her mother's, but she had her father's direct blue eyes.

"That's my hair she took from me," her balding father teased. She smiled shyly and sat down on the couch. "We have a younger daughter too, Alyssa," he said.

"Alyssa's really named after Jack's real mother," Lita explained. "Alyssa Gabi Elsa. We wanted to name Nicole Elsa after Jack's mother, but Jack's adoptive mother wouldn't hear of it. Jack said, 'I feel I would like to call her Elsa, I feel I must. I don't know her and I want to remember her.' And his [adoptive] mother said, 'No, you mustn't.'"

"My mother' won't accept it. I tried to explain to them—try to put yourself in the position of my parents who died. Would it be such a terrible thing, to name a child for Elsa? But she was adamant—she's a very strong-willed person, and I didn't want to rock the boat. I wanted to have peace. So what could I do?" he sighed.

"Perhaps one of your daughters will name one of their children Elsa."

"Maybe," he said blankly.

He brought some photo albums and showed me a photo of himself at about five, with his adoptive mother. "I used to think this was the first photo of me, but when we visited the Dann sisters recently they gave me these." There were several Bulldogs Bank pictures.

"I was very pleased to see how I look there, just like any other little boy. . . . One sees pictures of people coming out of those places, drawn, old, horrible young people looking old. From these pictures one can see that I didn't depreciate so bad." He laughed nervously. "I had visions of babies with malnutrition and so forth, and here I look like any other little kid, and this is very pleasing to me. . . . I know the Reds fed us in Prague after liberation before we came over here in the bombers. See there," he pointed, "I've even got a little potbelly and chubby chops.

"Here I am holding a ball, climbing around like an ordinary little boy."

Then Lita turned to me. "If it hadn't been for Jack's experience in the camp, do you think he might have made more of himself in school and so on? We've read that deprivation in the early years is very important in later achievement."

"I sometimes think it must have left its m-m-mark." For the first time, I heard the remnant of an old tension. "M-m-many teachers always told me I could achieve more . . . but I was a nasty kid like any other. . . . Still, one wonders if it left a mark."

"I think it's fair to say you've borne á special burden, Jack," I said.

"There's another thing," Lita said. "Jack would just like to see a photograph of his mother."

"Oh yeah," he said hopelessly. "I know there's almost a guaranteed certainty that there's not . . . The chances of me getting hold of such a thing are so remote that I say to myself, to console myself, since I consider that Nicole tends toward me, then I would like to feel that my mother may have looked an older version of my daughter. So that's my way of saying, that's the photograph, there," he nodded to Nicole, "the closest photograph I'm going to get." His eyes misted.

"If I ever went to Israel, I'd put an advertisement in the local press. That I'm in town, in such a place, and anyone knowing about the son of such a person could get in touch with me."

Lita spoke. "What you haven't told Sarah is that you calm down for ages, and then all of a sudden, out of the blue, a few months will pass and he gets this upsurge of wanting to find out again, and then it just dies away again. He gets a few unsettled days."

"I get one of my piques," he admitted miserably. "I don't know. I don't know if it's ever been portrayed among the other people that you've spoken to. But with all that I have, I could be in my taxi, or anywhere, and I could feel terribly alone." He looked down, resting his head in his hands, and fought for control as he said with effort, "It's hard to put your finger on it. It's upsetting. You look around you and see that everybody, well, not everybody, but most people around you, have got brother, sister, mother, uncle, aunt, whoever it is. I look around me and can honestly say with fair security that although I've got two wonderful daughters, my wonderful wife, my adoptive mother, a very wonderful family. . . ." The tears came. "I feel terribly alone!" he blurted out in deep, heartrending sobs.

Sitting across from her father, Nicole had been fighting her own tears as she listened to him. Now she too cried, but silently.

"This is what grabs me every so often," he said, finally surfacing over the wave of grief. "I don't know if I'm strange or something, but this is what happens. This is what you feel."

"I don't think you're strange at all," I said. "I think you're feeling what is natural to feel. Your whole family was wiped out, and you were left alone. No, I don't think you're strange. I think it was the world that was strange to have allowed it to happen."

When he regained composure, he reflected. "Still you've got to readjust, especially as you get older, it's a big adjustment. I raise my hands to heaven and say to the Almighty Being that has allowed me to live, and I say to my wife, if it all stopped tomorrow, I would regret nothing because I have been able to do something that others weren't able to do: *to live!* This is what I consider. I live for my parents that died." The words came on a wave of grief. He sobbed again, and now Nicole cried audibly with him. Hearing her jolted him into control, and he looked over to her lovingly, smiling sheepishly and trying to get her to smile. But she was unable to respond.

"It's a hard thing to see your dad whom you love and who takes care of you—" I began.

"Sit down and cry," Jack finished for me, now in perfect control. "I think it's an important thing for children to see parents cry and not think they're statues like they're made out to be." Nicole dabbed at her tears with a tissue.

"My mother is seventy-two and has had good health. Now she's losing her sight," Jack went on. "She's getting bitter and says, 'Why does it have to happen to me?' I tell her to turn it around a bit and say 'Why *didn't* it happen to me? What am I, something special? Whereas I used to say I was something special, having survived, now I say, why shouldn't it have happened to me? I say to her, thank God you've *had* wonderful health, and eyesight, a pretty good life. If a person can say this, then you've had more than most people. A lot of people. Think of the people who couldn't see straightaway, people who died with no chance.

"She says, 'Oh, my son, if only I could see you.' And I say, 'Look, you're born in this world with two arms, two legs, eyesight, hearing, speech, *if* you're lucky! And if you lose one thing, it's true, it's terrible. But, I said, people lose everything and still carry on. A person to be born into the world blind, it is a terrible thing! She can't turn around and say thank God for seventy-odd years: I had wonderful sight. I saw. I read. I've seen the colors of the rainbow, the colors of life. That's why I say: I came out of a hellhole. I've got this life given to me. I take it in priorities like this: *Biology*, life is first. *Health* is your second. *Love* is your third. *Possession* is the last."

We continued to look at his photo album. There was a series, taken every year on the day some of the London taxi drivers decorate their cabs and take underprivileged children to the seaside for an outing. In one, Jack had cleverly rigged his cab to look like an old airplane, like the old RAF bombers, complete with propellers, tail fin, and special lights. There he was, standing beside his plane, dashing in his pilot's helmet, goggles, jacket, and flowing white scarf. Four dark-skinned little children were beside him.

LEAH ROVELSKI CHOW

Sacramento, California, April 1980

After three years of searching for her, I was finally going to meet Leah. For her, liberation from Terezin and the flight to England had been followed by two new partings: a six-week separation from her group at Windermere because of a ringworm infection, and then, because she needed eye surgery, another separation from her only security, the toddler group. No familiar person was in attendance during her surgery and hospitalization, for Martha Wenger, the caretaker in Terezin, had been sent to a DP camp in Germany to await a visa for Australia. When Leah finally rejoined the toddlers she was reported to have been cranky and easily upset.

The educated couple who adopted Leah had no other children, and the woman, a schoolteacher in her late thirties, had, according to Alice, been determined to love and teach Leah.

Children were riding their tricycles up and down driveways bordered by petunias as I turned into the suburban street where Leah lived.

A little Eurasian boy on his tricycle pedaled across the cul-de-sac to ask me where I was going.

"To visit Leah Chow."

He looked puzzled. "Why you come here?"

"To talk to her. What's your name?"

"Donald. My mama's in there." He pointed to the bungalow with the oriental facade and pedaled away.

The door was opened by a smiling ten-year-old girl in an old gray bathrobe. Her eyes sparkled with excited intelligence as she bounced about and called out, "She's here!"

Leah entered, head down. "Patricia, take her coat!" she ordered. Her thin face was accented by the rows of tiny pink rollers on which reddish hair was tightly wound. Dark circles under her blue eyes and a drawn look disturbed the beauty there. She had told me on the phone that she did not go out into crowds except to go to church, so that she could meet me only at home.

"This is our first house. Probably the only house we'll have. The carpeting is new and the dinette is from Christmas," she said with pride. Patricia, observing us closely, sat curled up on the floor at our feet.

"How have the others done? Are they all right?" Leah asked. "There's one—in the States too. I can't remember his name, my memory has lapsed so badly in the last year. Him and I are a month apart in age."

"Berli?"

"Yes!" Her tired eyes lit. "We were a pair of demons together! I threw him into the pond at Lingfield. I was a complete brat. Is he married?"

"He was." I offered to give her his address.

"We were very close, very close. All I know is that there were only twenty-five kids out of five hundred when they came to rescue us out of the concentration camp, and I heard that only two of us got a settlement of money—him and myself—and that it was a battle. I don't know if you've met the lawyer, he died—Strons, he lived in England. He did the case, and I did not know till I was twenty-one years old. He wrote me beautiful letters, and he never drained one penny from it, very beautiful. Even his daughter wrote me after he passed away. I wish I could have met him."

"Do you get a restitution pension now too?"

"Patricia!" The sudden loudness of her voice startled me. "Make some tea and warm up a piece of pound cake." Patricia got up obediently and skipped to the kitchen. "And bring me water!" She turned back to me.

"Yes. I get it every month from Germany, but they're slow at it. I never wanted it. Let's face the truth."

"Don't you think you deserve it?"

"No, I don't think so, because to me the life is the life. You can't bring back what has been taken away from you, okay? A brother, a mother, and a father. That cannot be replaced. Money cannot replace it, okay?" Her voice was strident. "I had to explain that to my [adoptive] parents, and she got very upset. I do not have animosity. I do not have hate, which I don't know how the other kids feel on it. They may have a lot of hate for what's happened—the destroyed families. I never did.

"'Cause I told my mother at the time, 'Well, it's happened,' and she said I should hate them, but I said 'I don't hate them.' *One* individual forced them to do it! But life is like that. In ways I'm glad I have the money, because it does help me out to buy the kids extra clothing and whatever, because it's so hard with four kids here, on my husband's salary. In fact, they're supposed to raise it, because I've got Donald, but they haven't done it yet. This month it's $343. But for Donald, not yet. Every year I have to file a paper that I'm still living, and that I still have to get the pension."

"Do you have to have a medical exam for that?"

"I have to see Dr. Z——. All the way to San Francisco. They're ridiculous. Have you heard of Dr. Z——, German man? I was under him for a couple of years, and I gave it up. I didn't care for him, and this Dr. X——, I just saw him in January, and the questions! They asked me 560 or 580 questions, written on paper. I had to sign. I thought I was going crazy. Then about an hour oral. I thought I was crazy when I went in and when I came out I was three times worse! He told me I should go back to therapy. I didn't want to, the last two, three times I'd been to see him. He debates if I'm eligible to get my pension higher, if I'm worse or stable or whatever he wants. So when I went in last time, he said I was no better than before, that I should go back to therapy maybe twice a month. That's what he suggested. But I didn't want that."

"Why?"

"Oh," she sighed, "I don't know if you'll understand it."

"I'll try, I promise."

"You promise, okay." She smiled. "I'm raised in the Jewish faith, but I'm not a strong one. But in [the] Christian [religion,] when you accept the Lord, there's many miracles He will do for you. And I feel strong enough—it must have been the Lord's hands which kept me from getting killed at six weeks old. You know, you're taken away from your mother, naturally you need the milk, the nourishment, for three to four and a half years—and so when I became a Christian, it turns your whole life around. You accept. You go up and down the hills with the Lord. There's one verse in the Bible: 'I can do all things through Christ, He strengthens me.' Sometimes He'll do a miracle healing there and then, sometimes He'll do it later, you know, slowly."

Patricia came in, bringing a china cup, green tea leaves brewing inside. "I told you to get me water! Go ahead!" Leah barked. Then turning to me, she spoke more softly again.

"I feel the Lord made my mind and He can cure it. It's us ourselves which put ourselves in this predicament. My life, well, it's been a tragedy, yes, but I feel there's worse things in life than what I went through. The Lord says, 'Don't dwell in the past, Look for the future. Go every day at a time. With My help you'll make it.' So that's the way I feel because Donald is a miracle child. I wasn't supposed to have him."

"Really? Why not?"

"Because two months pregnant my water bag broke. Oh, and I cried. And it was shown to me that I was going to have another boy. My husband didn't believe it, but I knew it."

"You just felt it?"

"No, the Lord had told me. And the pediatrician came in and told me that ninety-eight percent of the children that were born that way were retarded, and they found him one hundred percent normal. They're all smart, all the kids. They all take after their father. He's a very intelligent man. He's a high-school math teacher."

"And you, why do you put yourself down?"

"I'm a very condemning person to myself. That's me. Because I've been brought up put down all my life. It's the way I've been told so many things."

"By whom?"

"Oh, school, and my mother was hardheaded to get along with. We're different personalities. She did her best. She tried to show her love the best she knows how. My parents worked, and I feel they didn't have time for me. When I was eleven, I told my mother I didn't want her to go to work. I resented it. I used to have tremendous migraines as a child. I still do get them, if I get tension. I suffered very much as a child, maybe once a week I'd come home, and they'd last a couple of days. One time it was over a week. They didn't know what was wrong. That's when they discovered I had it."

"How old were you?"

"I was about thirteen or fourteen. I couldn't go through high school and university. Now when I see these kids—they got the brains to go, and they don't want to go—that gets me really angry. I was a very bad learner. I was put in a school for a couple of years. I don't know what they call it, maybe a backwards school, I guess, but that didn't bother me, you know. Maybe that's why I put myself down so much among people. But you know, we the non-smart people can do really good in ways."

"Have you ever thought to finish school now?"

"I don't know. I might go into the Lord's work. Maybe in convalescent homes. Talk to the old people. There's so many people in there that nobody knows they're there. Talk about the Lord. Read to them. Tell them they're loved. Listen to them. I'm a good listener."

"Do you have people who listen to you?"

"I'm a very inward person. When I'm hurt about something, I'll keep it to myself. There's a couple of people in my church; one girl, she's black, she's partially blind. We get along really well. We talk. I help her, and she helps me. And I have like a mother here too. She's been very helpful. She's made a lot of my clothes, too."

"How did you find her?"

"I had an accident with my foot, and Bea came over to the house and started talking to me and praying for me. I fell in love with her, and then I started going to that church. Something possessed her to ask me, have you accepted the Lord into your heart? Did I know about salvation and all this? She told me about salvation, and I dedicated myself to it. She's from the same country as I was—my parents were. She's Polish descent. In fact, she has a daughter the same age as me, and we have the same birthday. April 24. And I know Berli's in this month, May 24."

"How old were you when you parted from Berli?"

"I was five and a half."

"And you remember his birthday!"

"That's the only thing I remember. I don't know if he'd remember me." She sounded wistful. "I feel bad, but he's the only one I think about now. I wonder if he goes for therapy. There's a lot of people who came out with trauma and have psychiatry the rest of their lives for that."

"Does your restitution money depend on your going for psychiatry?"

"No, it's not a threat to the money as long as I go for my two- or three-year checkup. No. It's a threat to your own self. But first I have to pay the money. Then they pay me back. Sixty bucks now, that's a lot of money! And my husband wouldn't like it. Sixty bucks is outrageous. We got into a hassle about it. That's one reason I quit. But you know, when you don't care for somebody it's no use going. You got to go where you're comfortable, where you can talk to a person. I didn't care for either of them. See, they make you go where they want you to go. But this last psychiatrist told me I could go where I wanted to go. If I went I'd go to a Christian psychiatrist I saw on TV."

"How long did you go to this last psychiatrist? The one you didn't like?"

"Two to three years. But see, I've been under psychiatric care from the time I was seven and a half till I was eighteen, till I left England. I liked the one I had in a child guidance clinic there. I always went up and had a treat up there. They were very good. I was a naughty little girl, I guess. I gave Mother a hard time. You see, they say the first five years of a child's life is very dramatic for them. They learn to love you because they learn that you're the security for them, the mother and father, especially the mother. And with the first five and a half years, being put away for so long and then coming out, I was a rough child. Excitable too. I used to hit the other kids, not meaning to. I gave my mother a hard time, but I needed the love and the attention. I needed a lot. I wanted a brother, and I asked her why she didn't get me one. And she said, 'You were too much, you'd have been jealous,' which I don't feel I would have been, 'cause I'm not a jealous person now."

"What do you know about your natural parents?"

"My [adoptive] parents were very secretive, and I feel a lot of it were lies."

"How?"

"Oh, they would say to me they didn't know nothing about my parents, and then as time went on there were bits and pieces, and it got me kind of mad. When I was in my early thirties I got a letter from Germany with two hundred dollars stating my father was a professional man and this was all he had left, and it took them thirty-one years to find out that I was sole heir to his inheritance, and it got me really wanting to go—to dig into it and find out more. My husband said, leave well enough alone, don't dig in, and then the psychiatrist I was going to had a book that this old lady had done, and she had written my birth date, and that I had a brother and that my father was unknown, and that was wrong.

"Now this is a coincidence. When I was pregnant with the first one, we had the girl's name picked out and the boy's name picked out: Paul for a boy and Mary for a girl." She grew excited. "So when I was pregnant with Mary, they got my birth certificate for me. They finally found it." She sounded disgusted. "And I was sitting at the table, and I opened it up and started screaming, and my husband wondered what had happened, and there, believe it or not, Mary was my mother's name! So I'd named my daughter after my mother, which I'd had no idea. So Mary is really named after her *real* grandmother!" She looked happy for a moment.

"It's too bad I never had a picture of her, but what can you do? I know my father's name was Moses, and my brother was three and a half years old. All I know was, I was six weeks. The only question I asked was why my brother didn't live and I did? And I guess it was the Lord's will that way, that's all I have to look at it. I never hated, to my knowledge I never hated. The past is the past. I've got my children to raise, and I don't want them hating, you know.

"My mother hates it that I go to church. When she comes, she wants to have things her way, and my husband tells me to give in to her, but I feel I've never had a chance to be my own boss. She says if my dead mother would know I was a Christian, she'd die a thousand times in her grave. But I wasn't raised strong Jewish, like Orthodox. If they raised me strong, that would be different. Now I take the girls to church on Sunday and Wednesday to Missionettes. But my husband won't let them go to all the socials. So I say, Chen Jung, one day these kids are gonna run, you have to let them go. They're supervised. They're not doing anything wrong. He wants them to study all the time.

"He's twelve and a half years older than me. He's not saved. He has his life. I have mine. He doesn't fool around, he provides. He's not a wifebeater, I don't fool around. We trust each other. I go to church and nowhere else."

"Do you go out to the supermarket?"

"No, not right now. Not in a big place. I have to be where I can see the exit. You have to go through it to really understand, because people might think you're really psychotic when you say something like that. I know another woman who went through it, and she's helping me now. You start feeling you're going to pass out, and everything is closing in on you. You have no air. See, I can't take the loudness of a whole lot of people anymore.

"Chen Jung's family fell in love with me. We get on so well. Every time they come out, they spoil my kids rotten. And they push me to church. They say, 'Go on, Lee, it's time, we'll do the dishes, you go ahead.' They treat me like family. They don't even question my being different. They have a lot of respect for me, and they told Chen Jung, you treat her nicely, she gave you four beautiful children, that's what they told him. I'll do anything for them. Maybe I feel the love and the warmth. They're always excited to see me. They bring clothes for me and the kids."

Donald came in from outdoors with a little friend. "Go upstairs and watch TV," she directed. He whined for a moment, doing a petulant shake with his sturdy body, but Leah held firm. She turned to me. "When he starts school in September, I'll be alone too much."

"So what will you do?"

"I'll watch 'PTR Club.'"

"PTR?"

"Praise The Lord. That's on at eight A.M., every morning. I like that. I'll watch for two hours. Sometimes they have real Christian psychiatrists, and they're real good. It helps you motivate things and think about things, what you should be doing, things like that. And they use the Bible. And in God's eyes we're all equal. We're all his children. See, the Bible has all the answers you need. Now I have to find out where the place is and read it, and the Lord will administer to you in different ways: it'll go through the pastor, it'll go through a friend, the TV, whatever. One day I said, 'Lord you know me, you created me, now you know what's my inner being, you know what's bugging me, show me.' Well, I never should have asked it, because one thing after another it's been shown what is within me, and boy, some of the things can really hurt. But Lord help me through it."

"And so what did the Lord show you?"

She sighed. "I needed forgiveness. See, I'm an oversensitive person. I have to ask the Lord to help me not to be so oversensitive. I have withdrawn from a lot of people. I keep away from them, and that is real bad. But I can't help it. We all have errors. The Bible says, look at yourself. Are you pure? Are you clean? No way, because nobody's perfect. Help one another. Pray for another. And of course, the Lord will show you the people which have gone through the same as you, which can help you and you can help them. You can go through what that person's been through, you can be compassionate and help them through it."

"So is that why you think of someday working in a convalescent home?"

"Okay, to me, we're a very busy generation. I hate the words I have no time. I hate it. To me, I have four kids, okay. I do the sick list at church. I can't go to the hospitals right now because right now I can't go through a hospital. It's just the fear of going in there. I'd pass out. But okay, I visited this woman there one time. She had broken her leg and the pastor had come in. They were talking about time, and I got so upset, I told him, 'I hate the words *I don't have time.*' What would happen if somebody called you up, and they say, 'Do you have a few minutes, Lee? Could I talk to you?' And you turn around and say, No, I don't have time right now, I've got to go to the store. Call me later." She slowed for emphasis and looked me square on. "I do not know the mental state that that person is in! God forbid I turned around and heard that that person was so desperate that they took their life! That would be on my shoulders for the rest of my life!"

Her voice dropped to a fearful whisper: "The Lord might say: 'Lee, remember that woman? she wanted help that time. Well, I don't have time for you, my child, because you never had time for that person when I sent them to you.' Wow!" Her voice trailed off.

"But if you ever got really desperate, do you have somebody to call?"

"I guess so. Well, sometimes, somebody will be led to come to me. But I'm a bull, very hard to get through to. I keep everything secretive. That's what's got me into a nervous state many times. Bea says, 'Lee, relax, talk about it. Let's pray about it.' She wants to help me many times, but I back away. See, I'm a very hidden person."

"You've been speaking rather openly to me, haven't you?"

"Of course, you can tell generally if a person is being nosy or if they're really concerned." She paused. "You're very unusual for a Jewish person."

"Really?"

"Because to me a Jewish person is very outspoken, very blunt. To me a lot of them don't have very much understanding. I feel your warmth and understanding and love. That's the only way I can say it."

"Thank you. I appreciate that because I do care."

"Thank you. I'm that type too. That's very unusual for a Jewish person, isn't it? 'Cause don't a lot of them just think of themselves? That's what I've been told. I mean I'm not trying to be nasty and downgrading, there's good and bad in everybody. A lot of people are so prejudiced against the Germans, the Poles, the Jews, whatever. Me, see, I could have all this. But that's one thing I don't have, thank God, because I believe everybody is individually okay. It doesn't mean because a German killed that they can all be the same way. No. They were forced into it. So I have no hurt against them."

"And who forced them?"

"Hitler did, see? Just because of *one crazy maniac,* they were forced to do it. I've got a lot of reason to hate, but is it going to do me any good? I don't know how the other kids came out. If they hate because of what happened?"

"Some do and some don't."

"Oh, some don't? Oh, that's great. That's fantastic. Did some of these kids which made it, did a lot of their relatives come out, or were a lot without 'em too?"

"Most were without relatives."

"I wonder if they hold grudges. That would be interesting, to get together and find out how they feel, and how the Lord could heal them through it." She was sitting tensely over to one side; the dark circles under her eyes had become more noticeable. "The trouble is, I have no time for myself. I'm tired," she said.

"Do you have trouble sleeping?" I asked.

She nodded. "I've been like that a long time. Oh, yes. In fact, I'm tired now."

I got ready to leave, asking Leah if she could take a nap this afternoon. Patricia got up and skipped out purposefully.

"No, there's too much to do, they keep me busy. I've lost a lot of weight lately. I've got a nervous stomach too, and the trouble is, they get up with me and go to bed when I do."

Patricia returned with a large stuffed animal, a slate-blue, well-worn mouse with two black patches for eyes. Without words, she put it on her mother's lap.

"Whose is this?" I asked.

"It's hers," Leah replied, "but I sleep with him."

"When Mom feels tired or nervous, you give it to her?"

"No, I go to bed and she grabs it from me every night after I go to bed." Patricia smiled.

"My habit was—this may seem really weird—as a child, when any problem happened or I was hurt, I'd always go to a stuffed animal and say, 'Will you love me?' See, that was me. You love me," she leaned over, cuddling her face into the animal. "I guess I felt a very unloved and unwanted child." Then she straightened, sitting up with sudden eagerness. "I don't know how the other kids came out. Did they feel rejected, or did they feel loved and wanted?"

"I'm sure most must have felt at some time like you."

My reply saddened her. She looked away, and then down at the stuffed animal. When she looked up again to me, she said with conviction, "Okay, I am what I am. The Lord made me this way. I am somebody. I am something. I am a child of God."

From Terezin: The Older Group

(DENNY) DENYS MUENCH

London, July 1977

Curly red hair protruded from under the visor of his Greek fisherman's cap. The jaunty angle of the cap was at odds with the anxious intensity with which he appraised me, sitting across from me in Bianca Gordon's garden. His round freckled face was boyish; only the thickened waist was a concession to middle age. We talked about teaching.

"This leads me to something about all of us in Lingfield," he said, "although we were brought up institutionally, we're not in any way alike."

"How do you account for that?"

"I think it's an achievement of Alice. I don't know how she managed to do it. We're not very uniform. She must have been conscious of bringing out individuality, and I think it's quite remarkable. That we all have different aspirations, goals. From my own experience with a class of thirty, I think it's an achievement to preserve certain differences in group upbringing.

"I've noticed a number of people who've grown up, even in fairly affluent surroundings, not just ordinary sorts of environments, but quite beautiful places, and yet they don't know where they're going. They have no real sense of direction. One feels that they're constantly struggling with themselves, or one feels their motivation is to compete with a sister or brother, or rebelling against the parents, and they don't realize that doing things for those motives doesn't achieve anything. So from so-called normal backgrounds or even better, I've seen people come out in awful condition. I think our growth then is remarkable.

"I think if you didn't see us together, or know Alice had brought us up, you would never know we grew up together, since we're all so individual and so unlike Alice. A couple have even carried this individuality and perhaps confidence to be themselves so far as to break away.

"It's interesting," he probed a frustration, "my contact with Alice is a strong one, but in another sense it's slightly impersonal. I don't mean this in a derogatory sense at all. Although I've felt close to Alice, I've never felt her as a mother. Maybe I was supposed to have felt that she was a mother, but I don't feel this was the case."

"What would she have had to have done for you to feel that was the case?"

"Well, up until my mid-twenties, perhaps I did feel more that if things were really bad, that there was someone you could turn to without having to swallow your pride. Whereas with other people connected with Lingfield, one couldn't do that. So in that sense she may have been like a mother."

He paused, looking away. "Perhaps what I felt a mother ought to be wasn't well defined. I never really knew my mother, even though I had some recollections of somebody who was supposed to be my mother, precamp period."

"You do have such recollections?"

"Oh yes, of somebody who called herself mother."

"Why do you doubt she was?"

"Um, because she didn't resemble me physically at all, for one thing, that must partly be the reason."

"You have such a strong image of her that you remember what she looked like?"

"Oh yes, I can remember quite clearly."

"Did you ever see pictures?"

"No, but I saw her, I can remember roughly what she looked like. You see, there was no physical resemblance *whatsoever*. She had black hair, mine is red . . . And as I say, I was scattered here there and everywhere, I didn't know where on earth I was a lot of the time."

His desire to discount the possibility of this relationship made me sense his need to stay aloof from the pain of sure loss.

"Yet couldn't it be that you resemble your father?"

"Possibly. She may well have been my mother, but somehow I'm not sure because there was no one there to verify it. I wasn't old enough to verify it, I mean, being two years old . . . there was no way to be absolutely sure. She had dark hair, black hair, rather on the chubby side, red cheeks, but no resemblance to me whatsoever, at least not her physiognomy. She may have been someone in one of these places looking after me—I mean I was in these group situations, this is what makes me doubt."

"Still, someone in the situation gave you enough nurturance that you have strong enough feelings to remember what she looked like."

"Oh yes, I called her Mother, whatever language it was. . . ."

"So whether or not she actually was your physiological mother, there was someone there with whom you were closely entwined."

"Well, I remember it was one night in some place or other, I remember she said something about . . . that she was never to see me again, and she was actually in tears, and I didn't understand it, and I almost laughed at her for crying. I couldn't understand why she was crying. She said, I'll never see you again. And she didn't."

"But now doesn't it tell you someone cared very deeply about you?"

"She must have, yes, that's what it must have been, whether she was my mother or not. But to be honest, whatever happened to me after that was so completely unconnected that it no way affected me subsequently. I mean, I couldn't get any emotional support from it."

He paused. "Maybe I might have been subconsciously aware of this. I can't be sure. Perhaps this might have been the one thing that kept me reasonably sane, though I was a very neurotic child, you must have heard. But compared with so many messed-up adults that I've seen, I think I'm reasonably normal. I don't say I'm free from all anxiety, I certainly can feel things strongly, but it doesn't interfere with my functioning. I can meet people rather easily now. I choose my friends carefully. I'm a Scorpio," he said, in a rare flash of humor.

"What were you like as a child?" I asked.

"I always walked fifty to a hundred yards behind the others. I was a daydreamer. I spent a lot of time on my own. I had little control of my aggressive impulses. I think I caused disturbances. I know I slept alone in a room, for several years, I'm not sure why. I had insomnia, it took me a long time to get to sleep; I kept toy guards at the door. I know I had an obsessional fear of death, I remember, when I was eight years old, shortly before I went into treatment with Alice."

"With Alice?"

"Yes, I used to come home from school at lunchtime for a special time with her. The others stayed at school for lunch. At any rate, I had a fear of dying and used to listen for my heart to beat. I knew if you ran around the block you could make your heart beat faster, so I always used to run around the playground just to be sure it would keep beating. I was also enuretic, and because of this obsession with death I used to like Alice coming to wake me up at night, because that meant I wasn't going to die that night. This was a comfort, to be waked up at midnight, because I knew there would be somebody. At that age I was scared stiff, even if there were boys in the same room. I couldn't feel secure. I couldn't sleep in the dark.

"Now I can't sleep with a light on. But then I was absolutely terrified at night. I used to have dreams about a devil under my bed, and one night I dreamed we were having a meeting, all of us together in the staff room, where the white piano was. And I was in with the crowd but not in with it, because I knew that something horrible was going to happen, and the devil was some lady or other in disguise. Immediately I saw her, I knew it was her, and she came up to me and grabbed my hand and I woke up because I knew she was going to take me to hell.

"Gradually I got over it. Because with adolescence I found I had a lot of problems with life, rather than death, that life is really complicated. The piano became my interest. Then I got a piano teacher who really helped, John Keith. And Alice let me quit scouts to have more time to practice the piano. I was a terrible scout anyway, the worst."

"How did John Keith help?"

"Well, there never was a permanent male figure in Lingfield, one who was there all the time. Wolf Blomfeld came on weekends, Ben Helfgot also on weekends, to do athletics, but John Keith was a highly perceptive kind of man. He helped me sort things out. He was sort of a musician cum mystic, sort of man you don't meet very often. I was eleven or twelve. He was fundamental in stopping me from drowning, with his relationship. It was more than a piano lesson. I believe before I met him I was on the verge of becoming a delinquent. Perhaps music helped sublimate energies."

"Is he still alive?"

"Yes, he's still alive. He stopped teaching music and became a priest, and then he became a monk. I have no contact with him now. He's not allowed contact with the outside world." He was impassive. "I think that probably people in our situation have problems in finding our identity in the world. It's obviously more difficult to feel established in it.

"I've been secretive about my life, my background. On the one hand I'm proud of it because I think the upbringing I've had is a lot better than what some people, even in family circumstances, have had. On the other hand, I feel ashamed of it, because of its being an institution. And this leads to another thing. I feel an irrational guilt about the loss of my family. I still feel somehow that I'm partly responsible for their extermination, in some way. Perhaps I feel guilty because I survived, and they didn't. And this is why, perhaps, I feel ashamed, because of that, and because of the Victorian attitude toward institutionalization and also my background, my parents having died in very unusual circumstances. Not just because they were ill or old, but simply because they were murdered. As I say, it is irrational because obviously I know perfectly well that I wasn't responsible but somehow there's something that makes me feel a part of the whole thing.

"I don't like to associate with anything German. I don't even like the fact that I was *born* there. I'd rather be born *anywhere* but *Germany* —Poland, Russia, or anywhere. I don't tell people I was born there, I tell them I was born somewhere else, because I feel ashamed of having a sort of German background even though I'm probably mixed blood anyway—a lot of Eastern European Jews are.

"Whenever English people say to me, 'Oh, you look like a foreigner,' I say, 'What do you think I look like?' They say, 'Oh, you look Greek or Russian,' never German, which is a relief, of course, because being thought of as German makes me cringe. I've even had children in school, really horrible ones, who somehow pick up the fact that my name is German, call me Hitler. When I was at senior school people would call me German names like Jerry. There was one incident with a student teacher. Alice was furious that I didn't tell her about it. He called out, 'Muench!' and he looked up at me and said, 'Oh yes you'd look nice with a Gestapo hat on.' Things like that cut rather deep."

"Denny, do you know of any groups of people like yourself who've been through the Holocaust, who meet to discuss their feelings?"

"No, I don't."

"Because do you realize that you are not alone in these feelings?"

"Oh yes, I realize these kinds of feelings of guilt are fairly universal, and it is irrational. At the moment when I'm talking about it, the whole thing is intensified. I don't think about it all the time, but it's only on reflection that it becomes important. And I thought it interesting for you to know."

"Have you ever thought of changing your name? I'm not suggesting that you do that, but had you thought of it?"

"Well, yes, but what I think is that you keep it, because you feel that in a sense you're hanging on to something. You can't completely sort of divorce yourself from your background even though it's extermi nated."

"How would you feel about having this conversation in the book under your own name?"

"I don't mind. I realize these things I express are plaguing others, and as I say, I think I'm reasonably normal. Perhaps I'm cynical, but still at the root of the situation, you see, is this: I get people very often in synagogue, somebody who hasn't seen me for a long time, they'll say, 'Oh, I knew you when you were so high.' And that's all they've got to say to me. And if I say something that sounds halfway reasonable, they say, 'Oh, really.' And they act surprised.

"I sometimes wonder, did you half-expect me and the rest of us to be—somehow, did you, like some other people, feel, well, this person's been through this, he's been through that, he's had an institutional background, no family background—did you intuitively feel you'd meet someone perhaps a bit inarticulate, someone having some mental aberration?"

"Are you asking if my interest in you is real?"

"Believe me, I know that. But I'm asking you because I want to find out about other people. What do they expect? Do they expect us to be not quite right? I can ask you this, but I haven't been able to ask these other people, because believe me, they wouldn't even speak to me enough to allow me to ask this question. We've had people from the clinic, for example, hanging around here at parties, and they don't speak to us. They just hang around and look at us, and you wonder what they're there for, what they're looking for. They don't have any sort of personal interest. For instance, it was difficult for Alice to get the piano lessons with John Keith for me from the Committee. And when I needed a metronome because I was studying, it cost about three pounds. And this was about the same price as a pair of trousers, roughly. So what Alice had to wangle with the Committee was not the metronome, but a pair of trousers, and then I'd get the three pounds. This is in a sense an almost facetious example, but it was what Alice was up against. And once we were no longer children, they just really were no longer interested. There was no kind of help in terms of finding us jobs or finding us careers. When we were younger, they wanted to do their good deeds, see us fed and clothed properly but then they faded. When I became a teacher, basically I did it on my own."

"Did you have an 'aunt' or 'uncle' on the Committee?"

He hesitated, looked troubled.

"Well, they disappointed me, in the sense that when I grew older they just faded. There was no kind of contact after that."

"You didn't try to contact them?"

"I suppose in a sense I could have done that, but in another sense I felt I couldn't psychologically."

"Why?"

"Because they were no longer interested. When Lingfield stopped, they stopped, basically."

"Does that mean that over the period of ten or so years that contact was made, it was not very deep?"

"Yes, I think it was in a sense very superficial. One always felt rather awestruck going to their houses or flats. They were society people. I don't think I'd now be afraid going to them, but *then* I remember going to them in my early adolescence, and being very conscious of the differences between these two worlds. The differences were so enormous that I just sort of creased up, sat there in awestruck silence. When I got older, I thought of getting in touch, but I couldn't approach them about anything."

"They never gave you a phone number and said call if you need?"

"No, my contacts with them were always at their discretion."

"Did they have children?"

"No, they didn't, but they adopted a girl from Lingfield, you see. They, I think, wanted to adopt me originally, but there were various difficulties. I suffered from enuresis until the age of twelve, and I think that this was partly the problem. So what they did instead was, when I was about six, they adopted a girl, same color hair.

"Emotionally, you see, there was this terrible letdown. Perhaps some of the girls know this feeling even better than I, because some of them, I think, nearly became prostitutes because of this feeling of desertion. Yes, in late adolescence they lived in rooms in Hampstead, and all sorts of things happened. Alice may have a different version, but I see it as having to do with this feeling of desertion which I personally felt very keenly, when I suddenly realized that these people were just *not there*."

"How did you resolve this?"

"I didn't, I just accepted that I couldn't get any help from anyone—oh, perhaps a bit of advice, but no real help. I realized I'd have to go on, on my own, regardless. I had this restitution money from Germany which enabled me to go to college full time to prepare for teaching.

"At that time I lived with a family in Ilford. I became aware of the family pattern, how in a reasonable family the whole situation is geared toward everyone helping everyone else. There's psychological support, there's financial support, there's a constant vigilance over people's welfare. And I realized that for me it couldn't be that way, that whatever I would do would more or less have to be on my own. And it would take longer and be much harder.

"Sometimes I wonder why we weren't all adopted. You know, when I was preparing to teach, I came across a reference in a child development textbook to something called *An Experiment in Group Upbringing*, by Anna Freud. It upset me. Did they keep us together as an experiment? Hadn't the Germans experimented on us enough?" He spoke between clenched teeth.

I assured him that the reference was to the group of toddlers, that the title was terribly unfortunate, but that to my knowledge no experiment had been done; the toddlers had been kept together for a year to gain strength and learn English. My words sounded feebly apologetic, and I saw his troubled face.

Denny paced back and forth in front of the group of twenty eleven- and twelve-year-olds, his Sunday School class at the West London Synagogue. He was very much in command of the group, and they seemed fascinated, eagerly following his lead in the discussion.

"Tell me about something you've made. What have you created that has given you the most satisfaction?"

Lots of hands flew up.

"A boy: "I made a picture, and it won a prize."

"But was it the prize that gave you satisfaction, or was there any satisfaction in the work itself?"

A girl: "I wrote a poem, and I liked doing it because that's my favorite thing."

A girl: "I made a piano composition, and it gave me satisfaction because my teacher liked it."

Denny: "But didn't it give *you* any satisfaction before your teacher liked it?"

"No, because I don't like making musical compositions."

Denny: "Well, class, when you create something, do you create it out of nothing? What do you think nothing is?"

There was a long silence.

A boy: "Nothing is what you start with to make something."

This time the silence was punctured by the restless shuffling of feet.

Denny pressed: "I know this isn't easy at all."

"Nothing is nothing," another child ventured.

"Yes, but can you tell us more about that?" He paced back and forth intensely, then paused and looked past them, out of the window and said, "You see, in the Bible we learn that God created the heavens and earth out of *nothing*. Can you imagine what that must be? A great endless void? Endless total darkness? For billions of miles. Complete, unrelieved emptiness for as far as one can possibly imagine. No light of any kind, no stars, nor sun, nor moon, and no reflections nor any living person—desolation: not any living thing nor organic particle, and no firmament. Now that was the beginning, before creation, before creativity."

The children were fascinated.

"Now on this paper that shall be passed, you may create something, and note especially what your creative impulse feels like, because that is something wondrous."

SAMUEL SCHWARTZ

New Orleans, March 1978

The tall, handsome, sandy-haired man came toward me in the airport waiting room, wearing a light blue, open-collared shirt. He seemed younger than thirty-seven. Despite the strong gait and the firm handclasp, there was a shy vulnerability in his face. His eyes appraised me warmly and with surprising candor as we exchanged greetings, and he took my overnight bag and led me almost protectively to his car. He wanted to know about everyone in London I'd seen. Alice had visited him last summer, he said, and it had been hard to say good-bye to her. "She's so important to me, you know," he said softly.

On the drive into the city he spoke confidently about his work in a large computer firm, and about his new home. He invited me to visit there as soon as my other meetings were over. Then he turned to me with a sudden, pleading intensity that took me by surprise.

"I know you're going to see my mother. Penny [his wife] told me she had given you her number. Please do something important for me—I know you can help me with this. Find out about my father for me. My mother told me some things years ago, but it wasn't clear."

"Can't you yourself ask her?" I tried hopefully.

He sighed. "I haven't seen her for six years. I can't."

The physical distance of less than one hour's drive between them was mined by emotional barriers too dangerous to risk and too massive to circumvent.

"I can't," he repeated, and added, "It's better that way. Will you do it for me?"

"I'll try," I promised.

Gerda Nieman sat waiting alone at a corner table in the noontime bustle of the coffee shop. The brown polka-dot scarf by which I was to recognize her was arranged with casual chic around the neckline of her beige linen dress. Blonde, fiftyish, and attractive, she was indistinguishable from other shoppers until she spoke. The accent was still German. In answer to my question about how her son Sam had gotten to Lingfield, she began to tell me about her life. She grew up in an Orthodox Jewish family in Halle. Her mother died when she was nine, and she left home at fourteen. When she was eighteen, she married Sam's father, a Jewish butcher. When the baby was born, she chose his name from an approved list. "You couldn't name him Oskar or anything like that. It had to be a real Jewish name. The Nazis wouldn't let you choose anything else. His middle name is Tzadek, after his father's father.

"Sammy was about two weeks old when the Nazis broke into our apartment in the middle of the night, searching for something. They crashed around, broke furniture, threw dishes on the floor. We were scared to death. They read a paper, there was nothing you could do. They found one or two small roasts. Any self-respecting butcher would have had some meat in his house. They took him away. Sammy was in his crib. They didn't touch him or me."

"Did you see Sam's father again?" I asked.

"I visited him in a prison outside Berlin a couple of times. I had Sammy in my arms. He was a cute little guy, I felt safer going there that way. The last time I went there, they told me he was gone. Someone said he was shot. Another person said he died. Imagine a twenty-seven-year-old healthy man just dying," she said contemptuously.

"I went to work in DEGUFA—a rubber factory, the Deutsche Gummiwarenfabrik. It was slave labor, in exchange for rations. I left Sammy every morning at a Jewish child-care center. It was a long walk in the cold, carrying him there and picking him up every night. This went on for over a year. We had to walk in the gutters in those days," she said. "The Germans owned the sidewalks. One night I went to pick him up, and he wasn't there. The place was boarded up. There were no children there anymore. They had all been taken away. Women stood around crying. The police were there, shouting that you had to move on. They said they didn't know where the children were." The resignation in her face echoed the anguish of women unable to move on, rooted to the place where the scent of their children lingered.

"A few days later, a woman told me she heard the children were all taken to concentration camp, but that Sammy was in the Berlin Jewish Hospital with an ear infection. This was true. I went to see him. By this time I had a relationship with a very good friend, a German I knew for a long time. His mother was my dentist. They had a back entrance I could duck into. We decided to try to get Sammy out."

Her face lit with pride as she went on. "This man had guts. He was a real man. He dressed up in his full SS uniform, and the three of us walked into the hospital. He and I went upstairs and told them he was the baby's father and wanted to take the baby downstairs to see his grandmother. He told them she was too old to come up the stairs. But they wouldn't let Sammy out. The next time I went back the whole hospital had been evacuated." She sipped her coffee, without emotion.

"And you, how did you survive?"

"I married this man, and he and his mother protected me. They really stuck their necks out for me because I was ducked under [passing as a non-Jew]. When DEGUFA was evacuated to cattle cars for camp, they told us we didn't need any food, because we were going to be shot. I jumped out when the train slowed. Then I made my way back to Berlin and passed as Aryan. I was lucky that I was so blonde. There were some very bad times during air raids. I could not go down into shelters because they checked identification there—" She paused. "My friends helped me, German friends, sometimes strangers. Without them I wouldn't be here."

"After the war, this husband and I were blown apart. I took the two children I had with him and boarded them out. I went to work in a hotel as an interpreter for the Rainbow troops—the first American troops in Austria. I had to work." She sounded apologetic.

"When did you learn Sam was alive?"

"In '46 or '47, I think, the Red Cross told me he was living in England. He must have gone out in '45? Did you know him in England?" she asked me.

"No," I said.

"Have you met him?"

"Yes, briefly, yesterday."

"Is he well?"

"Yes, he's well."

"Miss Goldberger wrote me the children were there, and it was a lovely place but it was an orphanage, and she asked if I had plans to take him. For a while I thought to take him and wrote Miss Goldberger. But then what would I do with him? He spoke no German. I was still ducked under. I decided I couldn't take him. I had nothing, absolutely nothing. I had the two children boarded out, I was living in the hotel with other girls. It was no place to take a child to. The people who had the other two children couldn't take another child. I wrote to Miss Goldberger and asked her if she could keep him. Things didn't get any better with me, living from hand to mouth.

"Time," she paused. "Some years passed. Really, nothing happened with the situation."

"Did you write to Sammy?"

"No."

"Did he know that you existed?"

"I don't know, I don't know if Miss Goldberger told him."

"Did you think of writing to him during that time?"

"I considered, what would he think—I have a real mother and she can't have me. I was very torn. Here's a child who had been taken away by force, and I all of a sudden can't take him back. But the life he had there was better than the life I could ever give him in Austria. He had his daily food, clothing, education. In '47 I had nothing. It wouldn't have been fair. He would have come to a worse environment. Later I worked in the American PX, but still I had only my income to support myself and the two children. At that time Austria was in the ground—very poor. Today it's different, they have everything there.

"Then I got a letter from Miss Goldberger, saying that Sam had visited the States. I don't know how old he was then, thirteen? fourteen?—and that an American family wanted to adopt him. So first I thought, the people are well-to-do, this is probably the answer for him to have a decent life. It took me a long time to decide, but I couldn't do it. I couldn't send permission for the adoption. He was my child."

"Did you hope you would be able to take him someday?"

"I really didn't know. You see, when you live through a war like this, I think you lose your sense. You live from day to day. You don't think it ever will get better."

"There was no family to help you?"

"My father died in Buchenwald one day before the liberation of the camp. My brother had Parkinson's, he went to Sweden. To come to this country, I made some arrangements, with a man, by mail."

"Had you ever seen him?"

"No, it was a real Yiddish arrangement, I call it. I was strong then. I could do what had to be done. Now I'm like butter. I hate myself for it. As soon as I was established here I wrote to Sam. He was seventeen.

I don't know if Miss Goldberger intercepted the letter. She called him in and told him about the letter. I sent for him. I knew him right away. At first we were close. But it didn't work out. I didn't like him giving cigarettes to my fifteen-year-old daughter. He was young, stubborn, cocky. He couldn't stand me getting mad at him. He went into the Air Force.

"He married while in the Air Force. When he came out they stayed with us. And then I made a terrible mistake. He was unhappy just after his first baby was born, and I advised him to get a divorce before the baby was old enough to know him. That was a mistake. He lives with her, and that's okay, he doesn't live with us, it's his decision, but never to see his mother is not right. From work and to work, he went by our place twice a day and never stopped in."

"Have you tried to talk things over?"

"It doesn't work out. I say if you don't like us, don't deny the children their grandparents. But that's water under the bridge. I've lost an awful lot in my life, and so I've lost this too. I have to accept it."

"Have they said don't come and see the grandchildren?"

"No, I stay away because I got snubbed badly. It's too bad. I couldn't swallow it. You go through absolute hell for a child. Results, zero."

"But you didn't really raise him."

"That's right. If I had raised him this never would have happened. Believe me. He never would have shoved me aside." She was furious.

"But I will tell you something," she paused. "I have learned in life to take what comes, and if you can't change it, then that's the way it stays. You don't try, you accept it. Someday I would like to meet Miss Goldberger alone and ask her some questions."

"Yes, what would you ask her?"

"I would like to ask her about Sammy's childhood. About his development, about how he grew and what he liked. What foods did he like as a child? There is so much I don't know."

At the door of the meticulously cared-for suburban house were Sam's wife, Penny, and their three well-mannered children, Mark, eleven, Lydia, nine, and Robbie, four. Penny introduced me to the children as a friend of Alice's, which prompted Robbie to rush off and find a book I could read to him. I had brought a book about King Tut for the family, and the older children were fascinated with it. When Robbie returned with Dr. Seuss's *Are You My Mother?*, I remembered the little boy who was now Robbie's father, and his incessant question, *"Bist du mein?"* when he arrived from Terezin.

In the evening, with the children in bed, we sat downstairs in the den, Penny across from us, a bit watchful and protective.

"I feel I am terribly lucky to have come out of it all all right. Some people are affected, you know, badly," he whispered almost confidentially. "But I was so lucky to have survived, to have found Alice. . . . Why me? And why do I have so much? This beautiful home, a very nice wife, children . . . Why? Why don't some of the others have it this good? Life is so much harder for some of them."

Then: "Did you find out about my father?"

I told him what I had learned. He seemed relieved that the information I had brought was consistent with what he believed.

"Do you have any memory of Terezin?" I asked.

"Only barbed-wire fences and being locked up in a closet. I don't know now if I really remember this or if it was told to me. The same with the memory of sitting in the pilot's lap. I think I must have slept most of the way. But I do remember the lorries, those olive-drab army trucks that we rode back to Windermere in."

Penny, who had been sitting quietly, left to make tea. We were alone for the first time since the ride from the airport. In a hushed anxious voice came the question that has troubled him for a long time.

"You know a great deal about what happened to us when we were children—can you tell me . . . I mean . . . do you know if, if they experimented on us in Terezin?" There was a long pause, as if the difficulty of expressing that torment in words required a period of recovery. "It's something I have worried about for a long time, especially just after we were married and Penny began to plan, you know, when we were going to have children. For me it was a bad time then, because I thought maybe something had been done to me and I wouldn't be able to be a father. I didn't dare worry her about it. For three years, until our first child was born, it was really hard. I really worried."

I was relieved to be able to assure him that in Terezin, the camp that had been run to a greater extent than any other by its inmates, there had been no experimentation on children. We sat in silence, grappling with the enormous weight of the burden he had borne alone.

"You couldn't share your worry with Penny?"

"No. I kept these thoughts to myself. I didn't want to worry her if it turned out to be something else."

"You certainly kept a lot to yourself."

"I still do. I also am aware that this can over the long haul be detrimental inasmuch as you can just take so much, then comes the day when you get the straw that breaks the camel's back. I can get very upset. Sometimes I think it would be better if I could get a little upset more often. Some days I feel lucky I am where I am. Other days things look bleak, then I crawl into a shell. There are very few people I really trust. I think I have in my life been let down too often. It takes a lot to get my trust. Some who had it and lost it will never have it again."

"Do you remember learning that you had a mother when you were in Lingfield?"

"No, I don't remember that. What I remember is when I was about eight going round with a little note pad and trying to recall my German so I'd be ready to go to her in Austria. And then the whole thing went flat, and nothing happened." His voice conveyed disbelief and dismay. "Later I learned Alice found out that when I got to Austria, my mother was going to board me out. So Alice wrote her, 'Hey, if you're going to board him out, let it be right here. He already has a good environment here.' And that was the end of it—of going there. I never heard from my mother again until I was fourteen and learned that she would not give permission for me to be adopted. I didn't want to be adopted by that family anyway. I went there for a few weeks' visit. They had a kid my age who was weird. These people were extremely wealthy. Neither of the parents was home. The kid my age would ride his horse across the lawn, digging up the lawn and walk the horse right into the kitchen through one door, pick up a sandwich, and walk the horse through the kitchen out the other door. It was strange. If I wanted to go to a movie in town they would call a cab for me. Things like that were too much for me. If a fourteen-year-old kid wanted to go to a movie I thought he should damn well take the bus. Still think so," he laughed.

"Anyway I didn't want to leave Alice and the rest of the kids. Though when I left for America when I was fifteen to spend the summer with my American foster parents in Vermont, I was happy. My foster parents were two American psychiatrists—I had seen them several times when they were in England. They sent packages about twice a year too. In the summer all their clients went up there for the season and lived in houses on their grounds. There was a boy my age, and a handyman I liked very much. We got along well. Only one thing I didn't like—I felt like I was being observed by the psychiatrists. Still, I liked the place, I would have stayed with them. But the woman psychiatrist told me to go home, finish school, and then come back to

Chicago—their regular residence—and they would help me get started."

"I did go back, got in about one and a half years of technical training when a letter arrived from the States from my mother, asking me to come right then. Alice and Sophie pleaded with me to go first for a visit, not to quit school, but I was too cocky and thought I had all the answers. So I went. I flew to New Orleans via Chicago so I could see my foster parents. I'll never forget that visit." He shook his head in disbelief. "They told me that under the circumstances they thought it best to have no more contact with me. They said they'd always be interested in me, and wished me well. Then you know what they did? They handed me a slip of paper with the name of a *judge* in Chicago! If I ever got into trouble, that was the person to call! Did they expect me to get into trouble? I felt terrible."

Penny returned bringing tea and photo albums of Lingfield. We looked through them together; she knew everyone's names. "The children call her 'Grandma Alice,'" she told me proudly.

"You know," Sam began, "Alice had a talent for finding something you were good at and helping you to grow through it. She knew I was crazy about planes and arranged for me to meet with a real pilot several times. Things like that.

"Alice only cracked down rarely. For instance, if you hadn't written your foster parents—those letters were supposed to be in once a month—then you had to sit down and do it, and nothing else, till you did it. But she wouldn't stand for anybody bossing us around just for the sake of asserting authority. There was this guy who came to work at Lingfield House. Fritz and I were about nine, and he was going to run the boys like an army unit. Well, he didn't last, just a couple of days. Fritz challenged him to a fight."

"Fritz?" I remembered the image of the crippled boy in braces.

"Yes, Fritz had a real developed upper torso and could box—you didn't mess with Fritz, at first because Hedi would get you, Hedi could fight too, she was big and strong for her age, but then Fritz became quite a fighter—I would never mess with him. Well, Fritz boxed this guy out on the back lawn, pinned him down to the ground. We were standing around wildly cheering him on. Alice had that guy out of there by nightfall."

A picture of Sophie prompted reminiscence about her. "You could con Sophie out of just about anything. She's very high in my regard, though she was only the cook and she did our laundry. But it was more than that for her. It wasn't a job." His voice grew tender. "Like there were times I didn't eat. Of course, I'd get hungry after everyone was done. I'd go to Sophie, and she'd fix me something. Sometimes it was leftovers, sometimes she'd fix a goodie, like chocolate pudding." A small boy's delight at being treated with special affection lit his face across thirty years.

He reflected on what had gone wrong with his relationship with his mother when he first came to America. "I guess I had this picture that everything was going to be cozy, rosy, and warm, pure bliss, that the only word would be yes. It just didn't occur. Thinking about it now—what was I entitled to? But I think what happened is that Mother remembered me as whatever age I was at the time I was taken from her, and thought that was what she was getting. But that isn't the way I was. It was as if at one year and nine months, when we were parted, if she said 'Jump!' she wanted me to say 'Yes, and how high?' That's what she was expecting. But to me, if she said 'Jump,' I'd say 'How come?' Because I'd never been told to jump before. Bless Alice's heart. If she ever did anything wrong, it was she was too free with us.

"I have to say that I was far better off growing up with Alice and Sophie—I mean, I could depend on them. They gave of themselves. I have to say that I've come out of the thing better than if it had never occurred. Maybe it's cold of me. Look there were one hundred children that survived Terezin. So I was one of the one hundred. Right there if my whole life turned out bad I'd still be luckier than fourteen thousand nine hundred others. But no: I come out of there and I'm put in a good environment, better than many kids would find in their natural homes. Okay. Of course I can't blame myself for that, but again, I ask myself, why me?"

This feeling of undeserved exemption and subsequent guilt was also reflected in explaining his reluctance to press further claims for restitution money from the German government.

"But you did lose a parent," I said.

"I lost two," he corrected me.

Penny spoke. "Sam lets me take the children to church on Sunday, but he won't come himself. I hope and pray," she said, "that someday he will come with me." She looked at him pleadingly. Sam shrugged.

I asked whether to use his real name in the book. He blanched, began to speak, and then thought carefully for a long time.

"You know, there are still Nazis active in this country, you read about them. We've had phone calls where someone hung up when Penny was alone in the house with the children." Penny agreed that it was too great a risk to reveal his past. The name Samuel Schwartz is one he chose after long consideration. Its undeniable Jewishness contrasts sharply with his own real name, which gives no trace of his heritage.

SYLVIA GRUENER COHEN

London, June 1979

The office was at the top of a dark wooden stairwell. Sylvia had explained why she preferred that we meet here: her husband was a very private person, and it would be easier without the children around, two teenage girls and an eight-year-old boy.

I studied the B & G Locke Company from the inside and let associations come: lock, *Schloss* in German, "The Lock," and Edith Lauer's hushed voice when she had said those words during our interview the week before: "It was the place in Terezin from which there was no return. From there the transports were loaded for Auschwitz."

Sylvia came toward me, small and energetic. She looked much younger than forty, and her shoulder-length hair and the Peter Pan collar over her sweater emphasized the girlish look. The little girl wearing glasses—her head tilted forward in the old Lingfield pictures —was still there. A bit nervously, she showed me into an adjoining sunny room with a large desk and indicated that I should sit across from her. Then she clasped her hands on the shiny desk. She seemed to be enjoying a private joke as a smile broadened her face and her eyes crinkled behind the horn-rimmed glasses.

"Now what would you like me to tell you?" she asked formally.

"Is this your office?" I asked.

She laughed. "It's my boss's. He's away in Brussels this week. I asked him if I could use it when you came," she assured me. Her usual workplace was a small area of an adjoining room, she explained, and went on to tell me about the English office hierarchy: file clerk, shorthand typist, audiotypist, secretary, and then director. "I'm a secretary," she said proudly. "I wanted to be just a little office junior, but Alice put her foot down and said, 'No, that's not enough, just to do filing. You need a proper profession.' I'm grateful for it."

"Do you remember meeting Alice for the first time?"

"Yes, in Windermere. I was six years old, and we had cots, and she asked us, did we require nappies? And we said, no, thank you! We lived in one long huge building in Windermere. It was rather nice. There were little rooms, sort of bedrooms, but all our meals we had in this great long hall which was a few hundred yards down the road."

"Do you remember anything about the journey over?"

"Yes, it was a bomber plane and I remember I got nausea. It was a very bumpy ride. I kept wanting to play with all the switches and things. I was sitting quite near the pilot with a lady who brought me over, I think her name was Zelma. There was no separation at all between pilot and us. We stopped in Holland for about three hours. I think there were other children on that plane who weren't going to be under Alice's care. Probably about forty people. About eight of us came from Germany, others came from Czechoslovakia."

"Did you know these eight from Terezin?"

"No, but we soon became friends. Did you say Theresa?"

"No, Terezin."

"Oh, Terezin. I don't know if you could call this Terezin. I remember running. We could hear the planes. This was in Germany, I remember, when there was a shortage of food and we were near this orchard and I was picking cherries, and once they locked me in. I was four years old. I was hungry. I recall picking somebody's cherries, because I hadn't eaten maybe, and they locked me in a sort of cupboard but it wasn't maybe more than half an hour and that was all, you know."

She related this in the same good-humored tone with which she had described the secretarial hierarchy.

"Was this in Terezin?"

"No, this was in another, sort of a community place, where other children were playing, and this is what they did, before the journey."

"Were you in Terezin?" I was unsure as to whether she hadn't realized where she had been, or whether she actually had been elsewhere.

"When you're talking about Terezin, you're talking about t-r-e-a-s-o-n, what kind of treason?"

"T-e-r-e-z-i-n, the camp," I spelled it out.

"Oh, Terezin! No, no, I wasn't. I thought you were talking about treason! No, no, I didn't suffer or anything like that. Only my parents did."

Shock numbed me as her words spilled out. I was aware that only a moment ago she had told of being orphaned, running, hungry, locked up.

"I never knew my parents. I don't even know what they looked like. I think my mother's name was Ciwji. I don't know what my father's name was. But I think I had a brother. I'm not sure, but when I was about three I recall there was always a big boy in the house, but other than that I don't really know. It was very dingy, probably because of the fighter planes, they didn't want any lights to show out so that they wouldn't be bombed, so that the shutters were always sort of down.

"Then I was put somewhere in a home. A community place, I don't know the name of it. That's when I was in the German home of some sort. Slept in bunk beds. I remember the underwear they used to supply. One week you'd have a pair of pants with elastic, and the next week you wouldn't have elastic at all, you'd have a string. Such funny things." She laughed.

"I remember a woman used to scrub the floor at about two o'clock in the morning, who looked after us. They had wooden floor planks. They had the light on, of course. She used to use that very old-fashioned kind of bar soap. Sometimes we used to go out for a walk in our rain boots, used to slip all over the place. They had very bad snowfalls there in Germany. I used to hate going out in the snow."

"Do you remember anybody who took care of you?"

"I think I remember a woman named Zelma, middle-aged, she'd wear her hair back in a bun. If its the same woman I remember, she brought us over to Windermere, and left the door open when she'd take a bath," she laughed.

"So you don't know the name of the place you were in Germany before you came to England?"

"No, but it was mostly children, a few adults looking after us. That was where the thing happened with the cherries, you know." She looked up at me mischievously. "Poor little girl didn't have enough to eat. And I remember the stew they served us, mostly gristle, no meat. The food was terrible. I remember only once having a piece of bread with butter, mostly they put a bit of sugar on it. Ever since then I've always suffered with my teeth. I go for regular treatment but the dentist tells me my children's teeth are perfect. I look after them, because I don't want them to suffer the way I'm suffering now. I don't give my children sweets before going to bed, ever. They always clean their teeth last thing at night. My teeth aren't suffering so much from when Alice gave us sweets; I think it was from Germany when they put sugar on our bread. And the soup, it had a horrible smell as well. But in Weir Courteney and Windermere the food was fine. You know, Sophie's a very good cook."

"What do you remember of Alice then?"

"I remember a middle-aged woman. She wore a skirt and cardigan. I remember she had a room with clothes, given by charity. And we were each taken in turn to see what would fit us because we didn't come over with any clothes. I don't remember what I traveled in. I had an old rag doll with a *tsipfl-mitzer* [an old hat]. She lost her eye, I must have pulled it out. There were pretty little dresses. I picked a pink taffeta with black little flowers, and another one with apples and green leaves. Then I realized I was living in luxury, in Windermere. Alice made a room for a classroom, and that's where we learned *cat* and *dog* and lots of things."

"Do you recall how you felt then, toward Alice?"

"I thought she was somebody like a mother who would care for me. You know, and I still contact her regularly. I think of her as a mother. My husband knows that."

"Does your husband know about your childhood?"

"Well, no, not a lot. Oh, he knows that I was sort of an orphan and that Alice sort of came to look after me when I arrived in England. No, I haven't given him more history than that. I don't think it's quite any of his concern, quite honestly."

"Why isn't it?"

"I don't really know." She laughed self-consciously. "I think that's my business. Maybe because he's close to his sisters and brothers, and I don't want him to pass all the information on to them."

"What don't you want them to know?"

"Well, it's enough that they know that I haven't got any parents, or that sort of thing, but I don't want them to know. . . . I'd rather not. I'm not as close to my husband's family as I should be, but that's the way it is." By this small confession, she seemed to avoid being pressed toward the larger abyss. "But I still stay in touch with Alice. I call her, or stop by sometimes on my way from work. I'll get some coffee," she added, getting up and moving toward the door. "What do you take in it?"

Later she told me, "We used to have garden parties on the huge lawns at Lingfield. The London Synagogue Committee and their grown children would come. We used to decorate the tables on the lawns.

"There was also a little lobby house where two spinsters lived. They used to do a bit of washing up for Sir Benjamin, and I liked to go to their house alone. It was a little cottage, and they used to give me tea and make me bread and butter and jam on school holidays. Later on, there was Mrs. Spiegel. She used to give me five shillings when she'd see me. That was a lot of money then. She had a flat on Dollis Hill. Her son was training to be an architect at that time. I used to like to watch him work on his big easel making drawings of buildings.

"Once she held a garden party. And the tables were laid just like a

Buckingham Palace garden party, cakes and orange drinks. Then we'd eat and play games on the lawn. That was a very nice Sunday afternoon."

"Did your relationship with Mrs. Spiegel last long?"

"Oh yes, she came to the wedding, she witnessed the certificates. She came to visit me. At that time we lived in a very little flat. It wasn't much. It had no bathroom, just a little sink in the kitchen. I wasn't embarrassed then for anyone to see my place, as I would be now because it was a horrible place, although we decorated it and did everything we could to it. But it was terrible conditions and without running hot water. I brought three children up without running hot water. I used to boil it up." She smiled proudly.

"We got a hot-water heater later. In the beginning we were quite poor, really. In comparison to that, we're not doing too badly now.

"Mrs. Spiegel came once when my babies were small, and then a few months later she died of cancer."

"Do you have contact with her son?"

"No. Her son must be a top architect now," she said wistfully, but quickly added, "I've been to Churchill's house. Very nice. I'm now a member of the National Trust. I like going to houses. I go into all sorts of public houses to view them. . . . Churchill's house is in Kent, it's called Chartwell House. It's a great big house, with many paintings. He used to get a lot of gifts of cigar boxes. All his medals are displayed. All his uniforms that he used to wear are on dummies around the rooms, all the helmets he used to wear as well as his boots. He had, down at the bottom of the garden, a big brick shed, a sort of summerhouse, with all his paintings, because that was his hobby. You have to pay extra to see that. And on his grounds is a big huge swimming pool with a little bench that he would sit on. It's well kept. I like visiting people's houses."

"When you visit houses, is there any special thing that interests you?"

"Yes, the ornaments, vases, figures. Anything that's unique. Like the room with cigar boxes and medals in Churchill's house."

"And if you could build a dream house of your own, what would it be?"

She thought for a long time before she began. "A rock garden, also a little pond with fish. I don't like any too-small places, I think it gives me a phobia, which is why partly I want to leave this job. My regular space is with two men, and it's very small. I sit in a corner. I don't have a place to move around. I don't like to work in a corner. And it would have a greenhouse. And a summerhouse. It has to be spacious. I don't like anything that's too small or tight because it gives me claustrophobia, it makes you feel like you want to scream."

I wanted to ask if she had been able to scream that time in the "community," when she was locked in a cupboard, but her words raced past me, and I worked to make sense out of them and what had gone before.

"We don't spend or shop on Saturday. In fact, we have an automatic light switch for the Sabbath. We keep up all the festivals. We're having an extension built, and maybe then we'll have a sukkah. I think one's living premises should be very important to the individual.

"Another thing that should be important to the individual, especially in raising children, is education. That's number one, more than money, more than anything. I learned that from Alice, really. Alice mixes with educated people. We went to a party at Alice's, and I had my daughters with me. One of the ladies [of the Committee] came over and shook hands. She asked my oldest daughter what she's going to be when she leaves school, and my daughter said secretary. But if she had said she's going to stock the shelves at the supermarket, I would have felt ashamed. Because of all these years they've paid for us to be educated and educate our children. You know, through them we got our restitution quickly, so it wouldn't have been right to have our children grow up to work in Woolworth's. I'm grateful for Alice seeing to it that I have a proper profession. What I see from other families, even though they've got parents they seem deprived in some ways. Like there's one girl in my daughter's school, from a millionaire's family. She walks around in a T-shirt that says 'I'm a Twit!' I don't think she's anywhere near where my daughter is. When my boy was little, I'd leave my ironing and dusting and read to him just so he could read at an earlier age. Now he's eight and doing very well and sometimes helps other boys in his class."

"And what comes after education in importance for you?"

"Culture. And you need to be a bit financially well off, because otherwise how can you educate your children?"

"Anything else?"

"Well, I suppose love and affection, trying to lead them in the right directions, not to steal, not to spoil them. I don't think a child should be spoiled. There's one child in my Sunday School who lives round the corner and is brought to school in a car. Ludicrous, isn't it? I think they ought to be made to feel they should be independent later on. My kids always help me with the shopping, they go out now and they buy their own clothes."

"How did you feel about becoming independent after Lingfield?"

"The actual coming out was a problem, when I went out to the girls' hostel, I didn't want to leave yet. I was one of the first to leave. Gertrud took me to the hostel, and when I was taking my suitcases I was crying. Then when I saw the lady in charge of the hostel, I thought, oh no! For a while we used to go home to Alice on Friday and back to the hostel on the last train on Sunday. After a while I got used to it and accepted it. I think it was the Committee that decided we had to move out. They couldn't afford to run Lingfield anymore. So they had to break it up sooner or later, and I think they decided this hostel was a suitable place. It was Jewish, but what I hated most was it was in the East End of London, very dirty area, though the hostel was clean and nice inside. There were all these bric-a-brac houses on the other side of the road. Very old-fashioned, compared to the good house we'd been living in. And some of the houses were bombed out and they wouldn't be rebuilding yet. It was depressing, I hated it and the matron had a lot of rules. She kept the place in order: two floors, twenty girls, sixteen single rooms and two doubles." She went on with a detailed description of the floor plan. Finally she said, "I was glad to get out when I got married."

"What about the man you married?"

"He's a very private person. He shies away from photographs, even at weddings."

"What is his work?"

"He's a clerical officer, tells people where the mail goes. He works night shift a lot. . . .

"In Lingfield on Wednesday we'd have an art class, or a bit of music. There was always something happening. I miss that sort of thing. My husband likes to watch wrestling. He's a do-it-yourself man. Oh, when we go on holiday we look around at things, he likes that. But I write poems. Done it for years."

In a cheery voice she recited a poem called, "What Is a Perfect Secretary?"

Back in California when I listened to the tape of Sylvia talking about Theresa, treason, Terezin, I was disturbed again by the uncertainty about where she thought the "community orphanage" in Germany she spoke of had been. When I returned to London a year later and we met again, I asked her if she knew whether the German orphanage that she had told me about was in the concentration camp at Terezin. She did not answer directly.

"See, I don't know when my parents . . . I've never had any information."

"Have you asked Alice?"

"No, I don't think she knows. There used to be a solicitor down near the Finchley Road post office, and he had to do with compensation. He seemed to have records of things, going back to when I was twenty-one. He read it out to me. I don't think that office is still there. You got the information when they gave you the money. In those days they didn't have photocopies like they do now. Even if I'd asked for it, it might have taken someone three hours to type."

"Seems to me you might have been entitled to have that information typed, even if it took someone three hours."

"Like I said," she repeated, "that office doesn't exist now. But I know I was born in Vienna."

She had recently applied for a job in a large corporation. "They asked me a lot of questions, and I told them I don't know my parents' names. They acted surprised and I haven't heard from them since. Maybe they thought I was ignorant, but I passed my A-levels and all the exams I need for my profession. I think they want English people; you have to be of English parentage to work there. They supply airplane parts, fighting equipment," she apologized. "Maybe because I'm born a foreigner they didn't want to employ me." She said it casually, without rancor, as if it were just one more small annoying dark trap to be sidestepped and forgotten.

ZDENKA HUSSERL

London, July 1977

Alice greeted me at the door and took me into Sophie's room, where she introduced me to Zdenka, a slender woman clad in a rose sweatshirt and dark green ski pants. Thick curls framed an impassive oval face in which the dark eyes avoided mine.

In the busy clutter of Sophie's room, where the sewing machine was laden with work in progress, Zdenka and Sophie were silently reading the paper together while Budgie, the small caged bird, watched from his perch. Occasionally the scratching sound of his feet could be heard walking on the grainy floor of his cage. "He used to sing much more," Alice said.

"Don't you think it's time to put the strudel in the oven and prepare the vegetables, Sophie?" Zdenka reminded her. "Don't get up, Soph,

I'll do it. I know the way you want the carrots done, in fourths, right? The way you used to do them for the soup Friday nights?"

"Cut them small, *Zenkchen*—it will look nicer with the fresh peas and mushrooms."

"Wish we could have some of those fresh mushrooms we used to pick in Weir Courteney, Soph—remember when you used to take us across the woods to get them? You used to fry them up with onions. You don't seem to make them that way very much now, Soph . . ." she complained.

Sophie promised to make mushrooms and onions again soon. They went together into the kitchen. I turned to Alice and remarked on an array of small pots with thriving violets in them.

"Oh, Zdenka potted these for me. They had been in one big container and she divided them carefully and arranged them. She takes such good care of everything. She remembers the dates of everybody's weddings and birthdays. Zdenka has a marvelous collection of pictures of our children, very meticulously arranged in scrapbooks."

Zdenka was more at ease with me after dinner. "May I interview you?" I asked.

"Oh no, not me!" she protested. "I'm sure Alice knows more about everything than I do."

"But your experience is important too," I persisted.

We began in Alice's study.

"*We* were the *first* to meet Alice in August '45." She took pride in this. "The second group came in May, but we were the first. . . . That's why every year, on Alice's birthday it's . . . I don't know," she searched for words, "a bit touching.

"Our first Chanukah in Weir Courteney was in 1946. Everything was prepared for us. It was so warm, lights burning, everything lit up in this enormous house. It was lovely. I don't remember too much there. I do remember I loved my tricycle and Berli wanted it, so I gave it to him.

"But one thing I do remember, when I came to England, I remember when I arrived I was clutching a brooch. Did Alice tell you about that?"

"No."

"She wondered what it meant to me. But I didn't know. I couldn't tell you today. But I remember it more than Weir Courteney."

I started to ask more about the brooch, but she cut off my question quickly before I finished, with a loud, impassioned "I don't know.

"Also there was someone who came to England with us that I was very attached to. I sat on her lap on the way over. . . . But she went to America. She lives in Pittsburgh now. . . . She wanted to adopt me. Is this important? Do you want to hear this?"

I said yes.

"She wanted to adopt me, but it was very difficult to get in on the Czech quota through the American Embassy. They couldn't wait for my permission so they left for America. . . . Oh, how I cried, it was terrible. . . . After two years it finally came through, and by then I didn't want to go. I must have been nearly eight, and I didn't want to be adopted anymore. I was attached to Alice by that time.

"In 1961, after thirteen years, I went to America. My first stop was Pittsburgh. I arrived on the *Queen Elizabeth* in New York, and then I flew direct to Pittsburgh, because that was my main point of the visit. But I was *so* disappointed, I even cried there! As the plane came down I saw her waiting there, her husband too. I was so emotional and I couldn't wait to get there. But it was such a disappointment. . . . And, of course, gradually . . . she doesn't seem to write to me anymore, I don't know. Did Alice mention Mrs. Lauer? Very good friend." Her voice trailed off. "It would be so nice if she wrote to Alice for her eightieth birthday. But whether she will, I don't know. She used to write to me every year for my birthday. Now she doesn't write. I don't know how we met her, but she came over with us from Czechoslovakia. I was very attached to her. I suppose it was the feeling she could be my mother. Of course it's disappointing that she doesn't keep up with the writing. I think I feel more hurt than she does. You see, why she wanted to adopt me was that she didn't have children for something like ten or twelve years, and then when she had children, I suppose *they* were the focal point in her life, and I suppose I was grown up by then and I wasn't the little girl that she wanted to adopt. I don't know if I'm right. You know I've been through analysis, so I also see it that way.

"Are you going to use our real names?" she asked suddenly.

"That's up to you."

"Well, I wouldn't mind, I think it'd be a credit to Alice. We're individual people. Have you asked the others? What do they feel? Hedi? Fritz? I wouldn't mind. I mean, we have nothing to hide, *really*. After all, we can't help what has happened to us, and I feel there's no one better than Alice, why not?"

"Or better than you . . . in terms of knowing your experiences. There has been lots written about adults who survived camp experi ence, but hardly anything about the children."

"Why?" she demanded.

"I don't know. Maybe it's too painful to write about."

"But why shouldn't it be brought up?" She looked indignant over the conspiracy of silence which denied the reality of her loss.

Then she murmured, "The people I loved always died or went away. . . . That's the way it seems to be. . . . My first analyst went away to America. My second died. . . . It seems I'm always left. Even the people I grew up with, the ones who are far away, I remember their birthdays and write to them more than they to me. It's sad. One can't do anything about it. I don't forget people, I have always been reliable. When any of the children went away, they always asked me to look after their animals because I wouldn't forget to take care of them. But about my early memories there's some confusion. I know we came on a bomber and we landed in Holland. Now I have some friends in Holland, who told me this. When I told Alice she said we didn't land in Holland, we landed somewhere in England. But I asked Yezhek and he said, 'You're right, we did land in Holland.' But this stands out in my mind; it was an old bomber. People that came over with us, they sat on orange boxes and we sat on their laps. And I sat on Mrs. Lauer's lap. And we were sick, poor kids. And when we landed in Holland there were all these soldiers, and they waited for us with hot chocolate and fruit, and we all ate that because we were so hungry. Now this I remember and I asked Yezhek about it because he was about sixteen then, and he said, 'You're right.' But Alice said we didn't land in Holland, so there's a confusion there," she sighed.

"And what camp were you in?"

"Theresienstadt. Have you heard of it?"

"Yes. When I was in Israel, I visited a kibbutz where there are many survivors of that camp."

"Have you been to Jerusalem to see this Yad Vashem memorial?"

I nodded.

"When I was in Israel on a visit I went there to Yad Vashem and I met this person—he knows inside where all the books and files are kept. And he showed me because all the people that have been in camps, their names are recorded in this book. . . . He showed me my name is in there." Her voice flooded with pride.

"Luckily, I know when I'm born," she continued. "Shana and Esther have made-up birthdays, because no one knew. Alice gave them theirs; they had no birth certificates. . . ."

"So you were in Terezin for how long?"

"I think it was about two years. I know I went to the camp with my mother, and my father went to Auschwitz. Afterward my mother went there, and they died. Most people who went there died. But you know Shana, Esther, and Julius were there but luckily they are alive."

"Do you remember saying good-bye to your mother?"

"No. The only thing, I don't know if its' true, but you see this burn on my hand? That I think is not from the camp, I think I put my hand in the oven at home. But otherwise I can't say I remember her. Alice tried to see if she could get pictures of her . . . but it was impossible.

"After the camp we stayed in a castle in Prague. Again I don't know if my memory is right, but that's where I remember sleeping in bunk beds. And somewhere we ran around naked. I can't remember if that was in the castle or in the camp. Also I had my hair shaved. Now *that* I remember as if it was today!" Her laugh was one of surprise. "They put us between a woman's knees, and they put this towel around us and they shaved our hair off and I screamed! Maybe that's why my hair grew curly, I don't know, people say sometimes your hair grows curly if you've had it shaved off. You see, we had lice. But I don't know if that was in the camp or in the castle, but it was before we knew Alice." She paused, reflecting on her confusion, and concluded, "So you see, Alice can't really help in this because when I was younger I asked about these things, but she can't answer because she doesn't know.

"I don't think we could have been brought up better, had we had our own parents," she reflected. "I mean, we had what any other normal child could have: we had animals, bicycles, school; it's all through Alice and Sophie.

"Sophie was more domesticated. She could cook, sew, do practical things. . . . Perhaps that's why Sophie likes me around. I always liked sewing—did you see the chickens I embroidered on the tablecloth we made for Alice? I was good at sewing. When I left school I went as an apprentice for a dressmaker. Sophie taught me how to embroider, mend, sew, and iron. I always did more than my share."

"Some of the children went to Israel. Had you ever thought about doing that?" I asked.

"No, although I live in a bed-sitter, I feel my home is in England. And, I don't want to . . . really be far from Alice and Sophie." She paused to consider that. "Sometimes I think if I did live in Israel my life would be different. I've been there for a visit. I've been to America for a visit. I go skiing every year. But I like to come back here. It's a funny feeling. But it's home here.'

It was dark as we walked home from Alice's. Zdenka wheeled her bike between us.

She told me she had worked in a florist shop for a while before her present job as clerk in a large supermarket. "What are your favorite flowers?" she asked me.

"Roses," I answered, "and you?"

"Lily of the valley. It's Alice's favorite flower too, did Alice tell you? For her birthday I brought her a bunch of lily of the valley. She was so pleased. And it's Miss Freud's favorite—also Miss Freud's father. It's a bit of trouble for me to do it now, to get the flowers for Alice to give Miss Freud for her birthday, but I always try to do it for her, to get it through the buyer at the shop. Oh yes, I miss the flowers, now that I'm not working with them."

I asked her what flowers she liked for arrangements.

"Well, I like facing work mostly, sometimes all around but mostly facing. If it's lily of the valley time, which is about the end of April, regardless of what the arrangement is I tend to pick my favorite flowers. Once the girls said, 'Trust Zdenka to pick valley.' And I said, 'I can't help it, *I'm* making it, and if it's my favorite flower, I will make it better! You know, I think if you're working with flowers *you* like, the work comes out better. Another flower that I love and Alice also loves is gentians—little blue flowers. If they're about I tend to use those, like when I have to make cradles for a newborn baby at a hospital, for the mother. If it was lily of the valley time, of course I'd use that, but if it was September, for a boy I'd use blue gentians."

As we neared the corner where we'd separate, she told of a floral assignment that had been very important to her. "This big funeral that was the biggest job I ever had to do. People always feel because it's a funeral they'll put any old rubbish in, and a woman at the florist, she used to make us use up all the old flowers in this sort of work. Imagine!" She was indignant. "Did the mourners not deserve better? Sometimes the customers stated what they wanted. This time there was a sweet little heart from the granddaughter. She was only two. It said, 'To Grandad from Tanya.' It was *so pretty*, carole-roses, it didn't even look like for a funeral. But I always feel, for the mourners, that's the last!" She flared. "And if they've paid for it, why should you make rubbish? Well, in this shop they said that my funeral work is *too good!*" Her eyes twinkled as she chuckled. "But I always remember that little heart. From the wife there was also a heart. It was a complete thing of roses, nothing else, and it was a lot of money. No, I feel it's the last, and it should be done well. I've always felt so sorry for the mourners. And oh, some of the cards, you nearly cried when you read them. I always felt so sorry for what people expressed on their cards. . . ."

Intermittently the glow of a streetlamp illuminated the beauty and sadness of her face.

We walked silently for a time.

"I know you're leaving in a couple of days." We were on the verge of saying good night when she asked, with an unexpected rush of feeling, "When are you coming back again, Sarah?"

In the past year Zdenka's letters have brought news of a more responsible job in the supermarket, and a wonderful visit to the Kesslers in Australia. Recently she's moved next door to Alice and Sophie.

MARTA VINDFOGEL

Cologne, West Germany, July 1981

Our footsteps echoed down the long empty corridor to her room. Marta stood in the doorway, a small slumped woman in a shapeless dress.

"Greet your visitor," Nurse Maria coaxed cheerily as we entered the room where three metal beds stood with dolls in them.

"Guten Tag," she winced, eyes downcast.

I told her I was happy to have found her, that I had searched for her a long time. She listened, head down to one side like a bird. Then she looked up with large blue eyes, clear as a doll's, and asked, "Haben Sie mir ein Paket gebracht?"

I handed her the package with the blue Sunday dress she had asked for, the day I called the hospital, the day the Red Cross cable came. There was silence as she opened the wrappings.

The nurse exclaimed lavishly over the dress and insisted Marta try it on. In a moment Marta stood before us in her white cotton underwear, obediently holding up both hands over her head. I looked away. A large wooden crucifix hung on the wall.

"See how nicely it fits you. We just have to shorten it," the nurse said with real delight and encouraged Marta to look in the mirror. At the sight of herself she looked blank.

When we sat down together at the table, I gave Marta a small box of chocolates bought on impulse for her at the train station. She gulped the first few quickly, hunched over the box. "Sie schmecken gut, die Praline," she said many times in a whimpering voice as she ate, never looking up. Each time she said they were good I agreed.

When they were mostly gone she offered one to her nurse. And when Nurse Maria refused, saying, "No, dear, they're all for *you*," Marta beamed, grabbed her nurse's hand and kissed it. Then Maria left.

I asked which bed was hers and she led me to the bed with two dolls, a large blonde named Inge and a smaller black male doll named Petra.

"Haben Sie eine Puppe?" she asked me.

I told her no, but that I had three children, named Debi, Ruthy, and David.

Her voice was urgent as she said, "I need another doll. Bringen Sie mir ein Püppchen in einem grossen Paket?"

"What kind shall it be? Male? Female? Baby doll?" I asked.

"Eine grosse Frau [A big woman-doll]. Ein Püppchen in einem grossen Paket." She grew excited as she repeated "Ein Püppchen in einem grossen Paket."

"Yes, I'll send a Frau," I agreed.

She took my arm and we began walking from one corridor to another where silent old people shuffled past.

"Will it come for my birthday?" she asked.

"I don't know," I said, remembering that her birthday was in September and that she would be forty-six years old. "You see, it will come from far away. I live in California. That's in America, so it must come by ship or airplane."

"For Christmas then?"

"By Christmas for sure." She clutched my arm more tightly.

"Do you remember when you were far from here with Alice Goldberger?" I asked.

"Yes," she said, "in Berlin. I was born in Berlin."

"Do you remember Berlin when you were very little with Alice?"

"Yes."

"And after Berlin?"

She looked blank for a while and said, "England."

"If Alice can come tomorrow, would you like to see her?"

"Yes, oh yes," she nodded.

She was standing at a window in the long corridor looking out when we came up to the floor. She recognized Alice instantly. "Da kommt die Goldberger," she said, coming toward us. Her toes turned severely inward. Did she need treatment or different shoes? She threw her arms around Alice.

A nurse came and toured us around the hospital. Alice was pleased with the cheerful red tablecloths in the dining room, the plants and nice armchairs in the empty day room. Our guide told Marta to wait as we were ushered into the office of the hospital's psychiatrist.

"Can't Marta come in with us?" I looked at the doctor, a woman in a white coat, sixtyish and hard-faced.

"You don't really want her in here now, do you?" With a decisive movement Dr. Schmidt slammed the window shade down the length of the glass door behind which Marta stood. I was shocked by how easily I was silenced by this authoritative woman.

Her large office was all white and filled with metal cabinets. It was as intimidating as an operating room. From where I was told to sit I could see medications and hypodermic needles behind shiny glass doors.

Alice broke the tension with compliments for the cheer and cleanliness of the place. The doctor warmed a bit and told us that some of the inmates had their own furniture.

"What is your interest here?" She was curt and correct.

Alice told her about caring for Marta in England after the child's liberation from Terezin.

The doctor, shocked, sat upright in her chair. "Terezin? Where was that?" she demanded. "But that was in Austria, nicht wahr?"

Until this moment, she swore she had not known that Marta had been in a concentration camp, though she had been her psychiatrist since 1969. "Ich habe, davon nichts gewusst. It is nowhere in the record," she said.

"Now that you know this, would it be possible to apply for restitution so that Marta could have furniture in her room?" I inquired.

"Oh, no. She is already a ward of the state, and has all her needs met. Besides, she's in a different section, for the chronic cases. No one there has his own furniture. She is content, on mild sedation, very mild," she assured us and went to a glass cabinet and brought back a packet of Troxall.

On the train back Alice and I each sank into our own thoughts. For me the clacking wheels kept echoing Marta's urgent reminder when we parted, not to forget "ein Püppchen in einem grossen Paket. Ein Püppchen in einem grossen Paket."

From Auschwitz

SHANA TRAUBOVA JOSEPH

London, November 1978

The tiny entry hall of the old wooden house in the Chasidic section of London's East End was decorated with children's crayon pictures. Shana wore a kerchief over her hair in the traditional way. It framed a welcoming smile as she came forward, a light blue teacher's smock over her plaid skirt. She had two children in tow. The little boy clutched her skirt in one hand, with the thumb of the other in his mouth. The little girl folded herself into Shana's skirt. I heard the pleasant noise of children, and saw that about twenty of them occupied the open rooms on either side of the small entry. A large Hebrew alphabet occupied half of one wall. A few children painted at easels, while others sat at small, old wooden tables, cutting, pasting, coloring. The little boys' hair had not been shorn, and the fringes of the religious vests hung freely below their T-shirts and sweaters. Very much in charge, Shana took my coat. Introducing me to her assistant, she told her to move the children into story time.

"We always have that before lunch," she explained to me. "It quiets the children—then they eat better."

She began helping children to put away their materials. "You know, at this age they can't do it all themselves, so we have to help them." Then she came across a paper that had fallen to the floor, and picked it up with excitement. She gathered the children and held up the paper, its brown crayon scrawls barely recognizable.

"See the beautiful tent that Aaron made—I think it must be like Abraham's tent in the wilderness. We must not let this be trampled on the floor. Aaron," she addressed a frail blond child whose eyes were glowing with pride, "such a lovely picture must be treated with care, darling. We must put your name on it." She whisked out a black crayon from her pocket, put the crayon into his fingers, and guided his hand.

The smell of baking pita bread filled the air of the small brick townhouse. Shana, with the help of five-year-old Devorale, was preparing dinner. Talking energetically, she told about buying this house.

"We did it ourselves," she said. "Tsiyon and I, working and saving. I think when you grow up in a family like Tsiyon's you see your parents struggle, and it's not so foreign to you. For me it was very tough. We had clothes, food, everything in Lingfield, but not growing up in a family, you don't realize where it all comes from. Tsiyon, of course, as a Yemenite immigrant to Israel, saw his parents wrestling with poverty and learned how important it was to save and plan. For me it was new and difficult, but Tsiyon helped me."

We went into the living room, where Tsiyon worked quietly at a corner table on some architectural drawings. Devorale sat on the patterned rug near her mother's feet.

Shana talked about her work. "It is a private school, of course," she said. "There is general education as well as stories of the Torah. Torah is taught by my assistant. We have these young girls who go to the seminary to study for two years before they get married, and usually they're very sweet. I am basically in charge of the activities. I see to it that the paints and things available for the children are appropriate for their age and suited to their development. I'm also in charge of the separation when a new child enters."

"Would you explain that, please?"

"I have a system. The first day, mother comes, and we establish rapport. She tells me about the child, about his sleep patterns, food habits, etc. Child and mother stay the whole morning through dinner at noon and have dinner with us at noon. We have a nine-to-four day. The child is *not* left by the mother the first day. This way the child has carried away a good picture of school in his mind. I haven't pushed the mother away—the mother hasn't left yet."

"I wish we had this everywhere," I commented.

"Oh, it's cruel," she lamented passionately. "I can't stand it when parents aren't allowed in a nursery when the child is put in. It's so cruel to the children. It's such a traumatic experience. Really, they have to cope with it anyway, but I try to do it in a kind way. To be human with children is very important. I can't stand any rigid method. You've got to be very flexible—they're all different people, you know. So the second morning, the mother comes with the child and stays an hour or two. And then we tell the child that Mommy's going shopping. I always say to a mother, 'Say good-bye.' I never let a mother persuade me to let her slip out. She'll say, 'He'll be upset if I say good-bye.' I tell her, don't mind if he'll be upset, because *I'm* going to take care of him. And you should be confident that I'm going to be kind to him. So we're beginning to make a separation. And the mother goes for an hour. She might feel very anxious—usually buys him a little something, and then she comes back and stays with him. So there's a little separation. Sometimes the child will wait by the window. Some cry a lot. I put the child on my lap and I take him around with me and help them to make a relationship with me.

"The next day the mother leaves him for a whole morning, and that's the first long separation. I encourage the child to join in our day, and again I take special care. Some mothers get very worried or anxious when they have to leave the child. I tell them to go home and phone me up as many times as they wish. I'll tell them exactly what their child is doing. If he's screaming, I'll tell you, I say. And I'll tell you when to come for him. It seems to help them to know they can call me."

"You saw, our school is in a very old derelict building. You saw that, didn't you? But it's not the building that counts, it's people. And we must try to do things in a kind way."

Devorale held up her carefully detailed picture of a house, a tree, and flowers.

"It's beautiful," her mother said, and to me, "I used to spend a lot of time drawing when I was a child."

"Do you remember being separated from your mother?" I asked, as gently as I could.

"No, I don't remember that at all. I can't remember my mother or my father. And we had no papers, you know. I don't know anything about them." She folded her arms, stiffening a little as if to brace against further shock. "I haven't got any memory of my parents. No, none at all. We don't even know their first names. There were no papers—we just knew *our* names, Shana Traubova and Esther Traubova—they said we were about a year apart."

"Can you remember anything at all before coming to England?"

She brightened, smiling. "I remember a woman named Malka—I don't know who this person is—and I have a memory of being taught Czech songs, maybe by her. I feel I can pronounce the language very well now when I sing.

"You know, an interesting thing happened," she continued animatedly. "When I was taking my nursery training, we had a social worker working there, his name was Ron. He visited Czechoslovakia, and when he came back he told me that I reminded him of people there." Again she smiled. "He said it was my interest in singing and art and decorative skills. He said that, but," here her words slowed, "I really don't know if that really *is* where I came from. . . ." She looked up at me searchingly.

She went to the kitchen, where I heard the oven door open and close. Her quick energetic steps resounded in the silence. A fruit bowl was in her hands when she returned.

She talked about her earliest memories of Lingfield, of being taken into the orchards by Sir Benjamin.

"He loved children—his wife too—but I remember him better. He would take us by the hand, after we came home from school, and walk into the orchard. He would pick an apple or something and talk to us. He was an old man then, and I felt it was important to him to give us something. He had a big dog, and Sir Benjamin used to make the dog sit up, and it used to howl 'Baa Baa Black Sheep.' We loved it.

"I remember helping Sophie in the kitchen. In the summer we used to sit outside the kitchen in a little circle and shell peas and sing."

She brought picture albums to show me. A picture of girls in Alice's room reminded her of a childhood problem.

"I had a maths teacher that I didn't like. She was very strict, and maths was hard for me. I had great worries at night about going into that class. When I couldn't sleep at night I'd go into Alice's room to see her, and she used to talk to me. She had a little donkey in her room, a toy. You had to open it from the bottom where the tail was and it had sweets inside. We all loved that donkey. It was nice to be able to go into Alice's room when I had worries. There were periods of time when it used to take me awhile to go to sleep."

She took pleasure in reminiscing about people who were kind to her and her sister.

"Did you know we had a special auntie? To give us the feeling of having a relative in England. All the children had one. They were West London Synagogue members. They took us, my sister and me, for weekends sometimes. Their names were Auntie Sally and Uncle Oscar. They had a dachshund, and they loved this dog. It was their baby. We had very good times with them. I remember one incident. It was during the time of rationing in England. Everybody had these ration books, and our auntie had saved eggs for us. And I remember I made a terrible mess of it when I was opening my egg. I could see she was kind of upset that I was wasting it. Then she helped me to eat it.

"Mrs. Heilbron, my next auntie, always kept in touch with me. Now, too, if a certain amount of time passes and she doesn't hear from me, she'll call. Their daughter, Annette, was our childhood music teacher.

They've always shown an interest in me. You can feel it when people have a good feeling for you, can't you, Sarah? For instance, Tsiyon's parents, especially his mother. Devorale and I lived with them while Tsiyon was away in the army, and she speaks no English at all. But we got on. I could see she wanted to help me, to be family.

"It was during the Yom Kippur War in '73. Tsiyon felt he had to go back to Israel to fight. He's a tank commander. Devorale was an infant. I had never met Tsiyon's parents. I was scared. But Tsiyon said to me, 'You must call her *Ima* [mother] and she will love you.'

" 'But Tsiyon,' I said, 'what if she *doesn't* love me? She may not even like me at all. How can you be so sure?'

" 'She will love you because I chose you and brought you home,' he said.

"And that is really the way it was. She did accept me like a daughter, straight off, without question. I'm very grateful to her for that. I could feel them wanting to be good to me, to be family. We are very close."

Tsiyon, slight and fine-boned, was sitting in an armchair across from us, and drew on his pipe and nodded agreement. I asked him how it was that he was willing to go back to danger in 1973, and to take his wife and child.

Patiently but without condescension, he explained. "There is this sense of responsibility. We have to have it so that Israel will survive. Maybe as individuals, we ourselves won't survive. But if through our individual acts of courage Israel survives, then it will have been worth it."

Shana listened to him with pride, then continued leafing through the photo album. A picture of herself smiling at eleven brought reminiscences of a trip to America.

"The American Foster Parents group sponsored two children to come to the States for six weeks and make public appearances for their work. We were on the Art Linkletter show and Steve Allen. It was during that trip that somebody in the States tried to contact us. They thought that my sister and I might be their children. Their name was Traub too, and they had lost their children, as so many people did. They had little girls by the same names that had been in concentration camp. There was an appointment made for them to see me. And they came over to see me. But we weren't the children." She paused, and then spoke as if anticipating my next question. "I don't know how I felt. I think it was a bit of a buildup. Most probably it was terrible for them too. There were many children with that name. And they were like many people who had lost their children."

"But how did they know you weren't their child?"

"I don't know—maybe feature-wise. It was a couple that came over. It was terribly disappointing. For both sides." With sudden cheer, she asked, "What else shall we talk about?"

Later, she reflected, "It was only when we were older and the home broke up and we had to separate and find our own way into life that I can recall any emotional feeling of wanting my parents. There must have been feelings and questions, where's my mother, and so on, but it's such a difficult thing that I can't remember. Alice may remember, but it's a difficult thing to answer when there's nothing concrete. When all the information has been destroyed. . . .

"But you know, I don't feel I'm any different from other normal people. Recently I've gotten to know someone, a friend, more intimately, and she asked me about my parents. So I said to her, 'I haven't got any,' and then you see the person get very worried and upset—how are they going to cope with this if they've embarrassed me, which they have not, because I've learned to cope. I'm not emotional about it. I feel strong about myself now.

"Then she said she was so surprised because I was such a happy and capable person. I think it was quite a compliment. I know that for some people it has been a hardship not having parents. I'm very sympathetic. Some people haven't been able to cope with life. It's too hard for them to grow up, not having parents, to take advantage of life. They are very lonely people. It's very sad. Most people are not sympathetic to someone different like that, and they do cast away people who don't fit into their lives. Most people who grow up in a family are pretty confident. I've seen the girls who are my assistants when they're sixteen, seventeen. These girls are confident, not at all shy, and so capable. They know how to dress, how to go about life, how to cope. You can speak with them about many things. I compare them to how I was at that age, and it's really an amazing difference. I was very lonely, insecure, and things just didn't work for me. It took me a lot longer to grow up and sort things out . . . and to get over this feeling that people will think I'm so different not having parents.

"But the best medicine I ever took in my life was when I went to Israel to a kibbutz at twenty-one. It was the best thing for me in helping me become a person. The pace is rougher there. You relate to people, make friendships. You work hard. It's a healthy atmosphere. I made a few very good friends. There were Americans, Dutch, Scotch, and Irish on the kibbutz, I got to know people. It helped me grow up and become more confident. But when I came back here I was confused, depressed. I had to start over and settle down and find work. After a few salesgirl jobs, I took the nursery training. But the good experience of Israel stayed with me. Actually, Alice always wanted me to work with children. But there was a period where I didn't want to, just because she wanted me to. She knew I was sympathetic to children early on. It's like any mother who's in a kind of work. You find that, don't you, in a family, that one of the children will go into the same work?

"One of the things I love about my job is that people confide in me and have confidence in me, and that gives me a lot of confidence. I'm the pillar there. I enjoy it. I like the people, I like the program, I like the *davening* [praying]. Devorale goes to school there, and she loves it. I think she'll have a beautiful feeling of security in Judaism that I didn't have as a child. She'll have the Sabbath, a close community, a calm belief, and a pattern of observance. You know, in this place we don't pray to God. That is, we don't say the word 'God.' We pray to *Hashem* [the Name], *Hashem*, I think that's really beautiful, *Hashem*." Shana pronounced *"Hashem"* lovingly. She looked peaceful. "Religion is an important basis of a person's life, a firm foundation," she said.

"Do you want me to sing a song about *Hashem?*" Devorale offered eagerly. She sang with disarming intensity, forging ahead despite the occasional cracking of her voice on the high notes, sure of the pleasure on her parents' faces.

ESTHER TRAUBOVA MANDEL

London, November 1978

A bright blue ceramic tile plaque of oriental design had been placed near the doorbell of the Mandel apartment. On it, English letters spelled out *"Anavim,"* the Hebrew word for grapes. It is the kind of tile that can be bought in one of the ancient, musty stalls of Jerusalem's Old City marketplace. A fresh cloudburst of hard rain fell sideways onto the porch where I waited to enter. Esther took my raincoat and ushered me into the dimly lit living room. The lace curtains at the opposite windows gentled the view of hard gray fences and apartments lashed by rain. The slip covered couch and the doilies under lamps shared a soft, much-laundered look. But the Sabbath candlesticks sparkled on the plasticized white cover of the small dining table and caught my eye. A thick pile of Yiddish newspapers was on the coffee table. There was an intensity about Esther that was both warm and anxious as she apologized for the brief time we would have to talk. She had an appointment to see her doctor at 4:30. She was troubled by headaches and needed to get a prescription refilled.

We sat down at the table. The bangs of her dark, shoulder-length hair were visible from under the triangular kerchief she wore in the manner of Orthodox women. Her face was pale but animated.

I asked her about her work at the same school where her sister Shana teaches. She described it with enthusiasm.

"I help do the cooking and serve the children their lunches. They get a hot lunch there every day." She was proud of this. "And I also watch the children out in the yard. It's part-time work. I like it because I can be home when my children come home from their school and I don't have to leave home until *after* they go in the morning."

"Did Alice tell me that you trained as a dental assistant?"

"Yes. . . . The training was not easy. That is, the written exam part was very, very hard for me. I didn't pass the first time." Her honesty was winning. "There were some very nice people who helped me study for the exams, and then I did pass. I started to work as a dental assistant, but I found it was very hard to be *shomer shabbos* [an observer of the Sabbath] in that work, so I don't do it. Now, of course, in this job at the school it's no problem." There was pride in her voice as she spoke of her husband.

"When I was pregnant and I didn't feel well, he did everything for me. I did absolutely nothing. I had to just lie and rest. I had toxemia. He used to come home from work and he was up till one, two in the morning getting things done. He has always helped me, even before. He asked me to keep kosher before we were married, and so I do this. He was brought up like this. Very observant. We go up the road to the Litvishë Shul. It's on the top floor in someone's house—ever so nice! These people are millionaires—they could live anywhere. Yet they want to live here in this neighborhood! They treat their house like Abraham treated his tent!"

I recalled her sister's reference to Abraham's tent when she demanded that her little pupil treat his drawing with respect.

Her excitement grew as she continued. "He doesn't have anyone staying in that part of the house. Can you imagine? And the *shul* is built in it on top! The woman of the house, she's got ten children. She looks like only twenty years old! They're very wealthy. She has a cook, a nurse, a cleaner, absolutely everything!" She paused. "That's their life. . . ." She sounded wistful.

"And do you go there on *Shabbat*?"

"Yes, and Aaron goes every morning. Seven o'clock he goes to *shachris*. He goes to *mincha* in the afternoon at work. Our daughter goes with him on Saturday. She loves to go with him. Our son on weekdays *davens* at his school. He learns both Hebrew and Yiddish there."

When she left to make tea, I realized that I was experiencing a strong sense of déjà vu. The slipcovers, the curtains, the scent of old Yiddish newspapers, the candlesticks returned me to my parent's house.

I asked about her earliest memories.

"I remember Shana, of course. And then I remember a woman —Malka was her name, I think, and Julius, I remember him. I was three. I was the youngest in that group that came from Auschwitz.

"The grounds of Weir Courteney were beautiful. Sir Benjamin would take us round for walks and give us fruit from the trees. Peaches, he picked the biggest for us. We all had lovely dolls. . . .

"On *Shabbes* it was fantastic, all the tables were pushed together, everyone was home; we all ate together. And Alice was at the head table. We had to take turns to sit next to her. During the week there were eight separate tables, and Alice would take turns sitting at each one.

"We used to have chicken, orange juice, and little *challas* that Sophie baked for us. Now I do the same with my kids, that's where I learned it. I've kept all that. It was fantastic, really. We were always all home for *Shabbes*. And Sophie was busy in the kitchen. . . . I used to love the kitchen, and I remember Sophie used to say, 'As long as I have little Esther in the kitchen, I don't need anyone else!' " She glowed with pleasure. "I was very efficient. I loved the kitchen. I love it now.

"Another thing I loved was Alice putting us to bed. She'd sit on the bed and we'd say the *shema* and get a sweet—chocolates! It was unheard of; chocolates were rationed then, it was after the war. I used to love that, and I do that with my children now. . . . We only wanted Alice to put us to bed. If she had to be gone to a meeting and if she couldn't get back in time, we'd be very upset.

"People used to call me Gertrud's pet. I loved her. I liked her discipline too. She was more strict than the others. She used to take me to her parents' home for weekends, her parents were wonderful people, too. When I got engaged I went first to visit Gertrude. You know how you get attached to people.

"You know, now that I think about it, we all must have been terrible kids to raise. We all had problems, we weren't ordinary, easy kids. Some of us had a hard time, to adapt. X—— used to imagine her mother was alive, and a duchess."

"And you, did you imagine anything about your family?"

"Shana used to think we had older brothers. But I can't remember

that we had any. I do have a feeling, I think we came from an
Orthodox Jewish family. We must have been born in the camps. . . .
We had numbers on our arms, you know. At school they would tease
us; they would call us 'Hey 8, 2, 0,' you know. So Alice thought we
should have them removed. Alice came with us. We kicked up such a
fuss about staying in hospital at night that they had to take us out. It
hurt to take the stitches out. The doctor, he was a very old man, not
very good, I think. It's not supposed to hurt to take stitches out, but it
did. Alice was upset. It was a skin graft, the numbers weren't in a
straight line."

"You mean he had to remove skin?" I asked.

Quickly, she rolled up her sleeve and answered impatiently, disturbed by my failure to understand.

"Yes, of course. It was a skin graft."

She held out her right arm for me to see the contrasting pale
crescent patch marking the place where she had endured hurt and
shame. Her outstretched arm, supported at the elbow by the other
hand, made the universal gesture of generations of children asking
for help and comfort from adults.

"It hurt so badly," she said in a plaintive voice.

In a flash, I saw her as a small uncomprehending child, stamped
like a parcel. The thought of her absorbing this and making any
trusting sense out of the world filled me with rage.

But she had recovered. The plaintive voice was gone. I heard her
talking excitedly about her marriage.

"I had a fantastic marriage in a *shul.* I had everything I wanted.
Alice had her whole flat for me for the party. I could invite whoever I
wanted. I had a table full of flowers, an enormous cake and everything. It was a fantastic wedding. Mrs. Rubens came, Mrs. Pinto
[Lingfield Committee people]. Wolf Blomfeld gave me away. He had
introduced me to my husband. It was really fantastic!

"You know Alice *never* pretended to be our mother. She just made
things good and happy for us, and that's why I never felt I missed
anything when I was a child. Only later, did I realize, you know. . . .
When I was going to get married they asked me all this rubbish.
Where are your parents, they asked? And that made a problem to get
married properly. You see you have to have your parents' birth
certificate to get married in a *shul,* and we didn't have it. Don't laugh,
you have to prove you're Jewish to get married in a *shul,* and *I couldn't
prove it!*"

"And the scars on your arm weren't enough?"

"No! They said that they had *au pair* girls who had married, who also had had scars removed. They made it a nightmare to get married in a *shul*.

"My husband couldn't get over it. He insisted, because my children would later have trouble if I didn't get married as a Jew. 'It's your right more than anybody to get married in a *shul*,' he said. So we went to Dayan [Judge] Grossman, and he was wonderful about it." She smiled broadly. He said to my husband, 'I'm not worried about Esther, I'm worried about you.' He was terrific."

She paused thoughtfully. "Now I've got what I want and I've got more than what I want. . . . I used to say I wanted six children, but that wasn't to be. I had a Caesarean with my youngest and I was so ill with toxemia I was in bed for thirteen weeks. Alice came and sat with me for nights in hospital. I think my husband would have liked a big family, but it wasn't to be. I've got two and I'm giving them a good chance, like I had."

"You do feel then that you had a good chance?"

"Certainly! No question about it. I mean, we got out. And we had the best upbringing we could possibly have. We were lucky. . . .

"On the whole I just accepted my upbringing and I didn't think about it. But when I had children I realized how much security we had, how much had been given to us. I want my children to have all the chances we had."

"Chances?"

"Well, we had music groups and dressmaking and art, and we had the chance to develop what we were interested in, and people spent time with us. In a regular family home you have to fix supper, or the phone rings, or you have to do something else; it's not quite the same as a person who has the time to do a certain thing with a group. At home as a parent you can get pulled away in different directions. We had a good chance as children. I mean, we could have been sent to Norwood."

"Norwood?"

"Yes, that was another orphanage, but it wasn't like ours at all. Ours was really home in every way."

"What do you think made the difference between an orphanage and a home?"

"Alice was really there for us, night or day. She was never 'off.' I think that's what home is. She never criticized you. And she always understood everything. She didn't just say, 'Carry on.' But she tried to have us look at things in the best way and tried to help us cope with them. If something was our fault, she'd say, 'Look, you have to apologize and make it right.' And we were really all watched properly.

"Now that I'm a person and have my own family, I want to give my children a chance which I had. I can sort of take something and give to them. I think that's very fair. I haven't been to school and learned it. But even now I feel that Alice is behind me. And that's fantastic. There's no end to it: I know people who have parents who say oh my mom just doesn't understand. I'd never say this.

"We also had aunts and uncles, ours lived in Grosvenor House. That's like the Hilton. We visited there once. We were so upset, Shana and I, we never wanted to go again. I remember we were eating round this long table and they were cutting meat and sort of throwing it on your fancy plate, and they said, 'Here's ten shillings to spend,' and we didn't want it. We didn't need it. And they were so offended, they took us home in the car.

"There was another family that wanted to adopt Shana and me, I think. They were jewelry people. They came to visit us and they really liked me, but I didn't want to go without Shana. Alice said they can't just take me but they have to take us together. Well, they sent this big Rolls-Royce car. They gave us watches and jewelry, everything. But Shana was crying that she didn't want to stay. So I didn't want to stay either. So we sneaked out of bed at night in our nighties to a phone booth. We told the operator we had no money and we phoned up Alice. She said get back into bed and I'll send someone for you next day. I asked her to send Gertrud and she said she'd try.

"Well, when somebody came next day from Lingfield to get us, these people were so angry they pulled the watches off our arms. They pulled off the jewelry, and they sent us home by train. And Alice said, 'Well, if that's the kind of people they are, I'm sorry you ever went.' They're millionaires, they wanted to adopt us. They said they wanted to give us luxuries. They would have; they had maids even to open up the beds for you! Imagine! That is how we would have lived. I liked it. But I didn't want it without Shana."

"How much younger than Shana are you?" I asked.

"We don't really know, they say a year, but it's all made up. Did you see the photographs of us? When we came?"

"No."

"I didn't either. No, I haven't wanted to—for what?" She tossed her head. "We were so undernourished, we looked terrible. Everybody said how beautiful we were getting, so I figured we must have looked awful!"

There was an ironic, self-protective smile on her face, but it disappeared in an instant. She leaned forward, looking suddenly drained, pale, and when she spoke again, it was much more slowly than before.

"I tell you, still . . . we'd never buy anything German. We'd never go there. We'd never step on German soil, not even on the way to somewhere else. Someone once gave us a present made there. We took it back. I know Alice has a friend who still lives there. Her husband was an artist. She was very nice to us and gave us one of his lithographs. I know Alice has been there to see her. . . . Still, *I* would never go there."

She rose to clear the table. After respectfully moving the candlesticks to the far end, she brushed crumbs with a damp cloth into the palm of her hand. When her determined strokes had made the white plastic cloth glisten clean, she reached out across the table with both arms in one long graceful movement like a blessing and taking the candlesticks in her hands, planted them in the center.

LILLIANA BUCCI PERTOLDI

Brussels, Belgium, July 1979

She moved about the spacious modern facsimile of a country kitchen with the grace of a dancer. Slim and leggy, in blue jeans and high heels, she appeared taller than her actual height. She was baking a cake and I commented that she was using an unusual looking mixer.

"Yes, it's *Boche*. They make very good things." She concentrated on the blending of ingredients. "Anyway, we can't blame them all forever, can we?"

I averted her searching brown eyes as I sought my own answer. "Not *all*," I considered, "but for me, some still."

She said that her husband would be home very late—another meeting. He works for the Common Market. Her two boys, aged ten and twelve, would be home for dinner in a couple of hours. Her voice channeled warmth and a search for precision of expression. Her English was good, but she kept an English-Italian dictionary nearby to check occasionally on the accuracy of a word.

When the cake went into the oven, she led me out of the kitchen to the huge living room, where highly polished wooden floors gleamed between the beautiful oriental rugs. Despite its grand scale, the room was inviting and warm. She indicated the apricots and peaches ripening at the large bay window.

"I'm going to bake with these fruit tomorrow," she said, examining them. "I'm having fifty people over this Saturday."

"A special occasion?"

"No, no," she laughed, "only that I like these people and I haven't seen them for a while."

When we began to talk about Lingfield she said, "It was like a home. I have very good memories, a big garden, a big house and love. Really love, especially from Manna. She was always with us.

"I came to England in February or March, and left the following December. I was not afraid to see my mother, but when I saw my mother again she was for me, in that moment, a stranger."

"How long since you'd seen her?"

"Two years. Yes, two years, because in Auschwitz she was not with us. We were alone."

"Do you recall being separated from her?"

"Yes, I do, because my mother came each night to say good night to Andra and me, and one day she doesn't come, I don't know where she was in Auschwitz, and I thought that my mother was dead. Because we saw always many people who died."

"You did?"

"Yes, of course. And I remember this, and Andra, my sister, remembers some things that I don't remember, though she is two years younger than me." Her voice grew quiet.

"Before she stopped coming, my mother always said to me, 'Remember, your name is Lilliana Bucci.' Because I have two names, Lilliana and Tatiana. Everybody called me Tatiana in my family. But when I was born [1937] it was not possible to call me Tatiana openly because in Italy with Mussolini that was a stranger's name. So they named me officially Lilliana. But my parents call me Tatiana. Now I'm Lilliana only for Manna, Alice, Zdenka, and you: it's strange for me when someone calls me Lilliana."

"Would you prefer I call you Tatiana?"

"No! Lilliana is a part of my old life, my life in England, and it was a happy life, that name is part of my past and the past has finished well for me." She smiled.

"Why do you think your mother kept telling you to remember your name is Lilliana?"

"Why? Because on my passport it said Lilliana—all my papers were Lilliana."

"She must have known that she was going to be separated from you."

"Yes, yes."

"Did she say something like that to Andra?"

"Yes, Andra is Allessandra."

"So you did remember to be Lilliana. And what do you remember about Auschwitz?"

"When we arrived they wrote the number, and then I remember the Block—the house where we sleep—and I remember very well the chimney with the fire. Yes, very well. This I remember. . . ." Then she leaned toward me, her face lit with amazement, and exclaimed, "But I played! I played there with nothing! with the snow! with the balls of snow!

"And I remember being very cold and that I never eat because there was very little, and I was very difficult with food. Like my children are now. My children like only pasta. Once a German soldier gave me a cake. I don't know why, because there were many, many children there and I don't know why to me and not to another child. Perhaps I looked like his child."

"Do you know how long you were in Auschwitz?"

"We were in Auschwitz March 1944 until—I suppose, January 1945, because after Auschwitz we were in Czechoslovakia for a few months, and then to London."

"That you survived so long in Auschwitz is incredible."

"Yes, but perhaps because my father is not Jewish. He is Catholic, this is the reason. I don't know, because my mother, all her family are gassed. All are dead in Auschwitz. My mother and her sister, no, because my mother's sister is married with a Catholic man too. It's possible this is the reason. Because to understand the mind of the German people is very difficult."

Her Italian father had spent six years of the war as a prisoner of the English in South Africa. Lilliana had last seen him when she was two. "My mother sent to Alice the picture of her marriage to my father, and Alice showed me this photograph and I recognized my parents. Alice said, 'Do you know these people?' And I said, 'Yes, they are my parents.' Before Alice told me, she wrote to my parents to be sure they *are* my parents. My mother still has the letters."

"After your mother no longer came to you in Auschwitz, what do you recall?"

"We asked constantly where my cousin Sergio was—he died, I suppose. Because one day a group of soldiers came and one asked all children if there was somebody who wanted to go see their mother. And Andra and I—it's strange, but we say no! And he, my cousin, say quickly, yes, I will go. And I remember that Andra and me told him to stay with us. But he go! And he died," she whispered sadly.

"How did you know to say no?"

"I don't know. Perhaps the *blockova* told me to say no."

"Do you remember her?"

"I remember one *blockova,* she was very nice with me, I was like a daughter for her, and she give me always beautiful dresses and I suppose that she told us to say no."

"Did many children say yes, they'd go?"

"I don't remember. I remember only that my cousin Sergio say yes."

"What was his family name?"

"De Simone. He lived with my aunt in Napoli."

"Did she go also to Auschwitz?"

"Yes, she lived always in Naples before the war, and she came to Fiume always to see her mother, and that's how she got caught."

"Did you ever feel angry with your mother then, that she left you?"

"No, I saw always many people who died, and I thought she died too. For me it was normal—because every day I saw dead people. So it was normal for my sister too. This was our expectation. Perhaps my mother told us that she leaves Auschwitz. I don't remember."

"To go to a work camp?"

"Yes, Dachau, I think she told me, but I forget. We don't talk about this with my mother. Normally we don't. We talked only when we saw TV, the film *Holocaust.* I didn't see all of it, because I was not in Brussels each night."

"Would you have, had you been here?"

"Yes, I think so. But I was alone because my husband went to bed. He didn't think it was good for me. He was not agreeing I should see this. He told me, 'You can make what you want. I go to sleep.' "

"So you watched all alone?"

"Yes."

Stefano and Lorenzo came home for dinner, moving into the dining room like basketball players on the loose. They wolfed down their pasta, leaving the meat, and asked questions about the number of countries to which I would travel.

"Do the children know about your past?" I asked, when they were in bed.

"I told them last October before I went to London for the television program ['This Is Your Life,' honoring Alice]."

"And what was their reaction?"

"They said they hate Hitler. I think that's normal," she said. "They

say 'We are Jewish because you are Jewish.' I am not Jewish, really
Jewish. I am not religious, but I feel to be Jewish. Perhaps because I
was in concentration camps and my mother is Jewish."

"And your husband?"

"Is Catholic. But not religious at all. The children in school study
Moralité. There is a choice: Catholic, Protestant, Jewish, and
Moralité."

"Did your mother tell you you were Jewish?"

"No, no. We were baptized! But I knew she was Jewish. But after
Auschwitz, when we came to Czechoslovakia and they asked Andra
and me what we are, we reply we are Jewish."

"What made you reply that way?"

"Because we were in Auschwitz: everybody was Jewish there and we
thought we were Jewish too. In Auschwitz there were only Jewish
people. There were not Catholics. But when we finish Auschwitz, I say
I'll remember that I am Jewish. I still have my number. I would never
make a plastic surgery to get rid of it. Why should I? It's bad
memories. But it's *my* life. It's finished and I am here!"

"What is your number?"

"I don't remember! 774 . . . 843, I think." She rolled up the sleeve
of her navy pullover: 776484 was tattoed near a tiny Star of David.
"Someone when I was younger asked me if this was my telephone
number." She smiled. "Mama is 776482. Andra 483 and I 484.

"My mother is very strong. She has suffered more than I because of
the *Boche*. She was a woman separated from her daughters—now I
can understand, because I have two children too, and she's very, very
well, my mother. She can talk about it. She was very strong. We were
afraid of her in Auschwitz because she was ill, very ill. She was in the
sick place, Revere. And we were afraid to see her. All women were not
very beautiful in Auschwitz, don't eat, only work, and without hair
and no dresses, and to see her so changed was . . . we were afraid. It
was, I don't know the word."

"A shock?"

"Yes, a shock."

"What had she been like as a mother before Auschwitz in Fiume?"

"A good mother, a good mother."

"You appear to have done well with your life, to have put the past in
place," I reflected.

"I think my problems today could be like anyone's," she said. "Still,
something strange happened to me not long ago, about two years ago.
I was in a little town in France, not far from Strasbourg, and there was

a group of German tourists there, all men who sing, very well. They sang very nice folk songs," and when they finished the songs they begin to march like soldiers in rows of four, and I begin to cry and I cannot control it. I want to escape, to run. My husband understands at once what happened for me. There was a little road to the right and I ran away so not to hear or see them.

"I have German friends, they are not bad. They are like other people. But when they are a group . . . When they start marching . . . I am afraid . . . Now one reads that all the nations knew that we were in concentration camps, and nobody does something."

It was close to midnight when her husband arrived. He was fair and blue-eyed in a white cable-knit sweater. I was staying overnight and we turned in shortly after he returned.

In the morning, he drove me to the airport .He spoke German, I Yiddish, and we understood each other well.

"I think it's better she forgets all the past, what happened when she was a child," he protested to me.

"Gianfranco, can you forget your childhood? Is it not part of you?" He looked surprised.

(ANDRA) ALESSANDRA BUCCI PEZZONI

Padua, Italy, July 1979

"I don't like Americans," Tatiana, Andra's attractive fifteen-year-old daughter, told me even before the German shepherd had quieted after my arrival. "They never talk to you, don't want to carry on a conversation! All they want to know," she said mockingly, "is 'How much for this? How much for that?' " She had waited on Americans in a tourist shop in Venice owned by friends.

Classically beautiful, Andra, in an elegantly simple cotton dress, sat in a corner, eyeing her daughter with pride as Tatiana spoke fluent English to me.

"I've forgotten most of my English," Andra said apologetically in Italian.

"We'll do fine with Tatiana's help," I assured her. Tatiana looked pleased and cleared her throat, ready to begin. Andra huddled deeper into the couch. In the dim light of the dark wooden shuttered living room, a thin ray of afternoon sun played onto her fashionably blonde-streaked hair.

"I still have a doll that Manna gave me in England," she recalled. "When I first came to Lingfield, I saw a lot of toys, a big rocking horse and many dolls. I was told that I would get one for my own. Then we were taken upstairs to the bedroom and in each bed there was a hot water bottle to warm the bed, and I didn't want that.

"Every time I went to bed I wet myself, also when I was in camp and also in Czechoslovakia, and I was afraid to wet myself there. I stopped that in Lingfield."

"How old were you when you came to Lingfield?"

"Six, but I was small. All the children that came from camps were *piccolo*. I remember I ate a banana in Lingfield. I don't remember if I ever had one before. During the war in Fiume you couldn't get them and before that they were very dear."

"Do you remember Fiume at all?"

"No, I was too little—four. But I remember when the Germans came into the house and took us. I was sleeping with my sister in bed and my mother came to dress me and wake us up. And my grandmother, Rosa, was there talking to the Germans and crying. 'Leave the children,' she said. 'Take me, I am old, leave the children.' But they were silent. They took us downstairs in the car, then we were taken to the Risiera [the rice factory in Trieste that had been converted into a prison].

"I was in a little, little room, a cell, I don't know if I was only with the family or with others too. The door had a round hole. Downstairs there was a big room where all the people were. From there they put us in a train to Auschwitz. I remember nothing of the trip."[1]

"I was there at the Risiera last night," I told her. "Have you taken your children there?"

"No, no. I have now nightmares and if I went there I would have more of these—it would not be a good thing for me." Her voice darkened.

"When we were taken, my sister and I had measles and my mother bundled us up into many clothes because she was afraid the fever would go up. Also in Auschwitz I was in a hospital barrack. I don't know what my sickness was. But there I saw a lady who had a baby."

"Were you frightened?"

"No. This woman was crying. She was in labor and I was looking at her through the slats of my bunk. Someone came and told me not to look. But I looked. I don't remember if they killed the baby or not. . . ."

Church bells pealed outside. Now it was dark. She lit a lamp and continued, Tatiana echoed her mother in quiet, deliberate translation.

"When my mother was in the sick barrack," Andra continued, "I did not want to see her because they had cut off all her hair and she was very emaciated. It didn't look like her and it made me afraid. . . ." She sighed and hesitated.

"It was in winter, there was snow. Then the Germans took people and piled them in a big mountain. They were all without clothes. One German picked up by the arms, the other by the legs, and they do like that"—she gestured as if flinging a body onto the pile—"and they threw them. When a German person died—some of them died too, I remember—he would be taken to another part of the camp, away but covered with a white sheet. But when a Jew or a prisoner died they took them naked without any cover at all or a rag."

"Did you see this when you were in the hospital?"

"When I was out of the hospital I saw this all the time. I saw this with my sister. We were always together. I was always looking for her more than she for me," she said sadly.

"Since she was older, she was perhaps your security?" I asked.

"Yes. Once a *Kapo* punished all the women, but this *Kapo* liked me and Tatiana. She would say to us, 'Don't go near these women because they have lice on them.' I remember also a kind German who gave my sister and me chocolate."

"Was that one time?"

"No, many times—and white bread, because he loved us."

"Do you recall the name of the *Kapo* who was nice to you?"

"No, but I recall she was very, very bad with other people—she was nice only to us. But I think perhaps if she was not bad to the others the Germans would have done something to her."

"What did she do to others? To women or children?"

"To women: they had to stay outside with salt on the ground under their knees, kneeling, holding bricks up in their hands for hours and hours." She demonstrated, holding her arms up over her head. I saw that she still had her number on her arm. "I recall when Sergio, my cousin, went away. There was a train the Germans said that would take children to their mother. But the *Kapo* said to Tatiana and me this train would never arrive to the mother. We told Sergio. 'It's not true,' Sergio said. He wanted to go to his mother. They closed this train, a cattle car. This train left Auschwitz and then he was no more."

"You saw him go in this train?"

"Yes. They put planks of wood up to the doors so they could walk up. Sergio's mother had already been sent away before. My mother came to say good-bye to us before she was sent away. She cried. I remember her hugging me but I don't know what she said or what else she did. I was so little then, I didn't ever understand what was happening around me. Maybe I cried too, but I don't remember.

"I was outside all day long and remember only snow. There was a lot of snow in Poland—only snow."

"Did you have warm clothes?"

"Tatiana received pink gloves. I don't recall clothes. They took our clothes away when we arrived. Then they put the numbers. My hair was shaved all off with a machine."

"What were you afraid of in the camp?"

"I wasn't afraid. Nobody did anything to me. I saw the flames going outside but I didn't know what it was, I didn't see them burn children, so I wasn't afraid. They didn't touch me or the children around me. I don't remember if I was afraid. Perhaps I was so shocked that I didn't know what was happening. Perhaps I thought it was all only night-mares.

"When I arrived they took us all off the train. All the people were crying and running and then I was afraid."

"What was the hardest thing for you?"

"The cold. I was cold all the time. I don't remember if I had the right clothes or if I had shoes. I do remember that in the bed there was only a rag over me—like nothing. I told you I was a bed wetter. When we arrived, I was sleeping on the second tier over and Tatiana under. But there was no mattress, just a little straw, and it 'rained' on Tatiana, so we changed—she on top and me on the bottom."

"When the Russians came they gave us salami. I don't remember if I was happy or not—because all the time I was there I didn't understand what was happening, and when the Russians came I didn't understand that the war was finished, that I was free. I was only a child."

She unclasped her hands and brought them up to her face, as if slowly framing her thoughts, and I saw the numbers visible on her arm again. She noticed my looking.

"Yes, I keep it. For me it is nothing to have this; the people who have done this to me, they carry the greater scar; they must feel something in themselves, not I." She spoke with quiet dignity, without rancor.

"Bravo," I said.

"I think for me it's important to speak because it was not my fault that I was in camp. And it's not something to be forgot. I saw the film *Holocaust*. But my husband did not want to see it," she said flatly.

Tatiana, who had been translating all along with surprisingly mature reserve, leaned forward and said with rising irritation, "In Italy, it was shown once a week, and we closed the shop early and ran home to see it every night. But there are people now who say it never happened, who don't believe it at all! I can't understand this!" Her eyes welled with tears. "What do they think! Why!" It was not a question, it was an angry demand. "Why!"

Andra made no reply, but, lost in thought, fingered something hanging on the shiny gold chain at her neck. Then she continued.

"When we returned to Rome from England, there was a difficult scene at the station. We were the first children who had returned from the war alive, and there were many mothers there at the station with pictures of their children, asking us if we had seen them. 'Have you seen this boy?' 'Have you seen this girl?'

"Then we went to my mother's friend who was also in the camp with my mother, and there too a lot of people came with pictures like in the station—'Have you seen this girl?' 'Have you seen this child?' I was very bad. I was terribly tired."

"Bad? Confused, I would say," I protested.

"I was not nice with people after what I had passed through. I was nasty. I didn't feel like talking . . . so when these people asked me, 'Have you seen this person?' I would say, 'Perhaps I saw them.' Because I thought it was cruel to say 'I didn't see them.' "

"That was a difficult task for a young child—to tell a parent yes or no."

"I cried a lot when the woman Alice sent with us to Rome left us. I didn't cry when I saw my mother. Tatiana did. I didn't. But I did when this woman returned to England."

"Well, you were younger, your security was tied to the woman who protected you on the journey from England. You hadn't seen your mother in close to two years."

"I didn't really remember my mother. When Alice showed me the photo, I did recall her. But once in Rome, I was afraid of the new life I would have."

"What are your first memories of being at home again?"

"After Rome, we went to Trieste by train and I asked, 'How is my father?' Because I'd never seen him. He was a sailor and left when I was small. I was curious: how will he be? He was waiting at the Trieste station." She smiled. I realized that what glistened around her neck were three chains, not one, and that suspended from them were a green and coral jewel and a gold Star of David enclosed in a circle.

"So you wear a Jewish Star?"

"Two," she answered, fingering them. "This one is a gift from my mother—she has one just like it, only bigger. And this one is a gift from my husband." It was a smaller one, very delicate.

Tatiana broke in. "My father is Catholic but because he knows she loves this, he gave it to her."

"How do you see yourself and your children now: as Jewish? Catholic?"

"I was baptized as a child by my mother and of course my father is Catholic. But I don't think about Catholic or Jewish. If it weren't for my mother-in-law and father-in-law I would let the children be Jewish. But for my mother-in-law, this would be like killing her. For them there is only Church, Christ, God."

"And how do you think of yourself, Tatiana?" I asked the daughter.

"Catholic," she replied without hesitation. Andra excused herself to prepare dinner. Arnaldo would soon be home.

Tatiana spoke passionately. "I'm proud of my mother, that she was courageous and strong to go on and survive. Nobody passed through what she did. I will never kill another person. I know why the Germans have done this: because of the economy. It was all in the hands of the Jews. But why did they want to kill all? I heard that Hitler wanted to kill all Catholics too, because he said you must love only Germany. I heard also that Hitler was Jewish too. That he was without parents and he was in an orphanage. Perhaps because of that he didn't like Jews. I don't remember if only the mother or the father was a Jew and that he was all the time alone in his infancy. Still, I don't see why he would want to kill all the people. My grandmother remembers more than my mother. She told me about it, and I've read books. I'm very sensitive, and cry a lot in films. In *Holocaust* there is a scene where all the Jews are put in a synagogue where all the Jews are burned. I cried, so I couldn't catch my breath. It's impossible to think this happened, to think of people, of intelligent people in this world who did it. Why didn't they think before, not after! At the end of *Holocaust* the young Nazi who killed confesses that he did wrong. But he must think *before*," she was shouting, "not *after!*"

Arnaldo sat down to dinner with wine to his left and an Italian-English dictionary to his right. He was about forty. Bearded and handsome in his white summer business suit.

"Andra's mother is the key for Andra's and Tatiana's coping. I love my mother-in-law because she is a person who is pragmatic, who understands that what's important is to live. And the best way is to forget. She has a strong instinct to live. She wants to live—every day. She's a wonderful woman. Now this is the question," he said, rather formally. "Are you writing a sugar-book, sentimental, like the TV program in England?"

"I don't think so."

"Good. Then if you please, have some more wine." He poured.

After dinner they took me into a gallery where many paintings hung. Tatiana led the way. "These were painted by a Jew, and my father gave them to my mother for her birthday," she said proudly. One of them was a black and white litho of women and children behind barbed wire. One woman had been shot. "This is one I like very much," Andra said.

Early the next morning we met downstairs, Andra still in her robe, Tatiana dressed, fresh and bright. Arnaldo was not up yet.

Over coffee we talked about Tatiana's schooling. I turned to Andra and asked, "How did you do in school? What did you like?"

"I didn't like anything. The best school was in England. Here I was put with young children. I felt stupid. I was a difficult child."

"How?"

"I was a strange girl. I had no friends when I was little. I was closed in. I was difficult for others and for myself.

"Also now, I'm difficult, I'm always alone. I don't talk much with others. I'm shy, ashamed."

"Why do you think that's so?"

"I don't know. My sister Tatiana is not like me. She's more open than I am. Perhaps if there was not the war I would not feel like this. Perhaps I was shocked, so now I'm stupid." She smiled and broke into a shy chuckle at her own excuse.

"Andra, I don't think you are at all stupid. You have much insight," I said.

"I'm insecure. I'm always feeling I'm not doing right, I don't want to be seen. There's much inside of me, but I'm closed to others. I'm an introvert.

"Oh, I have some friends, more in Venice than here. But they are different from me because they are all the time happy."

"And you? Are you sad much of the time?"

"No, but I'm not as happy as others." Honesty lit her beautiful face.

(JULIUS) URI HAMBURGER

B'nai Berak, Israel, July 1978

The empty lot through which I approached the side entry of the huge concrete building where Julius lived was a neglected, desolate place. At the far left corner, silhouetted against the sun, stood a knot of men around the frame of an abandoned car. One of the men came toward me. He was small-framed, and the short sleeves of his faded light green shirt seemed much too wide for the thin, muscular arms. He was wearing it in the characteristic Israeli fashion, collar open and spread wide—in this case, drawing attention to his sunken posture. He straightened slightly as he shuffled slowly closer. *This can't be Julius.* I thought of the tow-haired boy in the photographs, taller, more erect than the other children. Wasn't this man too old? He came closer, and I realized that the sandy blonde hair could have once been towhead. His eyes were blue, and they sparkled with surprising fire as he said my name.

"You have a hard time to find me?" he asked in a deep voice. His English had no Israeli accent, but neither was it British. It sounded like a mixture, most heavily Slovak. He extended his hand and invited me in. Our footsteps echoed up six flights of stairs. Doors opened and closed as we passed. Cooking odors, some familiar, some strange, wafted out on each landing.

His wife, a short, dark, maternal-looking woman in her early thirties, greeted me warmly. The apartment was small and neat; there was nothing in it beyond necessities.

"If I wasn't just after an ulcer operation, I wouldn't be home in the daytime like this," he said. "I'm going back to work in two more days." He works for Chashmal, the big electric company in Israel, as a welder.

"And when did you come here from England?" I asked.

"Nineteen fifty." He was animated, but there was a forced, staccato sound in his voice.

"I've been here twenty-seven years. I was in England first with Alice. Then they sent me away to another hostel. Then I went back to Alice. And then they sent me to a family, but I didn't get along with them either. I ran away. Then Alice arranged for me to come to my brothers and sisters. They were here already. Alice came for a visit. At the same time she met them. I didn't know them except from pictures. So when I came here to Israel, Alice was at the airport with them. I had not seen my brothers and sisters since I was six or seven, 1943–44. That's when we were in the camp."

"I'd like to learn about that from you," I said. "Can you tell me about your experience in those camp years?"

He pulled a pack of cigarettes from his shirt pocket and turned to his wife.

"Bring a cold drink, Batya," he said authoritatively.

She smiled apologetically, saying yes, yes, in Hebrew.

Julius drew on his cigarette and scanned my face, as if to measure me in relation to what and how much to tell.

"Why do you want to hear this?" he asked.

I repeated the same explanation of the book that I had given in my letter to him. I wanted to learn from the people who had been with Alice about their experience, and that little was written about child survivors from their point of view.

He sat for a moment, preoccupied, then inhaled deeply. "I was in the concentration camp outside Bratislava from 1939 on. I was about a year and a half old when I went there with my whole family. They took all the Jewish families from Bratislava to that camp. We went with them in the roundup.

"My brothers worked there in the camp. We lived in a long hut, in a room with my family and there were other families in other rooms. I went to a *gan* [kindergarten] there—there was a school there, everything, only we couldn't go out, and there were soldiers or policemen there. I don't know if they were Czech or German. But I remember only one thing, my sisters, they were always scared of the policemen. And I used to run away from them. Outside the camp was a valley and I used to run outside to the grass. The first time I ran out I could not walk yet. I pushed a baby buggy and pushed it out. They say I was still going on all fours when I did that. Later on I used to go out and walk around just to look around. I used to sing songs and go to the same guard that my sisters were afraid of. I wasn't afraid—I used to sing, and he gave me a few pennies for ice cream. There were stores in the camp and a big kitchen where we used to get our food.

"When the war started hot in 1943 they opened the gates of the camp and told us to run.[1] Everybody ran away. We were twelve brothers and sisters there with my parents, and all my family was separated then. I went with my oldest sister Heyde to Bratislava. We hid with some friends there."

"How much older than you was she?"

"Seventeen years. She was already married."

"And the name of the camp you all ran from?"

"Sered. All the people ran away from there. But after a while of hiding in Bratislava I got caught. I was caught and I was sent back to Sered."

"How were you caught?"

"My sister says differently and I say differently, as much as I remember. As much as *I* remember," he underscored his truth with rising anger, "her husband gave me away."

He looked at me boldly, measuring my shock. His lips drew to a hard, angry line, and then he flushed with hurt and shame.

"How did he give you away?" I asked after a while.

"It was like this," he began, now calm with the sudden detachment of a lawyer building his case. "They got a letter. This is what I remember. The letter was supposedly from my parents, that they wanted to see me. I was excited about this. So one evening my brother-in-law took me out. He took me in the street, it was dark, to a place, to a house." His voice rose as he made his point: "He did *not* go in with me! He just took me to the door and he just told me, 'When I'm around the corner, then you go in.'" His look pleaded for validation. "He gave me away," he said with resignation.

I saw tow-haired six-year-old Julius, his eyes bright with the anticipation of seeing his parents again, standing at the door of the house.

He resumed the story almost mechanically.

"And I went in and there were Germans there, and there was a person there, maybe he was supposed to take me to my parents, I don't exactly know—but the Germans took me to another house, and I was there two or three days. My brother, who's now in Haifa, was also caught and came to that house. He ran away after being caught and then was brought back, and he ran away again. I stayed there for about a week and then they sent me back with other Jews to Sered—the camp where I used to live. But now my family wasn't there. I was alone. They kept me there about a fortnight. I stayed in the hut that used to be the *gan*, across from our old hut. I ran out to see our old hut one day but it was closed, empty. Then I was sent to Auschwitz. I was the only one in my family that went to Auschwitz.

"By train they sent me." He stopped, looking troubled. "My sister says I was caught on the street. That's what she says. But I remember it clearly. I remember different."

"Could your brother-in-law have told her that? That you were caught?"

"Maybe. That's why I never argue with her. What's past is past."

"Is your brother-in-law alive?"

"No, he's dead. He died in Czechoslovakia. I can't remember his name. He's got a son. He died before the son was born, and then my sister came here in '46."

"Did she know then that you were in Auschwitz?"

He shrugged.

"Can you tell me about Auschwitz? What do you remember?"

"We went by train. We stopped about twice or three times to, how you call it?"

"Go to the toilet?"

"Yes. It must have taken three, four days. I can't remember exactly."

"Were you in a group of children?"

He seemed impatient here with my ignorance. "No, it was grown-ups, families, and everything. There was a family that I knew from Sered. They came with me with their son. We were all the time together. But when we got to Auschwitz they separated us. The children were alone. The first thing when we got off the train, they put us in a row and started writing numbers on our arms. I had it taken off in England. All of us had it taken off there. It was B4141.

"Here in Israel I was in prison. I went 'off my road. In prison I met a person with one number after me. He was a teacher. He knew me. He was also from Sered. He knew my whole family.

"When I got off the train, the first thing they gave us the number, then they took us to the bath. But we got relieved because the whole thing [crematorium] got burnt after they took all our clothes off.[2] I had my best suit with me. I didn't want to give mine. Someone said, Throw it away." Julius chuckled at this point. "I kept it. I took it all the way. Then they took it and gave us others. Then they separated all the families. Everybody started crying, and I was alone. I started crying with them. From there we had a shower and they took us to the camp with the huts in them [Birkenau]. Each hut was very long. There was one that was a hospital, for grown ups and for children. At the end of the hut there were the women with the doors closed. I slept in a bed with the friend my age I told you about. His mother slept in a different hut and gave birth to a son that last day, the day the Russians came to release us. I heard that the boy who was my age is very religious now and lives here in Israel. People who were in Sered have meetings here in Israel once a year. I was told that he came to one, but I wasn't there. My brothers and sisters forgot to take his address and so I never saw him."

"How did you spend the day in the camp?" I asked.

"Most of the day I was in the hut. And once a week they came to take us for a shower, and I didn't like it. I always ran away and tried to wash myself."

"Were you afraid?"

"I don't know. I know I didn't like it. They always hit me after that. There were women who looked after us in the hut. And instead of giving me a shower, they gave me a wash in the hut in hot water and told the kids to hit me because I ran away."

"How many kids were in that hut?"

"Oh, a lot—maybe two hundred."

"And what did you eat?"

"A kind of soup, and I used to get a piece of hard bread. The younger children used to get hard bread with a little jam. And I always swapped with them. And if I was hungry, I used to find pieces that rats left. I used to have a bit of bread under my head when I sleep, and the rats used to come on the bed and eat. The boy there beside me was afraid. He used to wake up when a rat came on the bed. I used to chase the rat away. He was afraid. I wasn't."

"Then there were three or four girls in the hut who came to England with me [Shana, Esther, Lilliana, Andra]. I used to steal bread for them. I can't remember their names, but I used to get bread for them also."

"Where did you get it from?"

"Can't remember where. Maybe other children. I used to look after the little girls till we went to England. We were very close.

"Toward the end I was in the hospital, the hut exactly opposite my hut. I had typhus. I was very weak. I couldn't walk. There were a lot of people in there. I remember people dying there, they used to take them by the head and pull them out." He moved his arms as if to pull an inanimate object and fling it sideways. "Just throw them away.

"I had typhus, and my clothes got all dirty, so I had to throw them away. So I didn't have any clothes there. I didn't have something to change. I was naked when the Russians came. I think they burned all the clothes. They moved us to another hut. We heard a lot of shooting, the sky was red. They put us in a room. I had no clothes. And then they took us to the village of Auschwitz and they gave us all kinds of injections. My cousin who was there asked me if I want to go with him, but I couldn't walk. I was sick. So they took me from place to place with other children till I got to England. I was weak for a long time. I suffered from the typhus till I was fourteen: I wet the bed. They sent me to a psychiatrist in England. He asked me foolish questions. They gave me all kinds of tablets. But when I came to a kibbutz in Israel, I stopped. I was ashamed and I stopped."

"How long were you in kibbutz?"

"Five years. Then I left the kibbutz, got in trouble with the police, and then I went back again."

"What kind of trouble?"

"Stealing."

"You learned how in Auschwitz?"

"I was also stealing in England. There were grown-up girls there with pocket money, so I used to steal from them. Alice caught me. She knew. And I used to sneak into movie theaters."

"Did you steal in kibbutz too?"

"No. But when I left, I did. So I spent a year and a half in prison. Then I went back to the kibbutz till I got into the army, and then the woman I loved left me and I went crazy and stole again."

"What did you steal?"

"Houses. I used to get into houses. Then I got caught and again put in jail. Twice I was in for half a year and the last time I had to sit for a year and a half. I got out in '61. I got married, got a job, had children, then that life finished. I got back on the straight road. I'm not ashamed that I made mistakes. I paid for it. I sat for it. I'm not the same person I was then. I'm a father."

His daughter, Sigalit, arrived home from school. He acknowledged her with a distant nod. We talked about his childhood.

"I was a difficult child. I went to a different school than the others. They were younger and could start in class A. But I had missed too much, and I was difficult."

"How?"

"If I liked someone I would do everything, jump over anything for him. But, if I didn't like someone, he couldn't make me do anything. Then if he would tell me not to do it, I did it. They [in England] used to tell us to be in bed at a certain time. I didn't feel like it. I used to walk around outside, and if they closed the house I used to come in through the windows. There was a time when I used to sleep with the older children. But when Alice saw I was difficult at night she gave me a room by myself. She told me I was the older one, and I could go to sleep when I want to. So then I went to sleep earlier than the other ones." He laughed.

"I was difficult. I had no head to learn. It was hard for me. Alice sent me to a psychologist to try to help me. I had no head for it. After the accident they sent me to another hostel. There was someone there I liked, a woman. I got connected there. But she went away and I lost my connection."

"Do you remember her name?"

"No. After she left I ran away once or twice, and then they sent me back to Alice. And after that to the foster family. But I couldn't get along there. The woman there wanted to mother me, and I didn't like it. I began to stay away at night. I ran away. After that Alice arranged for me to come to Israel."

"You mentioned an accident. What happened?"

"We were walking along the road, a bunch of kids taking a walk. We were walking, playing, and a car came. Somehow, Ervin got hurt. His arm or his leg, I can't remember. I remember after, I used to get letters from my aunt. She wrote to me like she would be my mother. Then I learned that she was not my mother, that my parents were dead. Then I cried a lot. I remember every Saturday I used to go to my room and start crying. Alice used to come to talk to me. She used to try to find out about my crying. I felt very bad when it was new—that I had no parents. Then it got easier."

He rose, walked over to a wood cabinet, and picked up two albums, which he brought over to the coffee table: one was of his family, the other of Lingfield. The family album contained prewar pictures collected in Israel from other family members. The one from Lingfield had been given to him by Alice when he left England. He opened the family album to a picture of his mother, dressed in white, holding a small baby in her arms.

"That was my baby sister. She died with my mother. There were twelve children in my family. You see these small children in the picture? They died." He pointed to little boys in sailor suits and little girls in pretty dresses, all under six.

"Besides you and your sister, did any of the twelve children survive?"

"Three sisters and two brothers survived. All the rest died, all the youngest children. The only one of the older ones to die was my brother who stayed with my parents. He didn't want to leave them and he was killed too."

The youngest survivor was Julius.

"I don't call myself Julius here in Israel," he told me. "My name here is Uri. I don't talk about my past much. I'm a closed person. Even to my children I don't give compliments.

"I always find things I don't like. It's one of my bad sides till today. I don't get connected. I only get connected up to a certain point. It's not natural for me to give compliments. My wife says, why do you shout at them? Why don't you kiss the children once in a while? I don't know why. It's not natural for me. What is not natural, I can't do. I don't think about it much.

"On Saturday I'm giving a big party for my son, for his bar mitzvah. In a hall." As if on cue, both children came up: Sigalit, the little girl, coy and shy, Shimon, the boy, looking serious.

"He has your wife's eyes," I said.

"No, he's from my first wife," he corrected. I met her [Batya, his present wife] after my first surgery ten years ago. I was recovering, she was on holiday. I told her if she would not take Shimon, I would not marry. I wanted him with me."

"You look out for your kids," I commented.

"Yes, I'll never let them go. Outside, I'm strict. Inside, I'm different."

Walking me to the door, he volunteered an observation about Alice. "A lot of people in hostels are alike; from one hostel to the other. They are people who do their work. They say, 'That's my work, I'll do it.' But there are people who do it with all their feeling. That's two different things you see. You have to believe in what you're doing. That's Alice. Always children, children, children."

From Orphanages

HEDI FRIEDMAN CHARLES

Ma'agan Michael, Israel, July 1977

The magnificent sweeping view of the Mediterranean, framed in the far wall of the kibbutz dining hall, is unforgettable. Dramatically accented by a few floor-to-ceiling struts is a panorama of beach, marsh grass, and a long horizontal grid of man-made fishponds, each blue mirror rectangle edged in tall green grass. Beyond the fishponds, bursts of whitecaps move toward shore across an endless expanse of cobalt sea.

I followed Hedi's instructions to ask anyone in the dining hall to call her. Then I sat down to wait and watch kibbutzniks eating, smoking, talking. No one was alone. I turned toward the view and imagined a swim at the end of the sandy road leading to the sea. It would be easy to slip off one's clothing in the tall marsh grass and glide quietly into the cool, fresh water. I recalled that years ago the marsh grass had hidden survivors of the Holocaust, who came to the country "illegally."

Hedi appeared, dark and beautiful. Several people came over to her and talked seriously in rapid Hebrew. She listened earnestly, nodding "Ken, ken [yes, yes]," then sharing a knowing chuckle. Her laugh was hearty.

"Come, I'll show you around," she offered.

In a deep, husky voice, she inquired in detail about Alice, Sophie, the Lingfielders in London.

We walked out of the dining hall through flower-bordered paths to a bungalow whose porch was lined with baby carriages. "This is our infant house. Come in," she said.

We entered a kitchen-playroom. A radio played softly. Two young mothers, wearing shorts and holding their infants, sat beyond us in the farther room, drinking coffee and listening to the radio news. The *metapelet* [baby nurse] bustled about at the sink and welcomed us.

157

Hedi took me into each room filled with bright pictures of flowers and toys.

When we left, I exclaimed to Hedi, "It's not like an institutional nursery at all—it's so homelike!"

She looked astonished. "But it *is* home!" she said.

Across the way, two-year-olds were playing. "That's where I work," she said, and invited me to visit her there next morning. We walked to her apartment. Inside, book-lined shelves, a record player, and art prints gave the place a comfortable look.

Hedi's husband Zvi came home from the kibbutz plastics factory where he works as an engineering manager. Originally from England, he had first met Hedi in the kibbutz. The three of us communicated easily, and began talking about raising children in the kibbutz.

"Sometimes as a mother I feel the lack of having a mother when I was a child. I have to really think about things. Some things aren't automatic. Maybe I took the easy way out—going to a kibbutz where it's sure and safe, where I don't have to raise a child all by myself. Maybe it's natural for me, the way I can function now, under a protective umbrella, so to speak."

"But as a member of the kibbutz, aren't you, too, part of the protective umbrella for others?" I asked.

"Yes, yes, of course. I think it's a positive thing. I've learned to be protective of others, also of something I believe in: for people to live together, to learn to be more generous with each other, to try to put down their own wishes so the other person can put *their* wish forward. I really believe in the kibbutz way of life. Really, I think it's the most beautiful thing there is. If you can take it. If you really wholeheartedly believe in it, so you don't mind the pettiness, the gossip. The idea itself is so beautiful it's worth fighting for. And what it gives to the children, it's worth almost any sacrifice for. One of the big points for me was that I knew kibbutz education is very much like Alice's way. The liberal idea of letting a child develop in its own time and up to its own capabilities. I think it's practically identical to what Alice believed in and what she tried to do with us.

"The first day I was here, I immediately felt at home. The kibbutz had prepared a cake and a bottle of wine and put it in my room to receive me. I was accepted very fast. They needed a nurse, so as soon as I managed to learn enough Hebrew, I went to work. They accepted me as a full member in a year. I got to know the whole kibbutz. It tied me with ribbons of love to this place, that I don't think can ever be broken. I've become so involved, I'm happy about every grandchild born, every soldier that gets a good grade. But that was also the hard thing about being a nurse." She paused. "You know about everyone's happinesses, but when something bad happens, it's twice as hurting. In a city hospital they come, terrible, broken up. It's a tragedy. But then they leave, you don't see them. Here in the kibbutz, you see them twenty-four hours a day, every day for the rest of your life. And you remember how they were once. And that hurts very much, that's very hard.

"But you have the compensation of all the lovely things. Like when the children have their graduation or the bar mitzvah. That's a very big festival for the whole kibbutz. Suddenly everyone comes up to you and says 'Mazel tov, how your son has grown,' and you feel really part of a family. I feel I'll back anyone up here, and they'll do the same for me. They appreciate my good points. They give me courage. They give me strength. They believe in me and they accept me. And in return I give as much as I can, the best that I can. It's most rewarding. I can really say I'm fulfilled. This is what I've got, a warm, safe, happy, good home, even though it's very big."

"Aren't you now part of the leadership? The Education Committee? Alice mentioned—"

"Second class. The first class are the veterans, the ones who set up the kibbutz. Actually, I'm close to them in my outlook. But until the younger ones have enough strength and guts to decide that this is their home and this is how they want it, to take over the responsibilities, that's the way it stays. . . ."

She identified education issues under discussion whereby the old and younger leadership differed, taking care to present both sides fairly. "And how shall we integrate our adult sons when they return from the army? Shall we have them stay here for a year so we can get to know them again? Or shall we let them take a year off, send them to see the world before they make their choice—if to become a kibbutz member? These are the kind of things we struggle with."

Then she excused herself, saying that she had to dress for her part in a movie dramatizing the early days of the kibbutz. She was to play a European aristocrat, coming to the kibbutz when it was only a pile of beach sand in the early 1900s. Zvi rummaged around in a closet and was pleased when he found an old yachting cap and ascot, to fit the part of her husband. Hedi returned, wearing a long maroon skirt. As she tied the bow of her blouse, she told me that Fritz, her brother, had bought it on a trip out of the country. The final touch was a huge, wide-brimmed straw hat, with a red chiffon streamer. The hat transformed her from a tanned, earthy kibbutznik to an elegant lady on vacation.

We walked down to the shore, where the balding but youthful movie director was setting up his tripod in a sand dune. Near him, a little boy of about three scampered, his nude body reflecting the glow of the late afternoon sun.

"*Shalom*," they all greeted each other. The little boy wiggled luxuriously in the warm sand, then sat up and stared dreamily out to sea while his father, in heavy, Italian-accented Hebrew, directed the scene.

Hedi played the scene with enormous dignity and regal presence.

Back at the apartment, Chonon, fourteen, and Dorit, ten, Hedi and Zvi's two children, were waiting for us. Hugs of greeting were exchanged amid ebullient Hebrew which included excited repetitions of the word "pizza." Hedi quickly changed into a smock and asked Dorit to come into the small bright kitchen to help. Their deft fingers worked harmoniously together, slicing pepper, onion, tomatoes, as if from a memorized score.

A young couple in blue jeans dropped in and were invited to stay for supper. They were American volunteers to the kibbutz and Hedi and Zvi were acting as their kibbutz "parents." Zvi and the young man began setting up a chessboard. Chonon watched.

"Has Chonon moved into the new place yet?" the young woman wanted to know.

"In two days," Chonon said. "We're still preparing it, painting and cleaning."

"Chonon is going into high school now," Hedi explained proudly to me. "So now he moves into new living quarters with the boys from his group who are old enough to go. The boys get new responsibilities. They prepare their own living quarters. It's a big change. They are more on their own."

For supper we crowded around a small table, sitting close together. Hedi was pleased that we all fit. There was an appreciative reception when she brought the bubbling pizza to the table, and her slices were very generous.

"Not so much, please," the slim young American girl said.

Completely misunderstanding her intent, Hedi reassured her: "Don't worry, there's more."

Late that night, Hedi talked about her childhood.

"I remember in Hungary we all lived next door together to my grandparents and many uncles and aunts—including Magda. And I remember I was six and supposed to start school. I had just gotten a little satchel for starting school. It had Little Red Riding Hood on it. Then we were taken away from our home, to a prison. I took the satchel with me. We were hungry there, but my mother said not to eat anything. We were not allowed to eat non-kosher food. My mother said to suck pebbles until the rabbi came and said it was okay to eat the food. My mother, baby brother, and grandmother were there, but not my father. He was left in the house. He was a veteran of the First World War and he had a bullet near his heart. They thought the shock of sending us away would kill him. When it didn't, they sent him in a transport to Auschwitz. But he suffocated in the train. He had a heart attack and died. My uncles told me.

"But I think the Red Cross or Joel Brand made a deal with Eichmann to let out some children in exchange for trucks and money. That's when my mother packed the Riding Hood satchel for me. I'm not too clear on other details because my aunt won't talk about it. I think it still hurts her. I don't want to probe. She lost eight of her brothers and sisters. She was eleven years old, not a baby anymore when this happened. I remember she didn't want to leave her parents, my mother, and all the others. But my mother put her in charge of us, Fritzi and me, and that's why she went." She stopped and reflected. "She took that responsibility very seriously," she said with appreciation. "It was really something. If we didn't behave, such beatings we got! She had a very strong conscience, a knowledge of right and wrong. . . . We also didn't sit down to eat until she put her hands on our heads and blessed us."

"So she came from a very religious home?"

"Yes, we all did. That's how she knew to keep us on the straight and narrow path. She showed us by physical force what to do. She couldn't explain it. But she always seemed very much older than us, though she really wasn't. Her response was immediate. We did something wrong—a smack on the ear. I used to pinch sweets in Lingfield and never confess. But if Magda suspected I took something, I was in trouble.

"After we were separated from our parents we went to various children's homes after that for about a year. One was in the basement of a sawmill. We were there during air raids and bombings. It was frightening, I remember being terribly scared. Sometimes when I was already married I would remember that in my sleep and wake up grinding my teeth.

"At any rate, we went from place to place, one children's home to another. They were always moving us. Then we went to Theresienstadt, I think, for a short time. They fed us there. Then to Prague. My uncle got papers from somewhere to go to Israel for himself and for my aunt Magda, and papers for Fritz and me to go to England. But Magda came with us. She wouldn't leave us.

"We flew in an old bomber from Prague to Scotland. And there they examined us to see how healthy or unhealthy we were. I remember my aunt was outraged because they examined her to see if she was a virgin. I think that upset her more than anything—that they would think she wasn't! They found we had scabies and ringworm. They shaved off all our hair.

"When we first came to Lingfield we spoke only Hungarian, and Alice only spoke English and German, so in the beginning we couldn't communicate. We smiled a lot at each other. . . .

"Alice wanted us each to have a special person in the house, and Miss Pickhart was my special person. I liked her very much. She used to read to me. I remember the Frog Prince."

"Magda moved to a hostel of older girls in London after about two years. We sent parcels to her. We saved up pocket money to send things to her. Of course it was Alice who arranged that and added things herself too. Alice encouraged us to write letters to each other," Hedi reflected.

"She encouraged and developed so much of myself. She tried to get us to listen to good music. Not everybody liked it, but I liked it. When I was older she took me to see my first oratorio. We went either to a good restaurant or a Viennese café where they had coffee with marvelous whipped cream. She also took me to good plays on the West End."

"Did she do this just with you, or other children too?"

"That I don't know. I think that part she did just with me. But I'm sure she did other things that other children were interested in only with them. But she found out I liked good music and drama, and of course I was interested in the cream cakes." She laughed.

"You know that I think she did find something, a point of interest, with everyone. She encouraged my brother in sports, in table tennis. She didn't try to coddle him and say he's got a bad leg, he can't do that. She encouraged him to swim and play tennis. He's an excellent sportsman. Now he plays golf.

"Sometimes I used to be cross with Alice for days, and then I'd meet her eyes and we'd laugh like maniacs. She never held a grudge or reminded you of what you did or said.

"What I think I really admire about Alice is the way she fought for us. Fought for us not just to be orphans, not just to cover our backs for us and something to put in our mouths—but something extra: To be *individuals*." She spoke with great feeling. In a mock basso voice she boomed, "Miss Goldberger, you are extravagant!" She smiled. "The Committee used to tell her that. Because she always wanted something extra, not just the things you *needed*, but also the things you *wanted*. And she was quite stubborn about it. I remember her putting on her hat and her gloves and off she went to the West London Synagogue to a committee meeting to get things for us. She got me a violin and lessons, or someone else wanted roller skates, or another coat. So off she'd go to get it for us. She fought for that. Mainly I love that she didn't settle for us to be just orphans. And didn't make me feel like an orphan. I know I'm an orphan. But she didn't make me feel like a charity."

"You and the others must have given her something important too."

"I like to think so. I hope so."

The next morning I walked over to the children's house where Hedi was already at work. As large as she was—five feet ten inches tall and generous in weight—she seemed very much at home on the floor playing blocks with the two-year-olds.

"I enjoy this," she said. "Maybe someday I'll go back to nursing, but for now this is what I enjoy."

I began to say good-bye.

"Sarah, tell Alice we are waiting for her to come, that we all miss her and that she must bring Sophie this time."

"Is there anything I can send you from the States?"

She thought for a moment. "There's an old Ella Fitzgerald record, we danced to it in Lingfield House while we were still together, before we all went our separate ways. . . ."

A few weeks later, in November 1977, on a Saturday night a siren went off in Ma'agan Michael. Lebanese terrorists had landed on the beach near the fish ponds. Two dinghies, loaded with ammunition, were found hidden in the marshes. The kibbutz was on alert.

In the dining hall, to which people converged for safety from the perimeter of the kibbutz, rumors flew—that two kibbutzniks had been found dead in the fishponds; that terrorists had made it around the kibbutz to the main road and were firing at cars. Kibbutz members, including Zvi, armed themselves and proceeded to their emergency assignments. The high school boys were armed and placed on guard duty alongside the men. For some, like Chonon, it was the first time.

(FRITZ) ZVI FRIEDMAN

Haifa, Israel, July 1977

His voice was warm but not as deep as his sister Hedi's. Fritz, over the phone, inquired about Alice's health. And Sophie? Her arthritis? "Do you know if she's doing the exercises I showed her?" He gave directions for getting to his home with as much concern, attention to detail, and awareness of expected difficult spots as a teacher to a blind student.

"Now, if you get to the Lebanese border, stop. You've gone too far." He chuckled impishly, then added, "Seriously, if you get lost, call, I'll come and get you."

Winding around on Mount Carmel, one could see sunset views of the city below and the Mediterranean beyond. The apartment area where Fritz lived was in one of the newer sections of the city. When I rang the bell, I could hear two small children on the other side of the door, moving toys.

"Come in, come in!" Fritz opened the door wide.

I noticed his resemblance to Hedi, although he was small and more compact, as if the larger size he was meant to be had been compressed into a space so small that his energy exploded from it.

"Come, Pamela, she's here," he called to his wife. We shook hands. His clasp was very strong. He was wearing the typical Israeli open shirt. His upper torso looked unusually strong and well-developed. Short kibbutz-type cotton shorts unashamedly exposed the lame leg, thinner and shorter than the other. He loped over to scoop up his children, aged two and four, to bring them over to meet me. When Pamela came out of the kitchen, wiping her hands on an apron, I handed her the small packages Alice had asked me to take along for the children.

"These are from Grandma Alice," Pamela told the children. Joyously the gifts were opened.

After the children had been put to bed, one by each parent, Pamela spoke of how much she appreciated all that Alice had done for Fritz.

"You know, the children call Alice 'Grandma,'" Fritz said, "yet I never called Alice 'Mother.' Strange, isn't it?" Raising his eyebrows, he added, "Alice never wanted anyone to call her 'Mother.'

"Alice wasn't a mother figure to me, you see. I had memories of my mother. And I had a sister and an aunt. I had a birth certificate and a past. Some children just had a name—no past, no living relative. Nobody can confirm anything for them." He looked directly into my eyes as he said this, to be sure that I understood both his good fortune and the gravity of the problems for the others.

"What do you remember of your early life at home?" I asked, after a silence.

"I remember it wasn't happy. I had polio at the age of two. From then on I was different. I couldn't walk, I was carried. Or I was pulled on a sled. We lived in the Carpathian Mountains. I was spoiled in a way. We were very poor. My father had had a heart attack and couldn't work, and so we had a very low standard of living. He was a Singer sewing machine instructor. No big status thing, he showed the women how to use the machine. But he could no longer work. We were practically living off charity. And then we moved from one camp to another, one school to another, as we had to leave."

"But you *were* together with your family."

"Some of us. You see, my father died in a cattle truck. . . . On a transport with me. You know, we were all crowded into a cattle truck. We were all squeezed together . . . and he fell dead on top of me." The shock and the weight of that fall seemed palpable as he struggled to continue. When he did, the strength had gone out of his voice.

"I don't know where he died, where's he's buried. There's no way to find out. I don't know where they threw him out."

I waited a long time for him to go on.

"My father was the one with the sense of humor. My mother was the strict religious woman. She didn't have to die. Her death was purely unnecessary. This is why I stopped being religious. The Germans said to my mother in our transit camp, 'We are resettling the old people in a Polish village called Auschwitz. The parents have to go.' So my mother said, 'Well, according to the Bible, it says honor thy father and thy mother'—it says nothing about children—so she went with my grandparents to settle them in at Auschwitz and left us, Hedi and myself, with Magda, who was then ten. She took Robbie, who was a baby being breast-fed. She didn't have to go. Of course, I don't know what would have happened if she would have stayed." He stopped, and stared down at his hands, clasped and clenched between his legs. His lips tightened. "Well, I feel, I *still* feel that her death was unnecessary.

"I used to think about it a lot as a child, my mother and my baby brother Robbie going into the ovens. It used to disturb me quite a lot. I could see it vividly . . . my little brother, my mother. . . . In Yad Vashem there are a pair of baby shoes from Auschwitz. I took Alice there. She saw them—" His voice faltered and broke, plummeting him into fresh grief.

"At any rate, once, when we were children, I remember Julius was pretending to be a ghost at night. He used to scare the life out of the younger kids. He shut the door, made it completely dark. I was scared and I started crying. Alice came, and I was too ashamed to admit that I was crying because Julius scared me. I told her I was thinking of my mother and that's what made me sad."

"And you never called Alice 'Mother.' "

"No, she didn't want us to. I think I tried to understand that she wanted to spread herself around to all the children. After Frau Lauer left—I was very attached to her—I decided not to attach to anyone. It was a time of flux. You never knew if someone would show up, a relative, an aunt, and whisk you away. I decided to hang loose.

"I didn't get a lot of attention when I was small, quite frankly, because I didn't cause much trouble. I could more or less cope. I had no problems in school. The difficult children got the most attention. But I remember going to school in Lingfield and the teacher calling us 'the German children.' And you can imagine with my name, Fritz, how the English children hated me for being 'German'? Remember, this was just after the war. . . . It was ironic, no, it was insane to call us the 'German children'!

"I was still a minor when a compensation claim was put in. Do you know how much you get? Well, it's written. For loss of two parents, a hundred pounds sterling. I was a student, I needed it badly. I had left the kibbutz and needed it to finish my physiotherapy training. I was living on thirteen Israeli pounds a month."

"How could you do that?"

"Didn't eat much," he joked. "Did I tell you that in an orphanage in Hungary during the war, some boys skinned a cat? I'm not sure if I ate that. . . . I do remember running around with bits of wood in my mouth, pretending it was chocolate, when we were hungry. At any rate, when the compensation came through I wasn't going to refuse it. But when I read the actual terms I thought, well, I'm going to save up, get myself enough money, go to Germany and say can I kill two parents here, please?" The humor that had leavened the bitterness was gone.

"Is that a closed situation? Can that be reopened?"

"Closed. No. It was done while I was a minor. You need witnesses from outside your family to state the status of your family."

"But what if there are no witnesses? What if everybody was killed?"

"Well that's what happened in my village. Everybody *was* killed. So we had no witnesses. I gave my compensation money to an uncle to buy a house. The rest I used to finish my schooling, in physiotherapy.

It came to a total of seven hundred Israeli liras. My aunt Magda refused to touch any of it whatsoever." He said this with pride for his aunt, admiring her. "She said the money was dirty, she'd have nothing to do with it. She might change her mind now," he speculated, "because she's not well off. I don't mean spiritually, but materially. She hasn't enough money to buy her own house so she pays a high rent. But there's no way we can get her a house. My sister, Hedi, on the kibbutz, bought her a refrigerator and told her she could pay back when she could because Magda would never accept it otherwise. She's an extremely proud person and possibly the person I owe the most to."

"How is that?"

"Because I think she taught me the difference between wrong and right. She was very stern, because she promised my mother to look after us. She'd promised my mother that she would teach us the *Shema Yisrael*. So every night she would come to our bed and make us cover our eyes and repeat the *Shema Yisrael*. You see, Alice never hit anyone ever in the whole place. None of the kids were ever hit except me and Hedi—by Magda. We were her property. If I did something wrong, I got walloped. Hedi got walloped because she didn't stop me from doing it. I was put in one corner to cry and Hedi in another corner to cry. Then Magda herself would go in a corner to cry.

"I spent a lot of time in bed because of a series of operations. I drew lots of cowboys and Indians. But always on horses because they didn't have to use their legs. But after the age of eleven I didn't really have any trouble with my legs, the operations were successful. Until that time I wore braces and was pushed in a baby carriage or carried by Hedi. I was six and felt conspicuous. I think it's possibly one of the reasons I feel fairly sound emotionally, also possibly pretty heartless."

"Heartless?"

"Yes, I can be pretty heartless, ask Pamela. Pamela, am I not heartless sometimes?"

"Well, I wouldn't say heartless," she answered.

"It was because of the leg. From a very early age I was put aside, so I had time to think: Why am I not like the other children? Why have I got polio and they not? And why is my skin darker than all the other children? Why do I and my sister speak Hungarian and the others not? I didn't know it was Hungarian, I just knew it was different. Why me like this? I read a lot, and that was the real beginning of thinking. I think as a result of that I have the ability to shut off certain sides of my character."

"What do you mean?"

"I don't suffer fools gladly. I'm perhaps overcritical. If I see a problem and a certain solution clearly and I'm convinced that *is* the solution, and that solution isn't taken, I cannot have any sympathy for the problem which endures out of the solution not being taken. And that is what I think I mean when I say I'm heartless. If you change what I think is the best solution to a lesser one, one that I think not as good, I tend not to compromise. And that can be definitely regarded as heartless."

"Or strong?"

"Yes, but if someone's emotional needs are for my emotional sympathies, not by critical judgment, it can be a problem. I know this side of my character."

It was late. He invited me to visit him the next day at the big physiotherapy clinic in Haifa where he worked and then promised that, if I would not mind coming along for an hour to the home of a boy he had been treating, he would drive me north to the Ghetto Fighters Museum, Lohamei Hagetaot, which I had not yet seen.

When I arrived at the large modern wing of the clinic where Fritz was in charge of a group of technicians, an older man dressed in work clothes was just ahead of me. He carried two large freshly caught fish dangling from a string and presented them to Fritz, bowing profusely and thanking him. Fritz shook his hand and thanked him, urging him to come back if his shoulder started to trouble him again. Then Fritz, dangling the fish as he walked, guided me around. In midafternoon, we drove to a house at the top of Mount Carmel, where, despite all the accouterments of luxury, a twelve-year-old boy struggled to retain the use of his limbs.

This handsome, painfully thin boy was sitting up in his wheelchair waiting for Fritz, and brightened visibly when he arrived. In the game room downstairs, he and Fritz played Ping-Pong. At first Fritz hit the ball directly to him, then, very gradually, targeted it so that there would have to be increasing movement to return it. The change in the boy was dramatic. He was vitalized.

Ping-Pong was followed by a swim during which they pretended to be whales, spouting and bellowing in the indoor pool that the family had built for their son. When the boy suddenly tired, Fritz cradled him tenderly at the side of the pool for a few moments, and then began egging him on to a game of tag. "But tomorrow you won't catch me, I'll guarantee you," he teased after allowing the boy to win.

"It's very important to keep him moving," he told me on the way down the mountain. "All hell breaks loose if you don't. Deterioration, loss of function, pneumonia."

The road leading north out of Haifa was jammed with late afternoon traffic. But by the time we reached Acre, the traffic had thinned.

As we turned past Acre to the kibbutz and the Sharon Valley, a long row of continuous stone arches appeared. They seemed to stretch for miles.

"Roman bridge?" I asked.

"Turkish aqueduct," Fritz replied. "This place has been run over by just about everybody, but we've still kept it ours, haven't we?" From behind the wheel he glanced toward me, seeking affirmation, a defiant twinkle in his eye.

We were driving toward a large mesa, which rose out of a valley of green, cultivated fields. On top of the mesa, a massive rectangular stone building commanded the countryside.

"That building up there is the museum of the ghetto fighters," Fritz informed me. "Just below it, built into the slope, there's a beautiful amphitheater, but you can't see that yet from here."

When we arrived at the kibbutz it was almost dark. We began to climb the long stone stairway leading up to the wide terrace of the museum. The stairs were swarming with soldiers. They seemed very young, and unnaturally quiet. Assembled in rows on the terrace, they stood at attention and faced the vista, from the Hills of Sharon to the east across the cultivated valleys ahead, to the coastal plain of the Mediterranean in the west. We heard their names being called out: "Ofer Ben Shachar!" "Avaram Rubenstein!" "Yehuda Traister!" "David Tzipman!"

It grew dark. The mountains, the valley, and the sea could no longer be seen. In the dark, a huge chorus of voices spoke in unison, a pledge to bear arms to defend Israel. "*Ani nishbah! Ani nishbah!*" they shouted.

"They must have just completed their training; I've never seen this before," Fritz whispered. We watched, mesmerized by the ritual of the calling of names followed by the pledge.

Our footsteps echoed in the empty hall. Then we descended to the exhibits and were assaulted by the pleading eyes of men, women, and children—on loading platforms, in camps, at grave pits. We were alone inside, confronted by our own losses.

We did not speak. Who among these was my aunt Rivaleh? My uncles? The cousins my own age?

Before a model of the Treblinka camp, where the lethal gas Zyklon B was first pioneered by physicians for the explicit purpose of mass murder, we heard distant voices, through the thick fortresslike walls of the museum. The platoons of young soldiers above us were singing the Hatikva, the Song of Hope.

"You know, life in Israel is not easy," Fritz said "Do you think I like the idea of risking my Nimrod in the army? But for me it's the only place I want to live. After all this," he extended his arm, palm open toward the walls of the room, "my God, there has to be a place of our own to defend! Better for my son up there," he raised his eyes toward the singing soldiers, "than here," he said, looking back at the massacre as we left the room.

Several months later, in Los Angeles, I received a sheaf of poems Fritz had written.

A glass case in a dark hall
All
Around Voices
Modern uncaring
Scientifically explaining
Unhearing
The whimper of a child
His silence
The gift of death
In gas
He has
One small shoe
In memory

Zvi Friedman
(written after a visit with Alice to Yad Vashem
Martyrs Memorial)

I remember the war
All black and white
The only color, flames
Frames of windows
Glass blown out
Stark silhouettes in rubble
Stubble on a few men's faces
Left to us
Anyone not family was feared

Steered across a loveless land
Always leaving
Grieving for our dead
Came later

Zvi Friedman

(MAGDA) SARAH LIBERMAN KORNHAUSER

Tel Aviv, November 1977

Magda lives on a kind of street in Tel Aviv that is becoming rare, where little bungalows built in the 1920s and 1930s have survived the encroachment of large apartment buildings. The years have seasoned their original colors to a common dusty patina. Old fig trees still thrive in small yards, grape vines twine vigorously around front porches. The front door of Magda's house is partially obscured by shrubbery and bright red geraniums.

I recognized her instantly from the old photographs. Her eyes, large, dark, and tender, retained the same depth of sorrow I remembered from the pictures of her, her head shaven, on arrival in England in 1946. Now I looked down on the luxuriant mass of black, wavy hair that framed her face. The realization that she was short, less than five feet, came as a surprise. Influenced by the admiration of Alice, Fritz, and Hedi, I had imagined her tall, idealized in heroic proportions, like a Henry Moore sculpture.

She was graceful and authoritative as she showed me in, introduced me to her husband, and offered me a comfortable chair. She negotiated Yiddish as the language common to all three of us, and moved deftly back and forth to the kitchen, serving tea and a golden strudel. She was immaculately groomed and looked competent, maternal.

"You have children?" she wanted to know.

I felt her measure my worthiness for her trust as we became acquainted, exploring safe mutual ground such as the weddings of our daughters. Her son-in-law was in the army; her son would soon be old enough to go. Her daughter worked with young children, and would be here later in the afternoon.

When her husband excused himself, we began to speak in English. Magda's voice was a warm contralto. Something of the rich hushes of Hungarian had carried over into her English, giving it greater range.

"This is just the way I remember my mother made it," she told me when I complimented her on the strudel. I had never seen it made with such generous proportions of poppy seed filling to dough.

"And you remembered that, how she made it?" I marveled.

"Oh yes, I was very close to my mother. I was the youngest of ten children, my mother would not even let me go to kindergarten. She must have known I would be her last child, and she said she didn't have ten children only to be left alone. . . . There was a very strong bond between us. So I would help her. We were a very religious family, it was the way of the family and of our neighbors all around us in Pleshovitz."

"You were taken from Pleshovitz to the camp in Kistarsca?" I asked.

"No, we were first to a prison in Budapest, a horrible big place, and we were locked up with all kinds of criminals, prostitutes and everything. My mother tried to shield us. Hedi and Fritz's mother too, but you know," she said, "little pitchers have big ears—we knew what was going on around us. It was impossible to keep it from us. It was a terrible shock. We were a very religious family. We knew we did not do anything wrong, so why were we put with drunks and criminals together? It was from there we were taken to Kistarsca. . . . That's where we were parted from our parents."

"Did they know where they were going? Did you know?" I asked.

"We didn't know. It was May of '44 and I don't know if my father knew, but when he parted from us, he blessed us. He must have felt something terrible was about to happen because," she paused, and almost whispered, "I saw it in his eyes, when he blessed me. I shall never forget that look. It is in me today just as fresh as then.

"It was then that my mother made me swear three oaths if anything happened to her: To take care of the younger children, to teach them the Shema Yisrael, and to take them to Palestine."

"And so you became, at the age of twelve, a parent."

"I tried my best," she said sadly, almost apologetically.

I was shocked at the sense of failure in her voice. "How did you and Hedi and Fritz get out?"

"It was arranged by the Red Cross and some Jewish organizations to release some children under the age of fourteen. So that is how we were sent to a children's home in Budapest. Fritz and Hedi and myself." She waited, as if considering whether to go further. "And I had another little niece with me, I don't think Alice ever knew this."

So she was in charge of three, not two, younger children. Alice didn't know. A child is missing.

"This was my brother's child. She was a year younger than Fritz.

She was only three. Her name was Hedi too." Then Magda brightened a little. "We were bound together from then on. You know, sometimes children can be more for each other than adults. Sometimes adults are only for themselves." Anger had returned her strength and pride.

"What happened to this little Hedi?"

Magda's sigh was edged with frustration and contempt. "She died just at the end of the war, and that was because of a grown-up. There was a time toward the end of '44 when little Hedi and I were separated from Hedi and Fritz because they divided us up into smaller groups to put us in different children's homes. I was separated from Hedi and Fritz, my sister's children, because our last names were different. But my brother's daughter and I had the same last name, Liberman, so I told them she was my sister and they allowed us to stay together. But I still went every time we were allowed out to see Fritz and Hedi and also two brothers of mine who were in another children's home. That is, until I got sick." Her voice quavered.

"My little niece then was very run-down. It was in the last months of the war when the two of us were taken out of the children's home. The Germans put us with hundreds of children together with old people, and they marched us the whole day in the snow to the Danube. They were going to shoot us, line us up on the bank and shoot us into the river. When we came there to the river, suddenly a Swedish Red Cross official came on a motorcycle with a paper that said we were to remain alive.[1] It was already late and very cold. My niece was crying. An Arrow Cross man came up to me and asked why she was crying. I was very afraid. We were more afraid of the Arrow Cross [the native Hungarian pro-Nazi party] than of the Germans. I told him she was cold and hungry. He said not to worry, she will soon be warm. I knew then he was one of our young men who dressed in Arrow Cross uniforms and helped us.

"The next morning they took us away again and put us in a cellar. Here we stayed for a very long time. We had very little food, dried pea gruel once a day that was brought to us by Jews who had gone over to the Arrow Cross." She made an effort to continue despite tears. "I became very sick, and my little niece got dysentery. I wasn't able to do much for her because I was so weak, except give her my food. Then when I was better there was no food at all. It was in the last months of the war and she was by this time very run-down with dysentery. Then we were moved back to the place where Fritz and Hedi were." Now rising anger contained her grief as she continued. "An aunt of mine was there, working there as a cook. She took a look and said the little girl must be taken to hospital."

Now the despair that had been building in her broke through and she sobbed forlornly.

"I said I didn't want her to go to hospital. 'I'll look after her, please let me take care of her,' I said. Then the matron came and spoke to me and said, 'Look, you are only a little girl. Since your aunt is here, if she says the child goes to hospital, then I must do that. If she were not here I would have to listen to you, and I would try to help you.' I knew that we were going to be taken away to another town that was not so badly bombed as Budapest, and I didn't want to leave her. But they did not listen to me. She was taken to hospital, and the next day I went to visit her. As soon as I came in, she asked, 'Did you bring me something to eat?'

"I remember I had been given a piece of poppy-seed cake, and I had brought my part for her. I watched how she ate it. 'Don't they give you anything to eat?' I asked her."

Magda's eyes flashed as she repeated little Hedi's answer: " 'It's not enough,' she told me." She sighed. "She was not yet four."

"This was the last time I saw her. The next time I went to visit her, nobody wanted to talk to me, so I understood that something had happened. They said, 'Some people have been taken out.' But by that time I knew how grown-ups lie to you. . . . I went to the head nurse and said, '*Now* tell me, *is* she alive or *not?*'

" 'Nothing could be done for her,' she told me."

I watched the torrent of grief and anger engulf her. Her handkerchief crumpled as she alternately dabbed at her tears and clenched it between small tense fingers.

"Since then the aunt who had sent her to the hospital tried to write to me when I was in England. I wrote to her that I don't want to hear from her. I just couldn't forgive her. If she had only waited a few days, not sent her to the hospital so quickly! We were sent to another town, to a smaller children's home. There were many sick children there and they were taken care of, and they *lived*! And even if we hadn't been sent to that place, my aunt was the cook, she had food, and if she had wanted to, she could have looked after the child. Hedi wasn't so far gone that she couldn't have been saved." A long pause followed. "Some adults are only for themselves," she reflected soberly. "So you see, later, when groups were being organized, I refused to go in the group with my older brothers to Palestine. I knew I had to take care of Hedi and Fritz myself. I couldn't trust anyone else to take care of them. It even took me awhile to trust Alice. Only after I saw she was kind to them, then it was all right."

We talked about Lingfield.

"The gardens were so beautiful," she remembered. "Sir Benjamin liked me—I felt it. Once I remember he brought fruit, a big peach, into the living room and put it on the table. He said it was special for me. But you know, I couldn't touch it. It embarrassed me. I could not take it when he didn't bring for the others. I think what happened is that the peach just sat there. . . . It just rotted."

"Once I became ill. Alice put me in a room upstairs, by myself, because she didn't know what it was. Fritz and Hedi could only come to the door when they came home from school to see me. Sophie brought me her transistor radio so I wouldn't be too lonely. It was so good to be worried about. We were like a family there."

Her newly-wed daughter and son-in-law arrived with Magda's seventeen-year-old son. "These are my children," she said, her eyes glowing. Magda's husband appeared. She served more tea. The newlyweds sat close on the couch, and I saw that, in her solicitous moves toward her new husband, Magda's daughter resembled her mother.

"When did you come to Israel?" I asked Magda.

"After training at an ORT school in London, I came with a Youth Aliya group, around 1950. Later, when I was already married, Hedi came, then Fritz. Fritz was studying at the hospital and would come to me for weekends, and then when Hedi took leave from the kibbutz for further training as a nurse, she came for weekends too. By then I had my first child, my daughter, and we were in one room and a half, we slept all in the same bed, but there was room. There always will be," she added fiercely, as if renewing an old pledge.

Magda's daughter rose and went to a side cupboard, and returned with an album of wedding pictures. Fritz had taken them, and processed them himself. They had arrived only last week. I saw pictures of the proud parents, the bride and groom, the in-laws, happy guests gathered around tables, enjoying themselves. There was one of Hedi dancing, and another of the children of Hedi and Fritz, playing together.

"It was really a beautiful celebration." Magda and her husband exchanged a smile.

"I'm saving a special letter that Hedi wrote to me for my daughter's wedding. She writes so beautifully. From the heart. It means very much to me. Do you want to hear it?"

"Yes, very much."

She read it aloud. It was a letter in which Hedi thanked Magda for helping her grow up.

You have taught us right from wrong.

You have taught us to know honesty from dishonesty.

You have taught us to distinguish the important from the superficial.

From Hiding

EVA FOLKMANN GRAHAM

London, June 1977

From the first moment of greeting in the entry of her brick suburban home, I understood why the other Lingfielders called her Big Eva. She was imposing. Not in actual size so much, but in her straight-backed dignity and the self-assured, upper-class diction. It was easy to imagine her as the grand hostess of a garden party, sailing purposefully among guests and servants.

"My story, you see," Eva began, with dramatic charm, "is completely different. That's why I'm surprised you want it. I didn't come to England like the others. I was brought by an aunt, who was married to my mother's brother. He worked for UNRRA. I was seven and a half, and he found out I was alive. My parents had me hidden in a convent. That's the reason I stayed alive and they didn't. In fact, my father died in February 1945. Can you imagine surviving all those years?"

"Sad," I said. So many had died in the last days of the war, too exhausted by the years of struggle to make those last, final efforts.

"It is sad." She spoke without emotion. "And when they found that I was alive, I was brought to England. I arrived in March and my uncle died of cancer in June. So there I was, stuck with an aunt by marriage who had a four-year-old daughter of her own, and she had me, a child that was really no relation to her whatsoever other than the fact that it was her husband's niece. And that was all.

"Now my cousin was a very weak little child, and we had a children's doctor—ghastly woman. Even as a child I thought so. She was a cold dreadful woman, and she suggested it to my aunt that it would be a very good idea, here was this lovely house in Lingfield, and she could arrange for my cousin to go to the country for Easter or summer holiday. And I don't know if my cousin went once and I went the second time or we both went. But whichever way it was, for some reason I wanted to stay, then I didn't want to. It was arranged that it

177

would make life a lot easier at home if maybe I could stay in Lingfield."

The storytelling tone in which she had been speaking became more and more marked as she continued in a singsong, as if reciting an oft-repeated rationale.

"And after all it *was* in the country, and it *was* among other children, and it was sort of not chucking me out and shelving the problem at home because there wasn't a problem at home, because I assure you," she stated with dramatic emphasis, "that over the last thirty years, without blowing my own trumpet, my aunt had far more love and affection from me than she ever had from her own daughter! Even for flying the Atlantic for six weeks at a time when she was dying of cancer, and her own daughter couldn't even be bothered!"

"Anyhow, so with that I stayed [in Lingfield], and I used to go back home for weekends and holidays, and life sort of got into a pattern and I stayed put. But I did have the backup of a family, which most of the children there didn't have. I was sort of very, very different. I won't say I didn't have their problems. But I think I was probably more balanced.

"In what way?"

"Well, you see I had roots, *slight* roots, which nobody else had. I always felt very different, and I still feel I'm very different now. They always seemed to have more problems than I had."

"In what way?"

"I think socially, mainly. I was always a much warmer person. Alice will bear me out. If she needed someone to go around or show something, I would do it. And I'm very much like that now."

"What do you remember of your life in the convent before England?"

"It was in Žilena in my hometown near Bratislava. But I remember very, very little. It's the most peculiar thing, it's as if that part of my life never existed! I do remember peeling potatoes there. I can't tell you why.

"I was ill once. And I remember being in a room that had the curtains drawn, so I think it must have been measles. Also, it was a separate room from everybody else. And now the only thing that turns my skin," she was speaking rapidly, "is when I hear 'Silent Night' sung in German. Because I remember the German soldiers using the convent for Christmas." She tightened and shrugged. "It's just something that makes me . . . ugh!" She shuddered with her whole body. "But other than that, I remember very little, really."

"Was there anyone there to whom you were attached?"

"No." She was abrupt. "Don't remember anything at all, just the room where I was ill and the potatoes. And I do remember being taken out, so we must have gone for walks.

"I think the nuns wore dark, maybe blue dresses. And big white hats. We used to sleep in a great big dormitory, the nuns slept in one corner. I remember once seeing them without their hats on. They just had white scarfs underneath. I always wondered if they had hair underneath or not." She laughed. "I also remember having to scurry downstairs into a cellar."

"During what?"

"Presumably while the soldiers were around. I wasn't the only Jewish child there. There were quite a group of us. I don't know whatever happened to any of the other children.

"Odd, isn't it, I remember very little about the convent, but I could swear I could take you and walk you into every room of our old house in Žilena and all around it. And I could only have been four when I left it. . . . In 1972, when we visited Israel for the first time, we met one of my father's sisters who left for Israel in 1936. And when we looked through old photographs we actually found a photograph of our house in Žilena. It was a big house on the corner, and I remember it as if it were yesterday. Now this last time when we were in Israel, a few weeks ago, my cousin had photographs of my father as a child and his father and his grandfather!" She was excited. "And photographs of *my* father with *his* father when my father was twenty! It was the first time I'd seen them. A pity they're out being framed now, I'd show them to you."

"Apart from the photos of your father, do you remember him?"

"No," she said, very quickly.

"Your m——?" I started.

"Not at all," she snapped. "I did know that my father represented SKF, the Swedish firm that makes ball bearings, and that my grandparents, that's my mother's father, was a cheese manufacturer."

"Do you remember your grandparents?"

"Yes, oh yes," she paused, and her eyes softened. "Yet I don't remember my parents at all. Not at all. . . .

"My maternal grandfather's house was built around a courtyard. Part of that house was where the cheese factory was. In those days they used to make it like we have the cheese triangles now and I remember sitting underneath the machine and every time one wasn't wrapped properly it used to fall with the rejected ones. I remember eating them. This is what I mean when I say I was different than the others because I had roots. I don't know what they remembered, because we never discussed anything like this as kids.

"I also recall being made to go to school and running away, and my cousin confirmed this. She said, 'Yes, you were terrible. We used to drag you to school.'

"I tell you, one of the most difficult things I found as a child was remembering things and wondering if they really were as you remembered. In 1947 my aunt who had put me in Lingfield took her daughter back to Czechoslovakia. She couldn't take me because I wasn't a British subject. She was frightened that if she took me they wouldn't let me out. I remember saying to her, '*Please* go to where I used to live and just tell me that what I remember is as it is.' When she came back I was right.

"If you ask me, would I remember my father if I saw him walk in this room, I wouldn't know who he was other than the photographs that I saw. But I can remember going tobogganing with my father." Her words were gathering speed. "I can remember going fishing with my father and catching a little fish that was put in a sink tub and waking up in the morning and it had jumped over the edge and it was dead on the floor. Silly little things. I can remember." She was talking fast now, her voice compressed anxiously. "I don't think these are things that you make up, because I don't think you can make things up like that. But," she said now matter-of-factly, "I don't remember them as people. I don't even remember going shopping with my mother. I can never remember being cuddled by my mother. It just doesn't mean anything to me. Some coffee?"

She went out and returned with a tray.

"Do you have any memories of coming to Lingfield?"

"No, no. But it must have been good because I wanted to stay. You see, *I* had the choice of staying or not staying, and I chose to stay. I never resented the fact that I was there and my cousin was going back home. In fact, you ask Alice, she'll tell you, she had terrible problems making me go home one weekend in four!"

Still it was the aunt's house she called home, a place in which she spent little time when compared with Lingfield.

"At Lingfield we used to do leather work, cane work, embroidery. We made menorahs out of bottle tops and painted them. When I think now what my children don't do compared to what we used to do as children! We used to make notepaper—take wrapping paper, cut out flowers and paste them on paper. A lot of these used to be done for the Lingfield Bazaar."

"Are you still connected with it in some way? Alice mentioned . . ."

"No. I work in the same building that it takes place in, but that's just coincidental. I work for the Reform Synagogues of Great Britain, which is the overall umbrella organization for all the reform synagogues."

"What is your work?"

"A bit of everything. I work in the office and we have various committees that the office comes under and we have an executive. Outside my work, I'm the secretary of the committee of new congregations, to help them get started and to help those that have gotten started and have problems."

"I went to the Lingfield Bazaar a few days ago," I offered.

"Oh, when were you there?" Suddenly, she stiffened.

"Thursday."

"Pity, you could have seen me. I was in the same building. You should have come up to see me. Who took you?" she asked, trying to sound casual but clearly upset.

"Alice. She asked for you, but you weren't there."

"I *was* there," she insisted.

"We couldn't find you."

"She didn't ask in the right office." She was angry. "Actually, I *was* there. What time were you there?" she demanded.

"About two o'——,", I started.

She overrode me. "I was *still* there, up on the second floor," she accused.

"We were on the ground floor. We had tea," I offered placatingly, apologetic for having upset her.

"Well, if you'd come up one floor, you'd have found me. I *was* there. Because I didn't leave till about four o'clock."

"Tell me about Alice." I ventured, after a long silence.

"I see Alice very little these days. I have a terrible conscience about it. I've gotten lazy. It means having to go get her and driving her back. She's done a lot for most of the kids. She's been marvelous. I don't know what would have happened to most of the kids if it hadn't been for her.

"But I'll tell you," fresh indignation came over her, "Alice was good with younger children, but I had my period four times before I knew what had hit me. All right, the fact that I was ten and a half was neither here nor there. Whether you expect a child to get a period at ten and a half I don't know. What I know is that I made absolutely certain that my daughter was not going to go through the same thing. I remember using handkerchiefs. I really didn't know what had hit me until Gertrud actually found them in my cupboard...

Gertrud was my favorite. I don't know why. Perhaps because she was the one I would go to. She had a sense of humor. She was lovely. You knew where you stood with her. I also loved to be in the kitchen with Sophie. We used to make lovely chocolate balls from dried-up cakes and biscuits and put a nut on the top. Zdenka liked to be in the kitchen too."

"Alice tells me you said you would be the first to marry, and you were."

"Oh no," she bristled. "I didn't need to be the first. I was very happy. I had lots of friends."

"Were you trained for any particular work?"

"Hotel management. But I didn't need to get married. See, I can understand somebody in Lingfield saying that they're frightened that at the end of the tunnel the place is going to close, and they have to get married or make a way of their own. But I never had this problem because I always had another home to go to. So there was no necessity for me to feel this way. I had a home to go to, which was obviously a good home. My aunt expected you to do the right thing at the right time. She worked very, very hard. She was a private dressmaker, and she worked from home. And her daughter was alleged to be very intelligent, a very brainy girl, and it was always much easier for me to be the one to do the ironing and the cooking, and the helping and serving than to have my head down in a book. I used to hate school, just hate it. I could never keep up. It was always easier to get out of doing something at my aunt's by saying 'Oh, I'll wash up,' or 'I'll sew the buttons on.' Yet I'm quite capable of getting a book, and if it's a good book, sitting through the whole thing. So it isn't that I don't enjoy reading. I read for pleasure, about people.

"Today I look at things with very different eyes than I would have years ago. If you look at the people who worked at Lingfield, whoever got involved, they were mostly spinsters like Alice, similar to her in nature, in attitudes and even in build." She paused for reflection, then continued. "I wonder why does one do the things that one does? Does one do it because of others or does one do it because of oneself? Why do I work where I work? But why does one do what one does? Why did all those women work there?

"At one stage there, I don't know if they were school psychologists or what they were, but I remember being made to put shapes into things and being closeted in a room with somebody and going in like this," she raised one arm high above her head, "and coming out like that," she indicated a small space between thumb and first finger. "I absolutely feel that child psychologists are the worst things put on this earth. Honestly." She spoke passionately. "I don't know why, whether it's a hang-up from childhood. Yes, I'm all for going to get help if you have problems with your children. So many people feel if a child's got a problem, you send them to the Clinic. Not 'the parents have got a problem with the child.' But 'the child's got the problem.' You send him in the Clinic four times a week, and they are going to solve all the problems. And life isn't like that. I know a child who has been going to the Clinic now for four years, four times a week and there happens to be nothing wrong with him except he is rebelling to get his parents' attention. So they bring him to the Clinic and think everything is going to be taken care of. But it isn't!"

"Do you recall Alice's connection with the Clinic?"

"I remember always wondering what Alice did when she went there. I knew she had a blind child at the Clinic, one that wasn't born blind, I think, and I remember asking her questions and being very interested, because it didn't concern me."

"You didn't trust her enough to let her close?"

"I don't know if it was that or if she wasn't the type to get close."

"What do you appreciate most about her?"

"I've never thought about it. She's always been there. I know she's at the end of the telephone if I take the trouble to ring her. Nothing would make her happier. Perhaps the need hasn't been there for a mother figure because I've had a family around me and then I've had my husband's parents next door. They've been wonderful to me."

MIRJAM STERN McHENRY

San Jose, California, September 1978

Mirjam moved cautiously among the acres of cars that gleamed hot in the morning sun of the airport parking lot. I followed her as she plodded down one aisle and up the next, searching. She was short, with blonde curly hair, and her appearance oddly suggested both fragility and strength.

"I got lost here one night picking up Alice when she came to visit. Couldn't find the car. It was horrible. Poor Alice, with her suitcase." Her sad wide-eyed look somehow called to mind the photograph of little Mirjam seated among the Lingfield children and opening packages from America.

We finally found the faded blue VW, and she drove us to her apartment on the outskirts of town. It was inviting and cheerful, with plants and crayoned pictures by her nine-year-old son. He was away visiting his father, from whom Mirjam was divorced. We lounged on the sofa bed, sipping coffee.

"I was seven or eight when I came to Lingfield," she began. "I think the thing that lured me to England was that they told us in Prague we'd have chocolate. Alice did give me chocolate before I went to sleep, and I was nibbling and licking on it to save it. I guess I must have fallen asleep, because she told me when she came in in the morning I was covered with chocolate, all the sheets and everything." She paused. "I was not in a concentration camp—I was hidden by a family." Her look inquired whether I was still interested.

"For how long?" I asked.

"I don't know. One and a half years or a year. The last nine months or a year I had to be hidden upstairs. I couldn't go out anymore, like I wasn't supposed to really be there. This was a place my father found for me and my sister. My father also found places for all my cousins, and I think he paid a lot of money. In the place where I was, they didn't realize what it would involve or they wouldn't have done it even for money, because later they had to have German soldiers living downstairs—and the German police were always looking for the man of this house, I think because in this house there was always a lot of partisan activity. Several times when they came to look for him, they found me, but they never took me."

"Do you think they thought you were his daughter?"

"I don't know. Then I got diphtheria. I found this out much later; there was a Jewish doctor in hiding someplace, but he was afraid to come. And I was so sick! They called a Gestapo doctor, an SS officer. *He* came," she said proudly. "And I think he knew who I was, and it was my birthday, so he didn't even charge them anything. *He* saved my life! I think the soldiers downstairs knew I was there too."

"You don't think they thought you were these people's kid?"

"No, because why would a kid be up there and never come down? Eat up there all the time. They never saw me. I wasn't supposed to but I would always sit by the window, and I would stare at the rats in the garbage pile across the way for hours. There were people across the way who also had soldiers there, and they knew too."

"Where was your sister? Didn't you say she had gone into hiding with you?"

"Oh," she dismissed the question. "She went outside one day, we hadn't been there long, and she got caught. She was sent away to a concentration camp."

"Were there other children in the house?"

"This woman had four children, I think, and the youngest one was about fifteen or something, and they never came upstairs. Nobody came upstairs except to go to bed. See, the mother was afraid when she realized it was serious, it wasn't just like having a guest for a while. She wanted to give me up."

"How do you know that?"

"She would," she hesitated. "Well, she told me all about concentration camps. She was telling me all kinds of things because she wanted me not to, you know, to do anything to endanger them. Like she'd say, 'This will happen to you if you do this.' When somebody came I was supposed to hide under the bed. She told me a lot about concentration camps because after the war I knew everything about them."

"She got your cooperation by terrifying you."

"Well, see," Mirjam defended. "She was just a simple peasant woman and she didn't want all the family shot. When I was very sick, they thought I was dying. I think I *was* dying. She was standing by the bed, and she said she was really concerned how they were going to bury me because I wasn't supposed to be there. How were they going to get me out of the house and bury me, and I thought," she laughed nervously, "they'd bury me before I was dead.

"They had some water next to my bed and I kept calling. I was too weak to get it. I just wouldn't stop calling. I think it was," she gathered strength and pronounced each word loudly, "a will to live! If I had just stopped calling I probably would have just died." Silence encircled us, and she got up to reheat the coffee. Finally, she spoke again.

"I think I've dealt with those memories. I know if it weren't for Alice and the people around her, we would have been a lot different. I also think that I had a lot of healing through Jesus. They're now doing inner healing and it's not just Hail Mary and Praise the Lord—there's a lot of good work being done. I mean, people have things inside for years and years that blocks them and keeps them from growing. I feel I can talk about the past, but I don't have an anger or hatred. To me the past was a different life. To me, I could think it was somebody else that it happened to. And then the life in England was a whole different thing, and my life in New York, and then my life with my busband, and then by myself. It's like they're all separate. They're so different." She sounded puzzled.

Where had the path started? I wanted to know.

Kurima, the tiny village in Czechoslovakia, was where she had lived until she was four. "There was no electricity, no plumbing- We had the one store there, and it had everything. My father sold flour, yardage, everything, and we had some animals, cows, also fruit trees. I remember plums." She spoke quietly, in reverie.

"My father was really a special person, because you know, our life, the Jewish people and the peasants, it was like worlds apart. Yet at Christmastime we had a big Christmas tree in the house for the servants. I'd always been impressed, for a Jewish person to have done that kind of thing in that time and in that place is sort of out of character. But it was for '*them*.' And my mother, well, I was told that she read a lot and that she was a sweet person. I know that for Jewish women at that time it was unusual to read a lot."

"Do you remember her?"

"I was very close to my father, and when I remembered her it was like I was angry for something. I don't know if that was my age or really something. She made a potato soup that I loved and I was angry and I said that I wouldn't come in, but I stood near the door and oh, I smelled that soup. . . . I don't feel that I really knew her."

"But you felt you knew your father?"

"It's just that when I thought of her in my memories it seemed that I was always angry about something, but my father, he was always loving, he'd pick me up and carry me. I was the youngest."

"Of how many?"

"My sister Judith, she came with me to England after the war. She's about eight years older. But as I told you she was in hiding only a short time, and I had a brother. He died in the war, he would be about two years older than me. He was in a camp too."

"What was his name?"

"I think Otto, I'm not really sure. My sister doesn't like to talk about those things, so I don't ask her. And we had one older sister, I don't know if she was mentally retarded, I must have been about two or three, and I know that she was very sick, and I went to the door and I was told to go away. Then she died. She must have been about fifteen. We were a very religious family. Our lives were based on being Jewish. It wasn't something you did on the weekend. You lived it every day. We followed the commandments, the way they understood them. We had a kosher house. You didn't work on Saturday. We went to synagogue. But I think the first school I went to, they already had made the Jewish children separate from the other children so we were all in one room. . . ."

"When were you separated from your parents, about four or five?"

"Well, what happened was that my father sent us first to Hungary, to my aunt there. My father arranged that we be smuggled through the woods in threes. I was with my cousin, Elsa, and her brother and my sister and her brother with Elsa's sister. And we were supposed to be smuggled over to live with my aunt. Because I guess the Germans were coming to Czechoslovakia first. My sister's group made it, but we were caught. They put us in jail overnight, and I was so humiliated I wanted to die. From there they put us in a Jewish orphanage. I was there for a year. My cousin and I were together there for a year. Then my father arranged for us to be smuggled back to Czechoslovakia."

"How did he know you were there?"

"Well, it was around the corner from my aunt's. Sometimes we could go visit her."

"But she couldn't take you out?"

"No. Then my father arranged for us to be smuggled back. About two weeks later the Germans took all the children from that orphanage. Then when I came back to Czechoslovakia, I went to the hospital to see my mother. She was very sick. And that was the last time I saw them, my father and my mother. It must have been a Catholic hospital, because there were nuns and we had been brought up that they hated Jews, and I feared they wouldn't take care of her. Then from there I went to this family in hiding."

I waited as she gazed away.

"There was this clock there, when I was in hiding. And I couldn't really tell time, but it was there and I was always watching this clock and thinking. I couldn't have had such bad feelings about my mother because I was always thinking she would come and take me back."

"You didn't realize how sick she was?"

"I knew, but that was my dream, that she would come and take me. I didn't know she had died till after the war. Mother died in Sered concentration camp and father died in Sachsenhausen concentration camp.

"In this house, when they left, they had to turn all the lights off. I was really afraid because I had to be up there in the dark. They didn't know much about child psychology." Her small, thin laugh had a bitter twist. "What really frightened me," she went on, "was there was always a question of who was going to blow the bridge up, whether the Germans would or the partisans. Anyway, the house was close to the bridge. So I always thought they'll leave me there and they'll blow the bridge up and the house will go with it!"

Later, over lunch in a restaurant, she told me of her experimentation in the past with drugs—LSD, quaaludes, mescaline. She picked at her salad, "You wouldn't know if I was on something right now, would you?"

"Probably not. Are you?"

"Would you believe me if I said I'm not?"

"Okay, but isn't the important thing that you know that you're not?"

"I suppose," she said halfheartedly. "When I was in hiding I didn't really eat right. They brought me mushrooms, but I hated them. I threw them in the fire. They had a big bag of sugar cubes in the closet, and I would go in and take handfuls of that. And one time they had a Christmas tree hung with candy, and I took a lot of the candy. They brought me a little present, too. I wanted to go to church with them, but they wouldn't take me. They said my father wouldn't like it. After the war my cousin Trudy was in the hospital, and they put me with her. It was for malnutrition. But I can't say they didn't feed me. I think it was just that I didn't eat."

"Did you eat upstairs alone? Did they just put the food in your room?"

"Right," she said, looking down for a long moment. "My aunt was very kosher, and she would bring chicken soup and different things to the hospital, and that added insult to injury because I didn't want to be there and then on top of that, you had to have special food. I didn't want to be Christian then, but I still didn't want to be Jewish. In fact, I haven't really felt good about being Jewish, till now. Now I really feel proud; it's like I'm part of God's chosen people, and it's a real feeling. I have never wanted to tell anyone I was Jewish, even when I was already in my twenties in New York."

"Were you ashamed?"

"I think it's deeper than that, I think, to me—it may not be so for all the Jewish people from Europe—but I can see how Negroes feel being black. It's something that's ingrained, that you're not as good, and I really understand the psychology of the whole thing. I remember reading a book by Bruno Bettelheim in which he talks about [how] the Jews in camp would rather identify with the guards. And I know because once we went camping, youth hosteling, in England, and there were some German boys. Well, I didn't flirt with them, I mean, I was just a little thing, but in my head they were more of a hero. It was like they were the strong, the good-looking guys. It seemed that everyone had that feeling, to want to be identified with them."

"Do you recall anything happy about being Jewish as a child?"

"Yes, Friday night all the good cooking smells, then you'd go someplace to pick up the food where it was kept warm and Saturday afternoon my father would take a nap, then we'd go to synagogue, and I was the youngest, so I got to carry the books and wear white stockings and a starched dress. And there was really good food. And I remember the Passover I said, 'I'm not going to fall asleep.' I must have been a brat all my life." She laughed with confiding warmth.

We walked back to the car, passing the windows of several dress shops. She looked longingly at an attractive display of summer dresses. "I don't make very much doing housecleaning," she said. "But I'd rather do that than work in a place where you have to get too involved with people.

"My family, we were not wealthy but we were probably well off. Somebody would sew our dresses and we would have big bows, and somebody would say 'Here come the Stern girls!' and so being in an orphanage was humiliating to me after being like a princess. That's why in the orphanage in Hungary I 'pretended I didn't belong there like the others."

Back at her apartment, Mirjam talked about her life in England. "One time it was raining and we had gotten these yellow rain capes from America. And one day I just said I won't wear that, I felt like the Seven Dwarfs. It wasn't the cape: I always resented being together in a group that's different. And then when we got to school we were all soaked, because I refused to put that raincoat on, and the others followed me. Anyway, the teacher took us into the headmistress's office and dried our clothes. There was a fire there. Then later in the afternoon or next day she rang the bell and said, 'Will all the Geerman children come.' They'd always say that, 'the Geerman children,' and she took Hedi and me in her room and gave us a lecture about how some children didn't have raincoats. I resented that and having to be responsible for the younger children because I was older. One time, Gadi had an accident in his pants and we were square dancing and the headmistress made me and Hedi take care of him. I was really annoyed. He must have been about five or six."

"And you?"

"Eight or nine. . . . I still have a doll that was given to me in Lingfield. It was sent by Eleanor Roosevelt through the Foster Parents Plan. I called her Mella. Manna made beautiful clothes for it. It was really pretty."

"Were you attached to any special adult at Lingfield?"

"At first, Manna. I was really crushed when she went to Israel. She had a sister who had cancer. I thought it was pretty shabby of her to leave."

"How old were you?"

"Must have been eleven or so. Then we all saved up and invited her to come back for a visit. But it just seemed like she was different. There was a lot of tension between us."

"How long had she been gone?"

"About three years. Everybody had a lot of expectations, all of us children of her, and she of us. That type of expectation, I don't think it *can* ever be fulfilled, because I don't know if anybody even knows what they want. She'd gone through things. We had grown up some. You come back and it can't be the way you think and so I think it was a large strain on her. We, I think, were disappointing. She was very critical of me."

"Of what?"

"I don't remember the incidents. I was about eleven or twelve, Alice told me that Miss Freud didn't think I was very happy and would I like to go for therapy to get help. I don't know for what. I started to go to this Dr. X——. And at the time we thought everything American was supergreat, and here was this young handsome American. And I was with him maybe a year and a half, and he decided to go back to America. So I was really upset. Miss Freud wrote me a nice letter. And then I went to Dr. Y——, an older man in a wheelchair. I couldn't relate to him. After that I went to Dr. Z——, and I don't think I was a very good patient with her."

"Why?"

"I think I was angry that Dr. X—— had left. And I think she was a refugee. Whenever she would say, 'Tell me about this, see, I understand,' that would really upset me, because you don't want to be with someone who went through what you did. She didn't really go through what I did. But Dr. X——, the American, he was like the white guys, the good guys. And when she talked to me, like I didn't want to identify with the losers."

"She, Dr. Z——, had a son and he was about ten or nine. I don't know if they do it now, but there's so much secrecy about it. It's like the patient shouldn't see this room or that room or the family. When her son saw me coming, he'd hide behind the door like he was taught that and I'd just walk straight into the room. I think they still do that and I think the secrecy just reinforces people's inferiority feeling. I think it's a negative thing. Because I think therapists and analysts are people too, and if you see their bedroom or bathroom you're not going to think that they're not God. It really used to annoy me. But she didn't change her mind. And I just wasn't very helpful. I wasn't a little kid that I could play with child guidance toys, and I wasn't grown up enough to think that I wanted help."

"How old were you?"

"Fourteen or fifteen. It wasn't my idea to go. I knew that there were things wrong. I knew that I wasn't happy. I didn't care for school. After a while she went to America too. When Dr. X—— wrote to me after he left, he sent me a picture, and I'd go to sleep looking at it. They were like treasures from heaven, his letters. One time he said something like maybe someday you'll come. And I took it that he was inviting me. I told Sophie about that and she said it didn't mean he was really inviting me, and I was really hurt." She laughed bitterly. "His wife had a baby in London, and I was more excited about that baby than I've been of anybody who ever had a baby. I've never had that feeling. I was so happy.

"He would write to me and I think I must have written very negative letters, because he'd write things like 'Sometimes if we're not friendly and cooperative, we think other people aren't. . . .'"

"Did you ever see him again?" I asked.

She hesitated. "It wasn't too great. He had a house and he had an office next door and," her voice grew faint, "he had me come to his office. Just seemed kind of weird to me, 'cause it was a weekend, I think Sunday, and it was like, I couldn't see his house! I think I was hurt by that."

Driving me to the airport, she reflected that if she had not had the care of Alice and Sophie and others, she might have been different, much worse. "Still, I think they are disappointed in me, that I'm not as good as they thought I should be. See, I was in London with my son for a visit and I wore hip-huggers and ran around to be with my friends, while Sophie and Zdenka sewed my hems. I was feeling very liberated then. I thought my head had been opened up to a lot of new things. People now who knew me then think oh, what's happened to Mirjam, now she's gotten so square."

She swerved onto the freeway and accelerated rapidly as she moved into the fast lane, gripping the wheel tighter and sitting tensely upright.

"Most people," she raised her voice over the wind rushing through the open windows, "will not believe that there's really a Devil. We're too sophisticated to believe that there is really a Devil. But that's the Devil's greatest tool, that we don't believe that he's real." Her voice grew stronger. "And a lot of depression is spiritual and we can bind it and cast it out. There are not many people that are actually possessed —Manson was—but people like that can be delivered and they'll be safer than anyone you know."

"How?"

"Through the power of Jesus' blood, they can be delivered. Because when Jesus was walking on the earth He met someone who had an evil spirit in him. And He said to him, 'I know ye the holy one, the anointing one of Israel. Have you come to torment us before our time?' The evil spirits in people always recognize the Holy Spirit," she said fervently, elongating the *e* in *evil.* "We're trying to do everything in *man's* wisdom. But our wisdom is nothing! The wisdom, it is something you can't believe when you get wisdom from God!" She was glowing with excitement. "And the gifts of the Spirit are words of knowledge and wisdom and discernment, things like that. *You're* nothing," she shouted at me. "*You're* just a channel! When you have *God's* power, *God's* brain, you know it's going to be superior to what somebody's theory is, isn't it?" She didn't wait for an answer. "Because theories change all the time. My people perished for lack of knowledge, it says in Malachai when the people are going to reject the Savior. Now in Deuteronomy God gave us all the blessings, and He said if you don't obey you'll have all these curses, and I believe it. I see it.

I asked, "Do you believe that what happened to you, to the Jews in Europe, is part of that?"

"Yes. It says in the Old Testament how much grief and suffering they're going to have because they'll be blind and because of unbelief. When people say, well, we didn't crucify Christ, well, literally they didn't do it because that was a Roman custom, but they forced them to do it. Pilate and Herod, they said, what has He done? He didn't do anything. And in the Old Testament it tells you He will be falsely judged. So when He was crucified—I forget your question?"

"I asked about the Jews in Europe," I said.

"So they said to Pilate, 'Let His blood be on us and on our children.' Like they said, 'Do it and we'll take the consequences,' and we have. I mean, God has a covenant with the Jewish people and that will not be broken until His plan is completed. Otherwise we would have been assimilated many years ago, wouldn't we? What people has survived like the Jewish people? But to me the exciting thing is, see, when we say spiritual we say Holy Spirit. We say Holy Spirit because there are a lot of other spirits." Her voice rose. "I believe in Satan and I believe in his demons and his spirits. Satan will give you what you want. Oh yes, and then he'll get you, like Hitler and Mussolini."

Some weeks later a package arrived from Mirjam from a small Christian commune called Grace Hill. It was the King James Bible with Christ's words featured in red. There was a list of passages for me to read in Isaiah and Jeremiah and news that Mirjam had married for the third time.

When Alice and Sophie stayed with me in June 1980, Mirjam

brought her son to visit them. He was delightful, a very intelligent, poised, and charming twelve-year-old. Mirjam was no longer in the commune, and was training to be an aide to the elderly.

(ERVIN) SHMUEL BOGNER

Kibbutz Ein Herod, Israel, July 1979

His letter said that he was the head gardener in the kibbutz. Therefore I expected his place to be filled with even more fresh flowers than is customary to welcome the Sabbath.

Tan and stocky, Ervin filled the narrow entry. He had the appearance of an aging ram, large-featured and stubborn. When I followed him into the living room, his weary gait cancelled the first impression of strength.

The TV was on. Judith, his wife, nodded hello, and he sat down beside her.

There were no fresh flowers anywhere in the well-furnished living room, but there was a pale lavender and mauve bouquet of delicate fronds on the coffee table. I asked what they were.

"Aha! These are Al Mahvet. You think they are alive, yes?" He chuckled. "Al Mahvet means 'over death.' These flowers are almost two years old, but they still look alive. You thought they were alive, didn't you?"

Then he gestured around the room and said apologetically, "We don't have any children, so what would go for the child instead goes into the apartment." He added sadly, "My wife cannot have any children." Grief descended like fine gray dust. "We shall go to dinner now."

Judith went to change, and when she returned she stood silently to have her sundress hooked, her back to Ervin in a posture of defeat, her round shoulders slumped toward her abdomen.

As we walked, he pointed to a neighbor's yard, where grapes hung in abundance from lush vines. "Someday we'll be able to go out here in my yard and pick grapes and eat them too. He's been there a long time, many years. We are only here a short time. They wouldn't give us a new apartment because we have no children, even though everyone in my group was already getting them and moving in. I complained. They called a big meeting about it. I said, 'Why are you punishing me? Isn't it enough punishment that I have no children?

Why do you make us more miserable?' Then they decided to give us one of the new apartments."

The people next door nodded in greeting.

"Are you friendly with them?" I asked.

"Not too much—you see, they have children. They're always with them in the evening. In the kibbutz, the life revolves around the children with the families. If we had children we would have more friends. In the kibbutz, if you don't have children you are nobody." Though he spoke sadly, he ended with a forced chuckle.

He paused to move a hose and pointed to an adjacent lawn, explaining that he had designed the automatic underground sprinkling system for it. As we crossed the vast brown lawn near the dining hall, I asked about it.

"It's old," he said, "needs new topsoil. A lot of work and a lot of money. For three years I've been asking for the money for it. But I get turned down. Maybe next year," he shrugged.

We sat down at the table of the kibbutz's founding family. "Because we don't have any children of our own, or family, we sit here Friday night," Ervin said dully.

Ervin and Judith ate silently, methodically. The conversation with the others turned quickly to the purpose of my visit, and a handsome young man with a small girl on his lap, sitting next to Ervin, demanded: "Aren't you finding that all these people that you are interviewing are not normal?"

Judith blanched and lowered her head. Ervin's face flushed, as if he'd been slapped. Our eyes met. His pleaded for acquittal.

"What is normal?" I fired back, and added, "What impresses me more and more is how people are coping with massive losses." Judith looked up, relieved. It was the first time she had looked at me directly. Ervin smiled broadly.

Back at the apartment, Judith served tea and cake that Ervin had made. "My grandfather on my mother's side had a bakery and that was where I played," he told me. "I made small cakes there and put them in the stove. That was my nursery in my childhood—the bakery. And my grandmother, she did a lot of cooking, too. Anyone made a *chasene* [wedding], she was the one who made the cooking, all the dinner, the baking, everything. I remember she was very religious because she had no hair and only a *sheitl* [wig] on her head. And there was a big family—seven or eight children in my mother's family, two brothers and four or five sisters. I don't remember exactly the number. Most are dead."

"Where was this?" I asked finally.

"Lepta Svat Nicolas, the city of St. Nicolas, in Czechoslovakia. I was born there, my father was born there the same, and my grandmother."

"Do you remember your father?"

"Yes," he sighed. "The first thing I remember is that my father was taken away to a labor camp. I remember he took his suitcase and put many cigarettes in it and his clothes and he said, 'Don't be worried. I'm going to work, the Germans asked me to work for them.' He got a paper that said he was going to go away to work for them."

"And do you remember your father saying good-bye to you?"

"Yes, I was in the wagon and my mother took me to the train station and I saw him, how the Jerries took him away, took away everything he had, and put him in a wagon for cows. It wasn't a real train for normal people, with windows." Shame damped his rising anger. "I didn't know then. Now I grow up and I understand what I have seen, the picture that all my life is with me before my eyes like I see it yesterday, this train. The way they take him away and put him in a train for pigs! For pigs!" he cried out. "I always see that in front of my eyes. It follows me since I can remember myself and I was age four. I saw them take away his razor and things, and then they took the clothes off my father. Then my mother took me away. I saw them take something off his fingers, go like this." He brushed one hand roughly across the other in a pulling motion. "I have that picture in front of my eyes, but I didn't know what it is. When I grow up I understand what I saw then. It stays before my eyes. . . . When you are a child you collect all these pictures in your brain and when you grow up they start to come out and you start to understand what you saw."

"And your mother? What happened to her?"

He exchanged a knowing glance of disgust with Judith. "Oh, my mother, she did all right for herself. She learned to survive. After we saw my father taken away we came home and she didn't know what to do, and afterwards she got some information. Some people told her to go away if she wants to stay alive because they're starting to search Jews, that she should find a way to hide herself. So my mother started to travel with me from one town to the next, from one person to another person, to Christian people. My mother spoke German, Hungarian, and Slovakian, so she could always find someone who would give us shelter for a short time. Somewhere she got a small Hitler Youth uniform for me. It had a cap. She put it on me and we went around like that. She would speak to me in German in front of other people. I didn't understand German, but she told me just to say 'ja, ja' when she speaks to me.

"At first people took us in then we went into the woods. We were starving. We ate what we found: garbage, potatoes, wild berries, roots. My mother said I had a swollen stomach from hunger sometimes. And then the Russian army came and found us. And my mother started to talk to them and she told them she was Jewish. Well, among them was a doctor, a Jewish doctor, and he took her under his wing. Her legs were very swollen and she had rheumatism, I think. I don't know what else was wrong with her but he started to take care of us. They were killing pigs and chickens where we were because the Christian people [had abandoned their livestock and] had run away from the Russians. They were afraid.

"My mother said we did not have anywhere to run and that the Russians would be better to us than the German soldiers, and we stayed for a while with them. There was shooting there, the first time I see Katyusha rockets, and they put me in a cellar and I was crying because I wanted to be with my mother." His voice caught in the back of his throat as if he were about to cry, but instead, he was smiling. "See, my mother was sick, so she stayed in the room, but *me* they put in the cellar! And I came up to see her and a bullet went right over her head into the wall!" He chuckled.

"The Russians left to go farther to another village to conquer. Then my mother was caught by the Germans, because she didn't know which part was conquered by the Russians and which is still German. So they put her in jail."

"And you, where were you?"

"I was left behind in the village. She went out to search for food for me. Maybe I was asleep when she went out. She was in prison a couple of days, and I don't know what I did with myself all the time she was away. I was alone in the village, playing with mud, with nothing. Maybe there were other kids, I can't remember. She came back in a few days."

"Your mother sounds like a very capable person, inventive in the face of danger."

"Her life taught her how to—you know, some people who weren't able to do that, died. . . . Life teaches people how to adapt themselves. Who did, is alive, who didn't know how, is not alive anymore.

"When the war was over we went back to our own town. Somebody else was living in our house. My mother was sick, her legs were swollen. She was working in a place, washing dying people. Things were very hard then. I remember my mother was standing a whole day from morning till evening in a line to get me a pair of sandals. They were a piece of wood with leather straps on it, and that was shoes. This was at the Bata factory, famous factory in Czechoslovakia. I was playing near, watching and waiting for her to come out because she wanted to send me to school and they didn't allow me to go to school without shoes.

"Then she put me in school and then the children hit me, they said, 'What are you doing here, Jew?' "

"This was after the war?"

"Yes, because the Slovakians were always anti-Semites, not the Czech people but the Slovakians. One of the guys made me put a plum pit in my nose. They forced me to do it and then it got swollen. I had a lot of trouble later from that, polyps that had to come out. My mother had to take me to the doctor."

"Were you very attached to your mother, then?"

"Yes, at that time I was still attached to her. But then she put me in that place."

"What place?" I asked.

"In Kosice, where they collected children," he said with a bitter grimace, "to transport them to Israel. I can't remember if it was my mother or my aunt who put me in there. They thought the children will be sent to Israel and I had two uncles there. Maybe she thought they will adopt me."

"Were you told why you were going into this place in Kosice?"

"Who brought me there, my aunt or my mother, she said, 'Here you're going to have a nice time. Here are all children like you.' I saw some bicycles there and I wanted very much a bicycle. Some of the children said, 'You want to ride?' And they teach me how to drive a bicycle. I was very happy that I could ride on a bicycle. But I didn't know I was going to be left there. I was there for a while. I don't remember how long. Then they took us to Prague.

"In Prague they gave us food and took us to the plane, about seventy-five children. It was a big plane with four engines and we flew to England. I came with Julius, Hedi, and Fritz to Lingfield. We lived there for a while. One day a group of us took a walk on the road and I had an accident."

"How did that happen?"

"I was making a mark, playing with Julius, with a pen. I think I wanted to take off his numbers, on the back of his hand, and there suddenly came a car, pushed me and pulled me for a hundred meters, and I had a broken leg. I found myself sitting on the main road near a bridge and crying, and Julius came and said to me, 'Get up! Get up!' and I said, 'I can't, my leg hurts me.' The car stopped immediately. He came to see what happened. They told me I had a broken leg, and the man of the car took two pieces of wood and tied my leg and he took me to the hospital. Then I found myself in the hospital in a cast. I stayed there in the hospital for five to six months, then they took it off of me. I made much trouble there." He chuckled proudly. "I was a very wild child."

"What did you do?"

"I got off my bed with my cast on. I had a bar between my two legs, I could not put them together, and I got down from the bed when I wasn't supposed to. Or I'd go on a wheelchair and go around to my friends. I was always getting off the bed and making trouble.

"What could I understand? I wanted to enjoy myself! I wanted to live like every child wanted to live! I couldn't talk [English] so I couldn't understand what they wanted from me. My first English I learned in hospital. Then when I came back they found out I am not a good enough student to study in school like all the other children. So they sent me away to Oxford, a school for children who have difficulty to study. I studied there for one year. Then they sent me to a village, I can't remember the name, I lived there with a family. It was a school where three classes were in one class. I don't know how the teacher managed, but that's how it was. I was separated from everybody for three years. Only the last year I was together with them in Lingfield House, Isleworth. There I studied for one year, then Alice brought me back to the group."

"Was Alice seeing you all this time, visiting in hospital and then the other places?"

"I can't remember what kind of relationship was between us after the accident. I understand she must have known what was happening with me, because she knew I was in the village and she brought me back from there. So I think she knew where I was. So in 1948 I came to Lingfield House again and I went to school there in the same class with Julius. He was one of the good sportsmen in the class and I was one of the best students in mathematics, and in reading I was one of the best, so every second or third page I got a star. When the headmaster came around to see what was going on I remember the teacher would say 'Ervin, read!' He was proud that he had a good student in the class.

"After one year the teacher wanted to move me, jump me to 1B from 1D and skip 1C because I was such a good student. The teacher told me, 'You'll waste your time in 1C. You can learn in 1B.' But when it came time for me to go in 1B I came to Israel."

"And how old were you then?"

"Twelve."

"Do you remember that teacher's name?"

"Yes. Mr. White."

"Do you remember the names of any of your other teachers?"

"No, but I remember his name, Mr. White." He sighed. "If I had continued there I could have finished school in two more years and made something of myself."

"So even though you had missed a lot, you were starting to catch up."

"Yes, I was catching up very fast and I also had private lessons because Alice wanted me to be with my own age in school. She wanted to help us. Alice and Manna helped us a lot after school. But that finished when I was sent to Israel. . . . After that I lost connection with Alice. My aunt put an announcement on a radio program, or in a newspaper, that is how Alice heard that a woman named Rosie Bogner has a son my age and is in Israel."

"Your aunt initiated this, not your mother?"

"No, my mother didn't care about me, I think. I asked my aunt later: 'What kind of bad mistake did you make!' Because I was upset that I left England. I would have had a much better life if I had stayed there and finished school and learned some work that can help me in my life. And then come here, at age eighteen or twenty."

"What would you have liked to finish as?"

"I don't know. When I came I was in a camp." His laugh seemed forced. "Call it a refugee camp of children."

"Ben Shemen?" I named a large boys' refugee camp.

"Ramat Hadassah, it was near Tivon. But first I was in tents. All refugee children came there and from these they started to send us everywhere. To kibbutzim. First I was in tents in Kiryat Shmuel for two weeks in sand, with a few guys and we got food, that's all. I didn't know," his voice rose, "that three hundred yards from my tent my uncle lived! The brother of my mother!" The outcry lasted only a moment. Then came strange, moaning laughter. Something within him had gone awry; laughter was the only way out for pain. "*Only* three hundred *yards* from my tent, my uncle lived in his house," he chuckled. "My uncle Akiva."

"My God, and your mother, was she there too?"

"No, she was with her husband in Tel Aviv, but my uncle was living in Kiryat Shmuel and my tent was in Kiryat Shmuel. This was the younger brother of my mother. He was here already in Israel since 1938!"

"And your aunt, the one who sent for you, where was she?"

"She was living there too, near my uncle Akiva, only about half a mile from there. I didn't know that I had an aunt and two uncles and all the brothers of my father living in the same area! Half a mile from me!" He was shouting his rage. "And I didn't know nothing! And sometimes I was walking near the house of my aunt and I didn't know that my aunt was living there!" He inhaled deeply, then sighed.

"Then I sent a telegram to Alice to send me the address of my mother. Alice answered and I phoned my mother. She came and said she was surprised that I had arrived like this with nobody knowing. I was miserable, dirty. I had a suitcase of clothes but I didn't know how to change or take care of myself. Then my mother washed me and she took me and said, 'Do you know that your uncle lives here!' Then she took me to his house, and he said, 'Oh goodness, I remember you when you were a little tiny boy. Now you are a big man already.'"

"And you were then?"

"Twelve years old. And he took me to a restaurant and to see places. Then he asked me, 'Where are you living?' I answered, 'Here!'" He was shouting. "'You can see my tent from your house!'"

"'You are there? The son of my sister and I don't even know that! Okay,' he says, 'I'll take you back there today and the day after tomorrow I come to take you to my home.'" Sarcastically, he imitated his uncle.

"So I say 'Okay, I'll be happy.' So my mother goes back to Tel Aviv to her husband."

"Your mother didn't offer to take you?"

"Yes, she said she was going to come back to take me. Then the same day that my mother went away they sent me away to Ramat Hadassah. Then my mother came to find me so they told her that I was already in Ramat Hadassah. So she came in a taxi there. This taxi was her husband's. She came with him, his two grown sons and two daughters and another woman. He was a cripple, not able to work at all. One of the older sons worked the cab for him. And my mother didn't tell me the truth, that this cripple is her husband. She introduced him as a 'relative' and he's going to take us home. I was so happy. I didn't care about the 'relative' because I thought he's going to take me home. I had left my mother four or five years ago. So I was happy that I was going to have a home and a mother like every child has.

"She took me to Tel Aviv. She showed me the house. But I didn't tell you that I had a problem. I couldn't talk with my mother. I talked English. In England Alice wanted us to speak only English. I forgot everything else. Hebrew I didn't know at all. My mother had to get translated through her husband. He spoke English perfectly because he was in the British Navy.

"I was there two or three days and this man said suddenly, 'Do you want a father?' I said, 'Why not? It's nice to have, like every child has; it's the normal thing.' 'Well,' he says, 'you know I'm your father now.' "

"Well, welcome!" Ervin said sarcastically. "I see a cripple and *he's* my father now! But a father's a father, so what can I do! I can't complain; my mother chose him! Of course I would like to have, like every normal child, a nice father and a healthy father and not a man that had problems to walk."

"Did he use crutches?"

"Yes, and he suffered all the nights. He made awful noises. I couldn't sleep there in the same room with them. And not enough that he and his four children and my mother lived there. His sister lived there too, and it was only four rooms. And he explained to me that he'd like to have me in his house but there's no place for me to sleep because in one room there's two daughters. In the hall is his sister and in the other room the older brothers. And in one room he and my mother have to sleep. So we decided that I had to go back to Ramat Hadassah for a while and later he'll take me; they'll arrange it later on." He sighed and looked away.

"So they took me back to Ramat Hadassah and I spent there a couple of months and they sent me to Kibbutz Givat Chayim. After a while I understood that I had no chance to be back with my mother again."

"When did you realize that?"

"After one year that I was in Israel when I had my bar mitzvah in Givat Chayim."

"Did your mother come to that?"

"I can't remember. Then I got into trouble and then they sent me away from Givat Chayim."

"What happened?"

"Our group was on a vacation trip near apple orchards. It was after school ended for the summer and a few of us guys, we go and steal some apples." He paused as if to retrieve something. "You know, when we were waiting in France for the ship to take us to Israel, the counselors told us, 'In Israel there is fruit and everything good growing everywhere and you just take what you want. . . .' " Again the bitter laugh of having been fooled.

"Well, we got punishment from our teacher to go back to the

kibbutz because we didn't behave ourselves correctly, while the others continued their trip. So I decided, I'm not going to take that punishment. I decided to go to my grandmother's house in Haifa. I loved my grandmother very much and my aunt, the one who put the ad in the papers looking for me, lived with her too."

"Your mother's mother?"

"No, she was killed by the Jerries, this was my father's mother; she survived Auschwitz. I knew I'd get some pocket money, so I went there. When I came back to the kibbutz my teacher said, 'I'm sorry you don't know how to behave yourself. You are now thirteen years old and you have to behave as a man. And because you didn't take the punishment, you go back to your mother.' So they put me on the main road with my clothes and bus fare and sent me to my mother. I told her they threw me away from the kibbutz, and I'm home. I was happy because I thought, now's my chance to be home. But my mother didn't think the same thing, and she went with me and tried to get me back in the kibbutz. And this teacher said, 'No, I'm sorry, you take him back. If your son doesn't live with his mother, he's going to be a criminal. If your husband has four, then he can have five children. His place is in your home, not here. Because all the other children who are here don't have parents. He has a mother, so how can you think about not keeping him in your own home'?"

"And you heard all this?"

"Yes, I don't know if my mother understood it as I did because by then I spoke perfect Hebrew and she didn't. Anyway, she didn't want me. She went to the Sochnut [Jewish Agency] and begged them to take me. I was put with a family in the south, and from there I came here to Ein Harod."

"Was there ever a time when you wanted your aunt or grandmother to take you to live with them? Or your uncles?"

"Mm, no, I wanted to be with my mother. Every child wants to be with his mother. When I got married I wanted to have a family, because I realized I didn't have it myself. I wanted to give to my child exactly what I didn't have in my life. So that's why it was so important for me to have a child in my life. . . . So he'll not suffer what I have suffered all my life and give him the love that I didn't get. That's what I'm searching all the time, to get a warm house. The only one that I feel loved me was my grandmother. . . ."

Judith showed me into the small neat bedroom, where one of the narrow beds had been prepared for me. "This is the children's room," she said. "I tried for eight years with doctors, tests, surgery. There was too much wrong with me," she apologized. As I undressed, I saw on the shelf near my bed two dolls: a boy and a girl, dressed in hand-crocheted clothes.

The next morning, as we walked around the kibbutz, Ervin pointed out the names of the green mountains opposite us: Gilboa, Barkan Benyamin, the barren brown Har Haklala on the leeward side, and finally Mount Shaul where King Saul fell on his own sword. Ervin talked about his "trip of a lifetime":

"The kibbutz gives every member one trip, usually to Europe. But the kibbutz gave us Canada, even though it cost three times Europe; they couldn't say no because my mother was there. We thought four hundred and fifty dollars was enough pocket money because we thought my stepbrothers would take me around with a car there. But when I got there, they said I didn't have the right license. If they would have told me that before, I would have gotten it. In Canada the children my mother raised, washed and cleaned for, they invited me *once* for tea! That's *all!*" It was a howl of pain, and then he murmured the truth: "They were too busy for me."

We strolled through the modern, spacious art museum which had once been the dream of his art teacher, Chaim Atar. "Once this was a shack. This teacher really wanted to help us, to give us knowledge and understanding. He was a very good man. You felt warm with him."

"Of all the things in here, which do you find the most interesting?" I asked him. "Do you have a favorite?"

He led me to a tall wooden sculpture of a nude woman stretched against a stake, her hands tied above her head. She looked down at a small boy standing close against her, his head nestled into her pelvis, his arms reaching up to her. We walked closer. "Her hands are tied, but he keeps trying," Ervin said.

CHARLES AND TANIA (MUENCH) KESSLER

Sydney, Australia, July 1979

It was winter in Australia, and I was glad to have a sweater under my raincoat as I waited for Charles at the airport.

The maroon and white jacket by which I was to recognize him was flung casually over one shoulder. He came toward me quickly and lightly, a good-looking man around forty, slim and sandy-haired.

"I don't usually wear this jacket except to my team's games," he smiled a bit self-consciously, "but I figured it would make it easier to find each other." His smile was warm yet cautious. I noticed a tooth missing on his upper jaw, and wondered which of his four children's needs had come before his.

"What kind of games?" I asked.

"Rugby league—Manley is my team. I'm an avid fan. We go to all the games, Bongey and I. He's our youngest, we root for Manley. Michael, who is seventeen, roots for a different team, the renegade!"

There was an open charm about him. He was eager to talk, to find out where I'd been and whom I'd seen. Was I too tired to talk after my overnight flight from Singapore?

Their house in the suburbs of Sydney reminded me of the houses built in California in the 1950s, modest, solid rectangles surrounded by chain-link fenced yards. We chatted in the cozy living room, sitting around the gas fire. Tania had disappeared into the kitchen and would allow no help. "This is my job," she said firmly. When she served lunch, each plate had been separately prepared in the kitchen, stacked high with schnitzel and vegetables in quantities no one could hope to finish. "That's the way she does it," Charles shrugged, resigned. She would not sit down but stood poised, ready to serve, and moved with quiet grace when anything was needed.

Keeping her company in the kitchen after lunch—she had refused my help even more emphatically—I could see Charles and Bongey playing ball in the yard. The boy, warmed by his father's urging, shyly smiled as he stared down at the ball and kicked. The ball went askew over the fence. In a flash, Charles, using the same agile side-swing gymnasts use over horses, hoisted himself effortlessly over the five-foot-high fence. Bongey clambered up on a box to watch his father retrieve the ball.

"Good boy, Bongey! That was a strong contender, even if it did go stray," he yelled as he ran. When he returned, he tousled Bongey's hair, patted him on the back and buttocks, and handed him the ball for another try.

"All right, I'm finished now," Tania said, as she wiped the chrome counter clean. We went into the living room. Totally in charge in her kitchen a moment ago, she now seemed ill at ease. She rose to draw the blinds, dimming the afternoon sun, and stuffed a folded towel in the space between blind and window frame where the sun still streamed. "I'm not a deep thinker," she said flatly, sitting down. "I leave that to Charles. Mostly I'm quiet. I don't think much about psychology or the past." I noticed the heavy, almost theatrical eye makeup she wore, so at odds with her generally shy, reticent quality. I asked her what she remembered prior to her arrival in England.

"I can't remember anything at all about the camp I was in.

Therezienstadt. And before England, I remember nothing. But there is something at Windermere. We sat there at long tables and we ate there. Also in Wier Courteney I remember we pinched fruit in Sir Benjamin's orchards."

"What do you mean, pinched? Didn't you live there; wasn't it for you?"

"Well, he only *let* us live there, I remember we weren't supposed to touch any flowers or take any fruit. It was *his* private estate, you know. He was a very nice man to let us live there.

"I can't really remember very much. I know there were some things that happened to me that I wanted Alice to know about, but she was so busy, she had so many of us and I couldn't tell her. . . ."

"And what was that?"

"There were these raspberries that grew in a thorny patch. It was a hassle to get them. I loved raspberries then. Julius wasn't afraid of getting scratched. He said he'd give me raspberries if I would let him lie on top of me. He was about nine and I about six. I had no idea what it meant. I don't know if he did. Of course he couldn't really do anything. I did let him for the raspberries, but I think there was something strange in him to blackmail me that way. . . .

"At any rate, when we were in England recently I told Alice about it. I'd always wanted her to know. I thought it's something she should have known, and do you know, she said absolutely nothing! I was very disappointed."

"What did you want her to say?"

"I don't know. . . ."

I asked whether there was anything that brought her special attention at Lingfield.

"No. I was just ordinary. I got along with everyone, I remember. Maybe I was the best in dancing.

"Did you get dancing lessons?"

"Oh no, that wasn't necessary, no."

"And school, what do you remember?"

"We walked a long way to school, past farm fields. I remember the smell. Yes, it was a good smell. At school I remember we weren't allowed to take the [Christian] religious period. Alice wouldn't let us. We were singled out, sent outside, even in bad weather, and I felt terrible. I would never do that to my children. It's terrible to be made so different. It was bad enough we all had such terrible foreign-sounding names. Muench! We got teased for our names. No, children don't like to be singled out. When my daughter goes to stay overnight with her friend, sometimes she goes to church with them. That's all right. I don't want her to suffer being different as I did."

"Do you remember anybody you were especially attached to in Lingfield?"

"No, Alice was too busy. Manna was in charge of my group for a while. She was nice. . . . She once told me I had the nicest table manners, I do remember that. But I wouldn't say there was anything special. We all liked her."

"Gertrud?"

"No! Gertrud slapped me a couple of times. You had to watch out for her. She had a temper—like a witch sometimes—not that I didn't have it coming. I was probably rude or difficult, but I didn't like it, and I still don't like violence. I would never do that to my own kids. Charles and I have never hit them, and we'll never do that. I can't stand that."

"Do you remember anyone kissing or hugging you in Lingfield?"

"Alice kissed us every night. It was like a routine for everyone. Once in a while Manna used to say something nice, like about the manners . . . but then Manna went away. Later on we got these foster aunties we'd go visit, and I liked mine. She used to give me chocolate, and I remember once she kissed me. And she gave me pocket money sometimes. She was nice."

"What was it like in Lingfield for you?"

"I was happy, busy all the time, there were always people around and things to do. I liked the practical things like basket-weaving, and I liked helping Sophie in the kitchen. And Sophie had a special place she kept baked things. Sometimes we'd pinch some apple cake or plum cake. You asked me if there was something special? Well, when someone came—visitors, like the Committee ladies, up in Alice's room—I'd be the one to bring up the tea tray. I was always very shy, not that they really talked with you, but you felt you were being observed. The Committee ladies always looked so perfect, every hair in place, like real ladies. It made me very nervous. It was hard for me to just be myself there. . . . That's the thing that's different in a family home, you can just be free to be yourself. . . .

"I think they could have given us a bit more to eat. Don't get me wrong, we were never hungry, but we were growing kids, and the way food was served, it was put out in bowls and you could take what you wanted. But I always felt I had to watch myself not to take too much when food was served this way, not to be too greedy because you had to leave enough for the others . . . you see what I mean? I like to be sure my children have as much as they want to eat. Charles laughs at how I heap everybody's plates, but I can't help it. I can't stand for them not to have enough." Her face was devoid of emotion, but her voice was angry. My heart quickened as I recalled Tania's painstaking presentation of beautiful, individually portioned plates at lunch.

We had been sitting silently when Charles and Bongey entered, and Tania rallied.

"Some hot tea, Charles, right?"

"That would be nice," he said. I followed her to the kitchen.

"Can you describe yourself as a child, Tania?" I asked.

"I got on with everyone—no special problems. Later on though, there were things that were difficult, and I made some mistakes. . . ."

We sat around the table in the evening, dark, handsome Michael and strawberry-blonde Deborah hiding their curiosity behind a show of preoccupation with the homework in front of them. Charles brought a big cardboard box of pictures to the table. He held up a photograph of his father, one of a few that had been given him by his mother, who lived in England. It showed a blonde, wavy-haired man in his late thirties.

"I know some things about my father; my mother's told me."

"Then he didn't survive?"

"No. He died in Auschwitz. . . . My father was a very good soccer team player. He played for Hakoah in Vienna, position number seven. And I know that he played in the same league as Rapide."

"Rapide?"

"Yes, that's a first division team, Rapide. Probably it's the main team in Vienna today. When Hakoah played Rapide it was a sellout." He said it passionately. "There's an old man here in Sydney who actually saw my father play. . . . He's quite old and senile in some ways, but he remembers the games very well.

"When the inevitable happened in Vienna, the team disintegrated and my father took me to Brussels." He took out a snapshot of a young woman wearing a nurse's cap, holding a little child, himself as a toddler. "This was Suzanne, she took care of me. I think I was in a clinic, I don't know for sure."

The next picture with Suzanne was remarkable for the affection between them: her head inclined toward him, she was holding Charles's face forward, with one hand under his little boy's protruding abdomen. Charles appeared happy.

"She looked after me as if I were her own son. I think my mother was jealous of Suzanne. I remember a row between the three of them before my mother went to England as a domestic. I was very attached to Suzanne.

"It was after he took me away from Suzanne that my father put me in hiding, with a farm family in the country. I remember my father taking me there. It was in Mollen, outside Brussels. I remember crying when he left. In the beginning my father came there—several times. I remember he brought me two lumps of sugar and he took me out to a grassy place, a park maybe, and played horsie with me. He'd get down on all fours and I'd ride on his back. Then, of course, he didn't come anymore." He sighed.

"I hated it there. The people were very strict. At first there were a few other children there too. Then I was alone, in an attic room with rats. I'd be frightened and pull the sheet up over my head. This is the woman of the family that took care of me." He held up a snapshot of a stern, heavyset woman.

"What was her name?" I asked.

"Can't remember. She was a horrible woman."

"And how long were you there?"

"Let's see, between 1939 and 1945. Funny I can't remember her name. . . . I even went to see her in 1963 when we were stationed in Brussels."

He showed me a picture of a thin six-year-old in a large sweater. "That was my best jumper. I wore it only when the Jewish committee man came round to see that I was properly fed and clothed. That man's name was Mr. Pollack. He came round in a Citroën. I remember that, but odd, isn't it, I can't remember that horrible woman's name."

"What was so horrible about her?"

"Aw, strictness. Just cold." He was contemptuous. "She didn't beat me up, I don't think so, but I remember her being very strict. No feeling for me. He sighed. "I know I used to wet the bed and, by God, I was so frightened she'd find out. I'd lay there in terror that she'd come around, and sometimes I would try to dry it."

"How could you do that?"

"If you stayed long enough in it, you could dry it, body heat, I suppose. . . . I was so frightened of her coming round." His voice lowered, compressed with emotion, as he went on: "I also remember they used to kill pigs. When it was time to kill it they would tie its legs, each one, then they would drag it onto this straw, and then somebody would cut its throat. Then they would set it on fire—light the straw so as to kill all the fleas. We'd have these blood sausages afterwards for ages, and bits of pig hanging everywhere. That would be the half-yearly meat supply. I liked these blood sausages and once I think I ate too many and I was sick and soiled the sheets. Strangely, that time she wasn't angry. I couldn't understand that. I expected her to be more angry than when I wet the bed.

"I was alone a lot. And chickens played a very important part in my life. They kept chickens there. I must have been with the chickens for days on end and I got to know each of them. I could tell them apart, each one. They would actually come into my hand, some of them. I remember being with them day in and day out for weeks. And I remember collecting snails, buckets of snails. I used to race them against each other and watch flies and pull wings off them. I was alone a lot.

"After a time I went to a school during the day, a convent school. They were strict there too. I don't remember much about that place except people coming around who'd whack you in the face with these keys if you were doing something they didn't like."

"Do you remember being told to say you were a Catholic if anyone asked?"

"No . . . but I remember there was a cupboard at the farm right in the living room that I went into to hide several times when German soldiers came around to look for Jews. There was one time when I thought my heart would pound out of me. I felt I was going to suffocate. I must have been in there for hours and I heard them talking in German saying, '*Jude, Jude.*' I was scared out of my mind."

Michael and Deborah were no longer pretending to do homework. Their eyes, intent on their father, were moist. Charles, unaware, focused on the box of pictures and continued.

"I know I spoke French before I spoke Flemish, which was the language the farm people spoke. My mother speaks no French, having come from Vienna, so I know I learned to talk when I was with Suzanne."

"What does your mother tell you about being separated from you?"

"Well," his sigh was slow and painful. "You can't get any sense out of her. We tried when we were there this time in England. I said to Tania, let's try again, but it was no use." He sighed again. "She starts talking about *her* past, she gets upset and then that goes on forever."

"Those must have been very difficult days for her. What does she say about herself, then?"

"Well, I've often, probably wrongly, accused her of getting me out of Belgium and having me brought to England against my will. See, I was happy in Provensardt, the place I was in after the war, after I was taken out of hiding. I was in a children's home with a Mrs. Jaffée in

Provensardt. It was a place like Lingfield. Mrs. Jaffée liked me. I was doing very well in school and I was happy there. . . . Had I stayed there, I think she would have adopted me and I would have gone to university. I didn't want to go to England." He was fingering another picture of himself.

I became aware of Tania sitting opposite me, looking longingly at the box of pictures that preserved his past.

"Charles," she murmured, "you're lucky."

"But you have pictures in Lingfield, don't you, Tania?"

"No, mine start at five or six. There's nothing before that, Charles." She tried to sound matter-of-fact.

"I didn't realize that, I'm sorry." For a moment their eyes met.

"I'll make some tea," she said and went into the kitchen.

He pulled out an identity card that granted his father permission to be in the streets of Belgium. It stated that Arthur Kessler's identity was "International." We joked about his father being an International Jewish Banker.

"What was his work?" I asked.

"A clerk in a bank! Aha!" We laughed.

"Do you read German?" Charles asked, suddenly serious.

"Badly, but I'll try."

He handed me a letter written by his father to his mother while Charles was in hiding, asking me to read it aloud. "This was written the year before he got caught."

Dear Else   Aug. 27, 1941

I am overjoyed to finally receive some news from you as well as a smiling photograph which shows me that thank God you look well and your teeth are all right. I would like to ask you to send me sometimes a proper photo—not one taken in an automatic booth. Don't worry about money. I will manage somehow. Regarding Karli's clothes you misunderstood me: only in case you still have the clothes you bought sometime ago, send them. You don't have to buy new ones as he has enough to wear. . . . I would like to reassure you about Karli, he's doing very well. He's sunburned as he's almost all day in the garden. Maybe I can send you a photograph next week. He's gotten well used to the home and always says good-bye to me smiling. My deepest wish is that we may celebrate a birthday together. Maybe with God's help this might happen. . . . I do not know a football player named Prager. I only remember the name. He used to play some time ago for WAC. You still have not told me what sort of position you have. Do write about it next time. Now finally I have my laughing Else with me and I'm glad that you were so courageous. This photo makes me feel much calmer and I'm greatly surprised at how you look since everyone around here has gotten very slender—you are not in the latest fashion here. . . . And now I come to the end, dearest Else, don't worry about me. With God's help everything will work out all right. Someday you will be proud of Karli and we will all be happy again. May God continue to watch over you, I greet you and kiss you a thousand times. He who always thinks of you,

Arthur and Karli

We were silent until Charles spoke in mournful agitation.

"I was away from my mother for ten years, 1939 to 1949, and suddenly she sent for me. I didn't want to go and leave the place I was happy in with Mrs. Jaffée. But I had to go. I couldn't remember my mother. But I started to pretend to feel happy about going to meet her: fantastic, I've got a real mother. And suddenly there I am and she's all over me and I feel, who is this woman? Who is she?

"She met me at the station, my mother. We had no common language. Her boyfriend was with her." He spoke with disgust. "I didn't know who he was. And there was Ellen from Alice's place who spoke French, and I'm told I'm supposed to go with her! My mother went that way and I went this way with Ellen! She was sent to meet me because she spoke French. I wondered what the hell's going on! I wanted to go with my mother, of course."

"What did your mother tell you?"

"I can't remember. You'll stay with a nice family with lots of children; it's very nice there, okay? We got there about ten at night. I heard strange voices. I couldn't understand what was going on in English, and then I went up to bed. The next day everybody made fun of me, because I wore short pants way up to there. In England they wore shorts only up to here. And I couldn't stand the cornflakes. I never had cornflakes in Belgium. I think I was temperamental in the beginning, wasn't I?" He looked at Tania.

"I don't remember in the beginning very well," she said impassively.

"Aw, come on, Tania, *I* remember *you* very well the very first day!" There was the start of some pleasure returning to his face as he cajoled her.

"I remember your mother coming to visit you. You were ill. That I remember. She was worried about you, that you were dying."

"But I remember *you* from the very start," he persisted. "I don't think I was as happy there as in Provensardt, I suppose because I became an adolescent. You see, I'd had to move again, it was too many moves." His eyes scanned the pictures in the box. He drew one out, and his face lit with excitement.

"God, Tania! Aren't you lovely! Just look at that! How lovely!" It was a picture of a shy adolescent schoolgirl, fair-haired and very slim. He gazed from the picture to Tania several times, radiating his feeling for her. She smiled.

They roused Michael and Deborah who, unable to tear themselves away, had fallen asleep. We said good night.

The next day, I asked Tania about difficulties she had alluded to the day before.

"When I started my period it was sometimes a bit embarrassing: upstairs Gertrud kept all the medical things. The napkins were locked in a closet upstairs where the boys were, and you always had to go up there in the cupboard and get it. We weren't allowed to keep it in our cupboard or drawer where you normally would keep it. If you wanted anything you always had to ask, go up there and ask for each one, pretend you're getting disinfectant or something and creep up there and ask. It was very embarrassing.

"I remember also around that age getting my first bra. It wasn't a new one; it was one somebody had worn before. Gertrud gave it to me. They were horrible bras, uncomfortable. I didn't get a new one for a long time. Alice got it for me eventually."

"You mean you didn't go shopping for it yourself?"

"No, all our clothes, if we wanted something, we had to go tell Alice and she would buy it for us. There were so many of us she couldn't take each one of us out for a bra. For my confirmation I remember being taken by Gertrude to look for a dress in Marks and Spencer, but they were too expensive, it had to be a certain price."

"Tania, what made you happiest there?"

She paused for a long time. "I don't know, really. I don't think there was a special time when I was happy."

"Sad?"

"I just went along, always busy with activities and I made a friend at school when I was about twelve outside Lingfield and that I think helped a lot. This girl was very free, very mature, her mother worked in the Pears Soap factory and occasionally I stayed at her house."

"Did you ever invite her to stay at Lingfield?"

"No, I never thought we could."

"But adults like Yezhek and Ben were always staying over."

"But that was different. They were there to look after us. It wasn't like here; Deborah brings her close friend home to stay overnight. I encourage it. I think it's important to discuss things with your friends; there are some things you may not want to discuss with mother and father.

"After school sometimes with this friend I'd go to the cinema—she always had her hair permed and I admired that. We'd put on makeup. She tried to make herself into a lady and I liked that. No one in the house wore lipstick or makeup."

"Rose did," Charles interjected. "She used to help Sophie."

"I liked the way Rose looked when she was going out with her boyfriend," Tania said. "She wore lipstick and nice perfume. I always wanted to shave and be a lady and have a social life."

"You had socials in Lingfield, I understand."

"I hated them; they were with the young Lingfield Committee [the sons and daughters of the Committee members]. It meant not being quite ourselves. Oh, they danced with us, they tried to be nice, but I didn't like sitting around feeling awkward. We did have some nice records."

"Yes, I remember one," Charles broke in. *"Bread-and-butter woman, yeah/give me a bread-and-butter woman, I mean the real domestic kind,"* he sang, chuckling seductively. Tania smiled knowingly, her usually placid face showing rare pleasure. "I used to like that . . . still do." He winked at Tania.

"She was never married, Alice, was she?" Charles asked. "She's very secretive about that part of her life, isn't she? But I think there was someone she was involved with . . . ."

"Not in the way we would assume, today," I said.

Charles reflected sadly, "What an incredible frustration to live with all your life. Even all the things she's done for children, the dedication, I don't think can replace that terrible void in her life. It must be on her mind practically every day, the things she has missed."

"I don't know if that would be so with Alice," Tania said.

"I've always felt Alice was very interested in our sexual life," Charles said. "She'd ask me questions about Tania, about our life, but it didn't take much for me to understand her need, even then. It must have been difficult for her when we were adolescents. And for Gertrude as well. Gertrude couldn't stand messing around, [the] flirting between Tania and me standing waiting at the shower. She'd come around and say, 'Stop talking like that! Get out.' She couldn't stand it."

"She'd look at us and make what we were feeling nasty and disgusting, it was terrible," Tania said.

"Tania and I would talk round about—without ever mentioning

things—it was all very naïve, very innocent. We really knew nothing then, had had no experience."

Tania added, "But Gertrude was always on the lookout, always watching. There was only one bathroom upstairs and we used to go downstairs to shower. I remember I used to go downstairs a lot to shower, I don't know why," she chuckled. Charles laughed knowingly, heartily.

"I hated it upstairs," she continued. "There were always queues; there were a lot of children, and it was Alice's and Sophie's bathroom too. But there was this shower downstairs, and when there were queues there sometimes too, I used to see Charles in his dressing gown. Gertrude hated that. She would come around to see that we weren't hanging around."

"I think they were frightened, especially Gertrude, that something would happen, that there'd be babies," Charles said.

"But they made it appear that what was natural," Tania continued, "was not normal, was nasty. Gertrude especially, not so much Alice. I think Alice understood. But Gertrude used to go around like a Peeping Tom; she was always everywhere, even in the television room. It was dark there, Charles and I would be watching. She would come in and say in a mean voice, 'Go to bed,' or 'Stop talking, get out!' We weren't even holding hands, it was *so* innocent, and she made such a fuss."

"Well, things built up and I was actually sent away," Charles said. "I couldn't believe it. It was the most terrible punishment for me, it was the most miserable time of my life."

"What happened?"

"On weekends I went to my mother's, and Sunday night I'd come back quite late. Then I used to quietly sneak up to the girls' room and give each of them a kiss: Esther, Sylvia, Zdenka, and so on, but I made sure I ignored Tania!" He laughed heartily. "Well, Tania wouldn't let me then anyway, would you, Tania?"

"No, Charles, I was frightened. Funny, isn't it? I really wanted to let him kiss me, but I was frightened. It's hard to explain. I know we were young, fifteen or so, and people say that isn't real love. But there was something very strong there always between Charles and myself, and I was frightened."

"When I went in there to the girls' room it made a commotion and Alice shouted, 'Come on out of there,' but she wasn't angry. No, I remember she took it in a jovial mood."

"I think she understood it was all in fun," Tania agreed.

"But Gertrude couldn't stand it, and, well, it *was* hotting up. One day Tania wrote me a letter that she was going to come up to my room at ten o'clock."

"I only wanted to see him, to be with him, that's all. I didn't want to do anything."

"Well, *I* did," Charles broke in, "I wanted to, but Gertrude or Alice intercepted the letter. Next thing there's a knock on the door and I said, 'Come in,' expecting Tania. I got the shock of my life, it was Alice, and she knew how to be very dramatic. She said, 'And whom were you expecting?' I said, 'No one.' I tried to act calm, my heart was pounding out of me. . . . She said, 'I caught Tania going up the stairs,' and she pulled out the letter and said, 'This is wrong!' And it was right after that I was sent away. It was a terrible shock to me. Away from Lingfield House, all my friends, really my home.

"Shortly after that Tania was sent to America, to a couple who had lost a twenty-one-year-old son and wanted to adopt her. It was then, when she was in America, that I knew I wanted to marry her. I missed her so very much. Still, even when she came back, there was this barrier."

"I missed Charles too, we wrote to each other. There were boys in America, but I missed Charles. That situation didn't work out. Alice had told me these people wanted a nice, quiet, shy girl to adopt. She thought I might be the right one. They were wealthy people. When this man came to London he stayed at the Dorchester, I went there to meet him, had dinner with him there a couple of times. And then I went to America. But it didn't work out. They were always kissing me. I couldn't stand it. He would get up at six in the morning to go into New York and come into my room and kiss me on the cheek. I was hardly awake yet, I didn't like it. And she didn't want to ever go out. She was not well and she wanted me near her all the time. The only time she went out was to the supermarket, and I'd go with her and push the cart. When he wanted to go to a movie or out for a walk I'd go with him, she wouldn't go. . . . They were very nice to me, but it didn't work out. I missed Lingfield House. I wanted to come back, and after a few months I did. I'm not sorry, I saw some of New York, it was like a vacation."

"Then what happened between you and Charles when you came back?"

"There was still this barrier," Charles answered.

"I got a job and moved to a girls' hostel in Stepney Green with Esther and Eva."

"And I used to hang around, actually hang around the door of Marks and Spencer to catch a glimpse of her when she would leave work. Can you believe that? She wouldn't have anything to do with me."

"I was scared, Charles."

"But you were going out with lots of boys," he remonstrated.

"I could let others touch me, but not Charles. I think it had something to do with the way we were brought up in Lingfield. Yes, boys always liked me. I still don't understand it, but I know that of the girls in Lingfield House, I was the one the boys were always after, trying to try things and so on. I wanted experience, but with Charles and me I knew it would be serious and I was too confused and frightened, so I avoided him. Strange, wasn't it? I accepted all kinds of other men I didn't care about and took stupid chances . . . and I wasn't happy. I felt unworthy and stupid, but I felt that I had something special. Men liked me and gave me attention and I seemed to need that. I was very naïve, didn't know how to take care of myself. All of us girls in Stepney were incredibly naïve. There really wasn't anyone who could talk to us and help us."

"Alice?"

"Well, no. I remember once Alice talked to me and it made me feel very dirty. The way she assumed things I was doing, it was dirty, not natural, and it made me feel very small and hating myself. But I must say she tried to help, and I wouldn't listen. She said she would give me the name of a doctor, but I was afraid, I didn't want to go. I thought it might be Dr. T——. That woman made me very uncomfortable, we didn't like her, none of the girls. I didn't want her poking around down there."

"It's incredible . . . your marriage and what you've achieved, when neither of you had experienced normal ordinary relationships between men and women as a model: was there any such in Lingfield?"

"No, we knew Susie Tietzer [who had worked at Lingfield] had been married, but no."

"Perhaps if I had been raised more normally it wouldn't have taken me so long to overcome this barrier with Tania," Charles said. "But raised as we were, not knowing how to express these emotions, we were afraid somehow to be made the fool by showing these feelings."

"Yes, I could be all right, not shy with any other boy, but with Charles, where my real feelings were, I froze inside even though I acted differently, and I stayed that way for a long time until after our first child was born."

Charles continued. "I was unhappy then, when Tania wouldn't go out with me. I was working in a job Alice got for me, and I hated it, living in a London slum with my mother, whom I couldn't get on with.

I knew I wanted to go to Australia even then, get out of London, make my own life. But for three years I worked in this job I hated because I didn't want to disappoint Alice. Then when my army call-up came I jumped at it. I enjoyed myself immensely. Guys my age had lived! In regard to girls, for instance, they'd lived *two* lifetimes compared to me! I made many friends, learned how to understand all kinds of people. That was one of the best years of my life."

Suddenly, he made a serious face and boomed out in a deep voice, "*Mimi baka mimi zasa!* I want woman now!" Then he laughed rakishly.

"I've heard all that," Tania said in mock disgust, smiling.

"In Kenya that's how it's done, and the natives would stop work and go out actually and find someone for you. There were all kinds of people, from the roughest to the elite. It was an eye-opener, a wonderful thing for me. I say to myself in all sincerity, I'm so pleased that we've got four normal children, I mean with our background. I want nothing more than to have them marry and bring their children here to us. That is my hope."

Tania nodded. "That's right, we're very lucky. I'm very content now. There's really nothing I want that I don't have. Oh, maybe it would be nice to have a little bigger house and maybe a brick one if I were dreaming. But actually I've got everything I want right here now. . . . When the children are all grown up Charles and I would like a little farm, but until they finish school we'll never move from here. We think it's important for children to have the security of growing up without being moved about the way we were."

Later, Charles spoke about his work at the Shell Company. His sense of competence was clear as he described his middle-management position, supervising people and exercising responsibility for dispatching resources to various geographic areas. He felt confident about being promoted.

"I've had to learn to be more assertive," he said. "I had to grapple with that shyness and inadequacy that I think is part of all of us that were brought up in Lingfield. Oh, maybe not Fritz, but the rest of us. I had to face that in myself and make a tremendous effort to be able to confront people working for me and tell them they're not doing things right, even let someone go. This took some growing up on my part, learning you can't please everybody all the time if you want to get the job done.

"I've been thinking about death lately. Two people at work were killed in a train crash last year. Seeing Wolf all white-haired when we were in England last year, it's given me this deep sense of time moving . . . and a spiritual feeling of searching for something. Sometimes when we're out in the country, camping at night under the night sky with eons of stars, I think there's got to be something out there, something beyond comprehension. There's this guy at work, he belongs to a group, and we went to see Billy Graham. He said there are eight hundred billion galaxies and in each there are a thousand billion stars. There's got to be some greater force we don't understand, I believe that.

"This friend at work, I started to say, he's been trying for two years to convert me. He means well. He keeps after me to become a Christian, but somehow it's just not possible." Charles, who had been looking at me while talking, looked away. His forehead lined suddenly. "I don't know, it just doesn't seem right to me. It's like this, that once you've been a member of a team and played with them, you, you just don't drop it suddenly and run. I feel that would be like disloyalty to your team!" he exclaimed.

"You mean your team is still Hakoah?" I asked.

He relaxed, and broke into a frank grin. "Yeah, that's it." He looked at me square, grinning.

Peter Wagner came in the evening. He was a slight, dark, witty man whose hazel eyes missed nothing. Peter had lived at Lingfield between the ages of eight and eleven, when his mother had been unable to care for him, having come to England as a domestic before the war. Though he had been spared camps and hiding, the jagged fragments of his mother's life in the context of the war had created a special hell for him. From living together at Lingfield, the two men had formed powerful bonds. They broke into French easily with jovial bantering and occasional song. Peter's relationship to Charles and Tania was like that of a brother; he was like an uncle to their children.

Michael left for his after-school job at a big market, and Deborah, meticulously groomed, went job-hunting. Bongey, bathed and ready for bed in his pajamas and bathrobe, waited for a final briefing with Charles on the day's rugby league scores. (Their oldest boy, Charles, was already on his own, living in another city.) The table was set for three, and Charles, Peter, and I sat down. Only after I refused to proceed did Tania join us.

Charles poured Australian white wine, and proposed a toast: "To your safe journey home."

"To the success of the book," Peter added.

"To your lives," I said, and we drank.

After dinner the men sang songs lustily in French. Then it was quiet for a moment.

"You know, when I was in Israel twenty years ago," Charles recalled, "I remember this incredible thing; wherever you went people would know the same songs and they would sing at the drop of a hat, hardly knowing each other, with full heart. I've never seen it anywhere else; they would get high, absolutely high on singing! I'd like to take Michael there next summer," he said, "have him meet Fritz and Hedi, that would be nice."

We sang Hebrew songs, and then it was too late to drive Peter home. With quick ease a bed was created for him out of sofa pillows piled on the living room floor. Tania turned the gas heater off. Its glow persisted as we said good night.

When I came into the kitchen in the morning, Deborah, dressed in her maroon school uniform, was tenderly smoothing the collar of her mother's robe. Then she began helping her mother serve. Like Tania, she did not sit down to eat and had to be begged to do so by Peter and me.

Tania was framed in the doorway as we left for the airport. Charles was adamant. "You can't be in Australia for three days and see absolutely nothing but the Kesslers." He took me to the Sydney Opera House.

On the quay below the opera house, a flock of white, broad-breasted sea gulls surged toward us. Warmed by morning sun, we watched as the creatures suddenly turned, lifted in unison, and soared out over the water.

"Aren't they a wonder!" Charles marveled. "Alouettes," he said. "I used to see them in Provensardt. They were a wonder to me then too."

Then, quietly, he asked, "Do you think that being the youngest of sixteen children could have affected my mother? I know they were very poor." He struggled to see beyond the burden of his own blinding hurt to hers.

"Can't you ask her how it was for her?"

"It's hard to ask her anything; you never know what's going to upset her. I remember once suddenly she came to Lingfield or called, she had got a day off, it was midweek and she asked Alice for permission to take me out of school. I was about twelve. Of course Alice wouldn't hear of it."

"What do you think of that? Would you have wanted to go with her?"

"Hell, no, Alice was perfectly right. I hated missing school, getting behind and all that, and it was always difficult around my mother. She and her boyfriend would always have rows, I couldn't stand him. No, Alice did the right thing, absolutely. . . ."

In the car again on the way to the airport, he spoke with the urgency of time running out. "I didn't tell you the other night, but I know how my father died. I know this from a letter to my mother. He was part of an experiment in Auschwitz. . . . You see, the killing wasn't fast enough for them. They were trying to find ways to kill them faster. They injected chemicals in the veins. They injected him with cyanide. . . . It's not an easy death. It's slow and painful." His sigh joined us to that agony. "He died January eighth, 1942. He was forty-two years old. Just my age."

"The little you know about your father has been terribly important to you," I said finally.

"Yes. I built up a picture of my father. He must have been like me, I think."

A wind came up as we unloaded my baggage from the car. It fluttered and sailed the maroon and white crepe-paper streamers that hung from the door handle on the driver's side. Seeing that I noticed, he said, "Manley."

"Of course," I answered.

PART THREE

Reflections

Like a life-sustaining river, Alice courses through these lives, here a fundamental source, powerful and wide, there a narrow contributor stream deep underground, a constant presence through which to strengthen or against which to define oneself. And, at eighty-four, she is still there, through letters, phone calls, and visits. Still available for a bit of advice, a loan, news about someone. The apartment she and Sophie share has been the scene of five weddings and several reunions. The nest she provided is the one they left, and to which many still return.

If one asks the question outright, "Was Alice like a mother to you?" some will answer indignantly, "No, my mother would have been different."

"How?"

"I don't know, just different." For so many, the thought of replacement evokes feelings of disloyalty and guilt toward the murdered parents they may never have known.

"We were like a family," Alice says, but not all agree. It is a source of great pleasure to her that Charles, Fritz, and Sam are still in contact. Charles and Tania's son Michael visited Fritz and Hedi in Israel last summer. In family fashion, perhaps Alice's long commitment has generated a legacy of commitment among some of the children.

"I tried to treat each child as an individual," Alice says. "With children you have to be like a gardener, to find the right treatment for each one." That meant using not only her own talents but all that could be summoned. In the carpentry for Ervin, the music for Denny, the chickens for Zdenka, the tea-girl role for Tania, the plays for Hedi, and the hostess role for Eva, Alice consciously worked to heighten a sense of self for each child in her group, and to show children whose parents had been taken away that there were adults who could be depended on not only to be there, but to provide pleasure.

For personal, sometimes tragic reasons hard-won attachments were disrupted. Manna and three of the psychoanalysts who were treating some of the children left England, and one died. They left a wake of longing and turmoil behind them: wasn't this abandonment just one more predictably bitter outcome of closeness and loving? But other people's lives were not made to stand still, even for these children —only Alice's.

Her deep commitment to care for the children can be explained, Alice told me with characteristic humility, as "survivor guilt." It is the explanation I accepted from her that first evening in her London apartment. True, the face of her brother—who had been a disturbed child, and for whom she had great compassion even as a child herself—haunted her, as did the face of his wife, her little niece, and all the children she left behind. But I have come to regard the term as a simplistic one that often stalls its user in the past, foreclosing the search for other important motivations. To see compassionate acts, self-sacrifice, and social commitment as largely motivated by guilt for past behavior, or for survival itself, is too facile. The positive wish to act decently and express feelings of empathy, the desire to participate humanely in one's time, require no such guilt for prior acts of omission or commission. That this doubtful wisdom is often accepted by survivors themselves—who, after all, are not immune to what the authorities say they are supposed to feel—is a special irony, imposing as a new stigma the bitter equation of compassion equals guilt.

The major elements of Alice's commitment to the children go considerably beyond her past. Forty-eight years old when the children first arrived, she perceived a true opportunity to be more whole, to create a kind of family. It was clear by then that there would be no husband, no biological children, but with all that she knew and felt about children, she could create a haven of understanding and enjoyment for those who had suffered, a refuge where they could be restored to health. And in the process, she might even hope not only to give, but to receive love from this family.

The children presented Alice with an unprecedented professional challenge. She had been recognized as a person who was gifted in her ways of working with children, in creating programs and environments to support their favorable development. Here was work more important in its potential for helping others than any she had ever aspired to before; and here also was an opportunity to continue her treasured professional relationship with Anna Freud, around whose insight, wit, candor, and intellectual prowess Alice fell privileged to learn. Alice knew that Freud had been asked to work directly with the children, but had preferred an informal consulting role, one that

would not require her to work with a committee of synagogue people.
Alice understood that the extraordinary burden of caring for the
children would therefore not be underestimated by her mentor, and
working toward Miss Freud's appreciation was certainly a positive
motivating force.

None of this is to negate the existence of feelings of survival guilt.
We have seen how it haunts even some of those who were infants at
the time of the Holocaust, so young that they could not have been
aware of, let alone accountable for, acts of omission or commission.
This fact once and for all should destroy the absurd implication that
survivor guilt is somehow suffered deservedly as an actual conse-
quence of past action or inaction by people who were ruthlessly hell-
bent on their own survival, seen lately as heroic by Terrence Des Pres,[1]
or, as more often seen, pitiful or monstrous.[2] When even those who
were infants at the time anguish, "Why me? Why did I survive?" it is
clear that the guilt suffered relates to the fact of survival alone, at its
most authentic existential level. The question can be heard as an
urgent quest for the place of one's self in a meaningful universe. And
though it remains unanswered it may yet have the power to inspire
life directions.

No discussion of guilt can ignore the tragic dilemma in which
survivors of any age applying for restitution found themselves. The
terrible equation I heard over and over was essentially this: "If I take
this pittance called '*Wiedergutmachung*' [literally, "making good
again"] for the death of my parents whom I still long for, then I have
lessened the guilt of murderers while increasing my own." The
anguish of this situation is heard in Jack's cry that they should really
pay! No wonder some, like Magda, despite real need, refused to apply
for restitution. Alice never applied for herself, though she did in
behalf of the children.

It is not the purpose of this work to assess whether Alice succeeded
with the children. Do parents, under optimal conditions, unencum-
bered by the traumas of war, persecution, and separation, "succeed"
in measurable fashion with each child? Professional mental health
workers may be disappointed not to find tables of data in this chapter
answering the questions they have asked me most frequently over the
course of this writing: "How many of the people you have interviewed
are psychotic, damaged, mentally retarded, etc.?" I see these questions
now as sharing a common value base with the German scientists who
classified persons and races as superior and inferior on the basis of
criteria over which the person labelled had no control, while totally
ignoring the most essential criterion for humanness—the ability to

behave compassionately. The closest any professional has come to asking me about that is the occasional question, "What kinds of parents are they?" Has our eagerness for scientific evaluation of functioning restricted our criteria for valuing human beings and led us unwittingly to judgments of superior and inferior, via assorted categories of normal and abnormal? When Leah says, "We the non-smart people can do really good in ways," she brings down the whole degrading system and warns us to beware of participation in glib selections. Perhaps if anything is to be learned from these lives it is a profound appreciation for the individuality of each person's struggle not only for acceptance, love, and self-respect but to do some good for others. It is widely known that survivors overwhelmingly have avoided seeking help from any type of mental health professional. In the literature this has been largely accounted for by lack of trust and pathology on the part of the survivor, rarely to "professional" attitudes of practitioners which may not only exacerbate fears of being once again stamped, categorized, and made to feel inferior but, as Eva recalls with outrage more than thirty years later, make such fears a reality.

What are the problems that endure for child survivors? What are their unique strengths? What current ideas about human development bear new attention in the light of these lives?

One can hardly turn a page of most of the interviews without sensing the continuing burden of loss the survivors feel for parents whom they may never have known, a hunger for some link with the past through family connections destroyed or distorted, for traces of themselves buried in childhoods they dare not remember.

The loss of parents in early life means loss of the very nucleus of one's own identity. "Who am I?"—that question which it seems can only be first answered in its most fundamental sense by one's parents—can be so pressing when reexperienced in adulthood as to precipitate many versions of Jack's sudden flight to Vienna, there to search for the authentic place to address his grief, to verify the existence of his true self. Shana's delight in being told that she was like people in Czechoslovakia, Eva's joy at having correctly remembered the house in Žilena, give us some sense of the intensity of the yearning to affirm connection to those people and places from which one has been uprooted and severed.

Yet even the clear pain of loss can be clouded by gnawing doubt: is the woman of my earliest memory my mother or someone else? So Esther and her sister Shana wonder about the woman Malka, and

Denny reasons that the woman he remembers could not have been his mother, because she did not have red hair. Yet doubt and confusion about who one is at the very root of growth do not abort the struggle of building an identity. "Now that I'm a real person," Esther says triumphantly.

Clearly, losses that occurred very long ago continue to reverberate deeply throughout life. Leah still longs for her older dead brother, and Fritz for his baby brother, Sam for the mother who would not have abandoned him. Jack in his mid-thirties and Charles in his early forties reflect with fresh poignancy on how young their parents were when they were killed.

This unnatural phenomenon of searching for a parent who will always be younger than one's self was so common among survivors that in the sixties there was a popular Yiddish song (with words by Kalman Friedman), the refrain of which was: *An alter zun zucht zein yungeh mameh* (An old son seeks his young mother). And at every life-marking event such as their own weddings, or their children's births, bar mitzvahs, and weddings, there is for all survivors the vivid, jarring encounter with those dead who should have been there. The Jewish custom requiring the orphan to visit his or her dead parents' graves prior to the wedding ceremony acknowledges this basic urge to reckon "who should be here and who is not here that belongs to me?"

If no one really belongs to me, then to whom do I belong? Intertwined with the problem of loss and recurrent mourning is a haunting anxiety about belonging. The Lingfield children had, in their many prior uprootings, literally lost their places. Although the experience was different for each of them—Fritz and Hedi still had Magda, Sam had a dream of a mother, and various children had different degrees of claim on Alice and other adults—the security and certainty of belonging continues to remain out of reach for some, even for those who were adopted young. Some adoptees still struggle with the problem of belonging within the adoptive family itself. (When the watch of a dead grandfather was passed to a distant blood relative rather than to the adopted grandson, for instance, the raw hurt of insecurity and self-doubt were freshly exposed.) Even as adults, they dare not risk shaking their only real ties of belonging by seeming disloyal or ungrateful in asking the adoptive parents for crucial answers: information about what is known about their origins, or the address of a relative of the family of origin, who had once written a note. Not only does such a search risk the status quo, but it is laden with hurt and anger: "If there are relatives, why haven't *they* found *me*?"

We sympathize with the plight of adoptive parents as we imagine the enormous difficulties they faced, wanting so much to erase the bitter past of their children. Before the Holocaust had become an accepted topic for the media and popular discussion, how they must have feared the questions that would require them to recall the Holocaust and relate it to their children. It is understandable that silence often prevailed. Yet, if we may learn from their painful struggle, what comes through is that the enormous hunger to know about oneself becomes more unbearable with silence and that withholding information creates a barrier. Disturbing as the truth may be, at least the child can have the loving support of the adoptive parents in facing it bit by bit in accordance with his ability to receive it. The alternative is for the child to deal with sudden shocks, imagined horrors, ghosts and longings, all alone.

Many of the children who were not adopted profited greatly from Alice's determined effort to provide a home where everyone belonged. But we have seen that some felt more included than others, and that, once they were away from Lingfield, in school and even in synagogue (where they sat as a group apart), there were endless new challenges to feeling accepted. Growing up in a children's home, even for children who are not Holocaust survivors, has, as Denny has shown us, its own severe problems of feeling outside the mainstream. We can therefore understand Eva's reference to going to her aunt's house as "going home," although she lived at Lingfield and was a visitor at her aunt's.

Many mourn for the loss of the more ideal, accomplished self that might have been: the self that might have, under normal conditions, learned better in school, behaved more appropriately, achieved more. Ervin wonders what he would have been if he had not been uprooted from England, had finished school or attended a better one. Charles longs to know how he might have turned out if he had stayed in the orphanage in Provensardt and gone to an academic high school. Characteristically, they blame only themselves for not having accomplished more in school, ignoring the enormous impact of environmental restriction, uprootings, language barriers, and the emotional turmoil of deaths and separations. "I was a difficult child," forms a running theme in the interviews, and Leah alone, perhaps thanks to therapy, makes a connection between the turmoil and her difficulties.

Add this to mourning for a lost sister, brother, or the parent-that-might-have-been had that parent survived at all, or survived unharmed, and we see that what is mourned is no less than a lost world. When Leah asks, "Are the others damaged too?" she seeks affirmation that she does not stand alone in the world in having lost a more perfect self. After years of psychiatry, "special" schools, and social stigma, she finds in Christ acceptance without diagnosis or condescenscion: "He made me the way I am. He loves all His children."

Many of the Lingfield children feel the outsider, feel the fear of disclosing one's true past, a profound sense of insecurity and shame about being a child of the Holocaust. But such secrecy, shame, and fear of disclosure cannot be designated as "their" problems, the problems of survivors. For they are born in reciprocal relationships with us, whose stigmatizing attitudes and behavior set in motion a tragic process. Too often has our fear of contagion,[3] the suspicion that the survivor is a member of a different breed, and the subsequent distancing contributed to the burden of bearing loss in silent isolation.

After the televising of the film *Holocaust,* many survivors disclosed their pasts for the first time, taking advantage of the unusual opportunity for new permission to discuss a subject that had been generally taboo until then. For them the problem of stigma is everywhere, even in the kibbutz, where the educated man sitting next to Ervin at dinner lightly refers to survivors as hopelessly damaged outcasts. In such ways is the isolating quality of their experiences magnified and made even more difficult to endure. No wonder Jack looks up from his tears and asks, "Am I strange or something?" And Tania wonders, "What are you finding out about us? Are we a bit strange?" So it is that the feelings of being an outsider, engendered by uprooting, persecution, and murder of one's family, are too often reinforced by attitudes of suspicion, "self-protective disinterest,"[4] or pathology-seeking by those who would not consciously wish the survivor harm, but isolate him nevertheless. No wonder survivors have often withdrawn or formed their own groups, in which they can speak freely, integrating the past, without being stigmatized. Yet, for this, the psychiatric literature has seen survivors as being able to relate only among themselves. Many psychiatrists, themselves unable or unwilling to deal with survivors' experiences, bear a responsibility for having popularized too narrow a vision in attributing the "alienation" of survivors to a pathological preoccupation with the past. Fortunately this professional stance is now beginning to change.

To feel the outsider is a painful psychic wound at any age, but to endure this for almost two years, as Mirjam did alone in hiding, cut off from her family, was to exist in a sea of terror—she, the outsider, hidden upstairs, the SS downstairs. Here, loss and abandonment were compounded with overwhelming anxiety and mortal danger. Such an experience leaves the survivor exquisitely vulnerable to each subsequent loss, shaking the foundations of hope for security from self or others. For those who suffered the further losses of departing analysts or favored caretakers, the burden was crushing. And, as Julius has shown, loss embedded in betrayal endures for a lifetime, its bitterness and shame continually disturbing one's feelings of self-worth: it is an uphill battle to feel worthy if, as Mirjam and Zdenka assert, "all the people I love go away."

The sense of loss, interwoven with feeling outside, abandoned, and betrayed, plays such havoc with one's self-esteem that it is almost impossible not to blame one's self for being unworthy of their staying or for doing something that sends them away. Being to blame for something assumes at least some control or power over circumstances, which is preferable to the horror of being totally powerless. Self-blame is thus part of the strategy of those who tend to bury anger in sadness and resignation. To risk alienating others by expressing anger and asserting one's rights risks breaking existing connections and being alone and vulnerable again.

Feeling uncertain of their own true pasts, uncertain of their worth, outside the "normal" mainstream by virtue of their unusual histories, and unable to disclose them even to close partners who often wish them to forget the past and live only in the present, some of the Lingfield children have problems with intimacy. Those who watched the movie *Holocaust* alone, without their non-survivor spouses, lost an opportunity to share and discuss openly a past they both live with in secret.

Despite all, there is a general absence of conscious anger or bitterness toward the Germans, with excuses and even empathy for them on the part of a few. The great care not to hate all Germans stems from several sources. Perhaps the fears of overwhelming aggressors, imprinted early in life, may make assertion too dangerous. To express rage risks admitting powerlessless, a devastating prospect for many. And perhaps there is the ultimate humane lesson learned out of the attempted genocide of all the Jews: that hating an entire group can lead to the creation of yet more innocent victims such as themselves. Alice's humanitarian ideals, too, may have influenced this stance.

Those living in Israel seem freest to express negative feelings toward the Germans of the Nazi era. Living in a country surrounded by enemies, all expressed the wish to be active in their country's defense. In contrast, some of those who live in England and the United States expressed fear of a rise in Nazism. Sam keeps his Jewish identity secret, but Mirjam and Godfrey alone went so far as to blame

Jews for their very existence as a group thereby, as they saw it, provoking persecution. Godfrey identified more with the plight of his German nurse as a young Nazi than with his destroyed family. Clearly, continuing anxiety over possible persecution is a common legacy for those who were persecuted as children, as powerful a factor as their great hesitation to assert anger. Frequently they have referred to themselves as "closed" (Julius), "hidden" (Leah), "introverted" (Andra).

In spite of the anxiety and fear, and the tortuous detours often used to deflect them, a most striking quality about this diverse group of people is their affirmation of life. They have a quality of stubborn durability. They keep hoping, they keep trying to make the best of their lives. Given all they have endured, this in itself is a kind of heroism; no one has given up. There have been no suicides, only one person out of a whole group who came of age during the sixties had been involved with drugs, and only one lived for a time outside the law. Marta alone lives in a psychiatric hospital. Their hardiness of spirit and their quiet dignity are part of this persistent endurance. And enduring is, after all, most fundamental. This can indeed be regarded as a tribute to Alice and the milieu she provided, and certainly as a tribute to the parents of the adoptees; but, most of all, it is a tribute to the strength of the survivors themselves.

Bound with that strength is the group's second most striking characteristic, its members' ethical and spiritual involvement. For many, spiritual commitment—whether to a religion or a kibbutz —melds hope with purpose and provides established ways to live life meaningfully, respecting others and self. Joining with others in common concerns and religious involvement combats isolation, and also links the survivor's generation with that of the dead parents. Esther's assumption that her parents "must have been Orthodox" motivates her Orthodox way of life and creates a reunion with her parents across time through faith within the shared community.

The yearning to be part of some ongoing faith or ideal in their children was strong in those parents who sensed that they were about to die. As the Libermans did with Magda, many parents of that time swore their children to faith and to reunion in Israel, thus bestowing on them a sense of hope and purpose for which to survive. Neither Esther nor Bella have any memory of their parents, yet what they imagine were their parents' wishes, and their own strivings to fulfill them, give satisfaction and direction to their lives. Bella described beautifully this binding of child, parents, and community when she said that "having Jewish identity is learning about the history of

Judaism and the Jewish people. That way one had a continuity, and I suppose in a way that substituted for my lack of family: the whole Jewish history and race were my family."

Those who chose Christianity, who rejected the religion of their parents, were also coping with many feelings, including the fear of being persecuted again as a Jew, and anger toward their parents or others for going away. Mirjam, who was hidden and protected by Christians, must have come to regard their religion as the more powerful in providing safety. In addition, her warm relationship with Sophie may also have been a factor. Here was a Christian person and, for many of the children, the first one who loved them and chose to live with them.

To people like Leah, Christianity in its promise of the power to heal and cure provides hope for relief of continued suffering. Her religion has offered her what psychiatry and school failed to provide: a rightful place among humanity. And her hope must be respected as a legitimate way of coping, especially in light of the questionable statistics for positive psychotherapeutic outcome.[5]

An interesting pattern of affiliation by country emerges out of the lives of the Lingfield survivors. Despite some difficulties in feeling part of the West London Synagogue as children, all of those who live in England are affiliated in some way with Jewish communal life. Except for Mirjam's older sister Judith, none of the Americans have maintained active ties with Judaism. Two are Christian evangelicals. The two Italian sisters, Andra and Lilliana, have followed their mother's pattern of retaining Jewish identification themselves while marrying Catholics and not rearing their children as Jews. The Israelis remain Jews.

Whatever the specific choice, ethical or religious, communal involvement as a way of living is strong. Whether it is expressed by the words "we are like a family here," as Hedi said in describing life at her kibbutz, or by Leah's implication that we are all children of God, the aim is acceptance and belonging within a particular way of life.

We noted earlier that the way in which the unknown or little-known dead parents of the past are imagined and then seen to give direction can be a creative way of coping, where the survivor pulls himself up by his own bootstraps. In building an important part of his life around rugby, Charles imagines "my father must have been like me," although his father is one that he has created out of himself and the few facts he treasures about the past.

Sometimes what is felt to motivate one from deep within is the dead parent's need. "I live to see for my mother," Jack says. And perhaps his choice of work, driving a taxi, not only enables him to see a great deal, but to cope with that disturbing need to know more about his mute past by engaging in conversations with all the interesting foreign passengers who ride behind him. Who knows what may be revealed by chance?

Despite the severest deprivation in early childhood, these people are neither living a greedy, me-first style of life, nor are they seeking gain at the expense of others. None express the idea that the world owes them a living for all they have suffered. On the contrary; most of their lives are marked by an active compassion for others: Hedi's role in the kibbutz and her recent creation of a kindergarten for neighboring Arab village children; Shana's tender thoughtfulness in planning the process of parting mothers and children on entrance to nursery school; Esther's pleasure in making hot lunches for children; Fritz in his devoted care for the physically disabled; Eva in her synagogue work; Berli's adoption of the orphanage in Vietnam; and Zdenka in the care taken for the mourners' bouquets are but a few examples. Among those who were adopted young the examples are striking: Jack's outing with the London East End children; Judith's commitment to the Israeli war widows; Leah's desire to work in convalescent homes.

One of the group's most fundamental motivations is to have a family themselves. *All* who have children are caring responsibly for them, and Alice's example probably deserves a good deal of the credit. Where, for instance, might Julius have gotten some notion of concern for a child if not from the memory of Alice coming to comfort him in his room? It was her interest, offered at a distance less threatening to him than mothering, and the later care of kibbutz workers, that provided him with models for becoming a responsible parent.

Furtheremore, the ability of child survivors to function as parents goes counter to some popular notions that only people who grow up in "normal," "good," two-parent homes can provide good parenting, or that you cannot give as a parent what you did not get as a child. Perhaps we have underestimated the influences of other people who are felt to be caring and dependable: an older sibling (Aunt Magda was only four years older than Hedi), a piano teacher, the cook. Media and cultural models may play their part. Perhaps we are not prisoners of childhood to the extent that we may have previously thought. The possibilities for learning and expanding roles or creating them out of bits and scraps, including one's imagination, seem to be there for some; new sources of love and acceptance given by a mother-in-law or a friend (as for Shana and Leah) can open up new channels to enrich growth even in adulthood. Perhaps we have also underestimated the creative power behind a parent's desire (like Tania's) to make her daughter's experience better than hers.

To create a new family is to bring hope alive, to personify it. Each birth in the new generation symbolically replaces the lives destroyed and speaks to the dead, as if promising them: neither your seed nor your name nor your line has been destroyed. Naming a child after the dead parent is a symbolic resurrection. The name lives on, as do real and imagined resemblances in family faces. As Jack says lovingly about the face of his daughter, "That's as close as I'll ever come to a photograph of my mother."

A child can also be the way to restore one's own lost childhood, by giving to one's own flesh and blood what one should have had, as Ervin yearned to do. He and other survivors who long for children and are unable to have them are particularly bereft, deprived of purpose at the most primitive level: to live to have children and to live for one's children.

Not simply having children, but the very making of a home becomes a central and special aim for many of those who have been homeless or lived in an institution. A place of one's own symbolizes profound security and self-affirmation. As Tania puts it, it is the place we can truly be ourselves. As Ervin describes it, "to get me a warm house" is the intense yearning of the once-homeless. Roots, even "slight roots," as Eva says hopefully about herself, are coveted. Wherever it was, every home I entered, whether rich or poor, communal in kibbutz or private in a city, was a place akin to hallowed ground, "like Abraham's tent," as Esther said. And in every home (with the exception of the homes of those who had been adopted early), tucked away in a cupboard or on a special shelf, was an album containing pictures of Lingfield, the first safe home after the long time of danger. Sylvia has elevated her interest in home into a hobby, visiting wonderful mansions, where it seems that the inhabitants see all their dreams come true and live happily ever after.

Those who were old enough at the time of their separation from their parents to have been told to look after younger children were charged with awesome responsibility, but they were also given the gift of a coping strategy for remaining alert, effective, and, above all, humane. Twelve-year-old Magda's precocious dedication moves us at the core of heart and conscience. She won not only survival for Hedi and Fritz by her courageous dedication, but a moral victory against the Nazis, a victory of love over hate, of concern over indifference. Although she was not powerful enough to save the younger Hedi, her gallantry was inspiring: she did not revert under stress to a me-first, survive-at-all-costs strategy. She did not abandon Hedi and the crippled Fritz because it would have been easier to go it alone. In behaving as she did, she set an example for them and assured the continuity of a tradition of family love, of "being together *for* each other." No wonder that acts of devotion and appreciation rebound among them today, and so often extend to others.

Alice reinforced this sense of responsibility and devotion as well, encouraging the older children in protective relationships with the younger ones. Julius, who had already looked out for Shana and Esther in Auschwitz, sharing crusts of bread with them, was encouraged in his relationship to Berli, who tagged after him. The youngest were encouraged to look after their dolls, and later on caring for pets was stressed.

This strategy may have profoundly influenced the socially responsible plane on which so many of the group live their lives. Their behavior should make us consider whether we have gone too far in our child-centered families, in avoiding burdening the older children with care for the younger. Perhaps we have unwittingly deprived them of meaningful social responsibility, of the real foundation for developing a loving, responsible family. Many of the Lingfield children's lives today testify to the powerful survival value for the self in looking out for others. Judith Stern, who at fifteen was taken away from Mirjam and sent to Ravensbruck, found the courage to go on only when she remembered her mother's charge to look after her sister. Finding the courage to go on because of others is still true for Leah, who despite chronic insomnia and headaches, gets up every morning early; "I've got my job to do. I've got my four children to raise," she says.

In their adolescence, both the army and the kibbutz provided members of the group with important stepping-stones to cope with leaving home and making the transition into the wider world. For Charles, Sam, Berli, Ervin, and Julius, it was the army that provided training of some sort and assured them a ready place of societal acceptance. But just as critical for them as young men, joining the army meant receiving permission for overt heterosexuality and aggression, neither of which could be tolerated to any appreciable degree in Lingfield. Ervin and Julius were drafted into the Israeli Army, and Charles volunteered in the British, as did Sam and Berli in the American.

The positive role of the kibbutz in providing ideals, fellowship, and safe perimeters within which to explore relationships was meaningful in several of these lives, as it was for the thousands upon thousands of orphans brought to Israel after World War II. Julius was able to outgrow his bed-wetting and to give up stealing at the kibbutz. Ervin was able to finish high school. In their brief adventures in kibbutz living, Shana was able to open up to friends about her life, and Fritz experienced a useful transition. In total, five of the Lingfield people used the kibbutz experience in some way for growth.

The Lingfield group also, of course, reflects the defenses commonly used by all of us in everyday stress situations: withdrawal, social distancing, denial, intellectualization, repression, and amnesia. Given the overwhelming events of their earliest childhoods and the general tendency to loss of memory for the early years, the frequency of the last two is particularly understandable. When asked what she remembers from her early years, Leah says, "The Lord spared me that." Tania remembers nothing prior to her arrival in England when she was five. The dread of remembering became clear to me in the sighs of relief and the exclamations of pleasure of the youngest adoptees, the Bulldogs Bank group, on seeing a picture of the group that Godfrey had given me. How fearful it is to think of yourself as starved, even deformed, at the mercy of overwhelmingly powerful evil forces. Sam's question, "Did they experiment on us?" sums up the horror. And his way of dealing with it was characteristic of the group—keeping the fear to himself, the specter of self-doubt gnawing at his very core.

Finally, one way of coping that is common to a majority of the survivors is to own one—and occasionally two—German shepherd or Doberman guard dogs, the dogs so feared in childhood, whom they now can master and rely upon to protect rather than destroy them.

Among eleven of the nineteen living outside Israel, there are fourteen dogs, twelve of which are German shepherds. No Israelis own any. By the time I arrived in Australia, on my last stop, I had been prepared to anticipate a dog, only to learn that the Kesslers' German shepherd had been so vicious that they had recently given her up to mollify the neighbors. But Tania still dreams about breeding German shepherds one day.

Several current assumptions bear rethinking in light of the lives of the Lingfield children. The first is the concept that early deprivation unalterably determines the course of life. Were the early headlines by eager reporters—headlines such as "Miracle at Lingfield; From Fear to Smiles"—actually correct about the possibility of children being restored to laughter and health? The outcome seems surprisingly positive for a few, and it is certainly not as bleak as the psychological, particularly the psychoanalytic, literature would have us believe, stressing as it does the absolute centrality of the early mother-child relationship. For, despite the persistence of problems and the ashes of the past, what we note in the Lingfield lives are endurance, resilience, and great individual adaptability, characteristics that are consistent with a small but growing body of evidence based on long-term study.[6] For these people, the first five years seem not to have had the power to innoculate all alike for good or bad. Contrary to previously accepted notions,[7] we learn powerfully from these lives that lifelong emotional disability does not automatically follow early trauma, even such devastating, pervasive trauma as experienced here. Apparently, what happens later matters enormously. Whether it is the confidence of a teacher, the excitement of new sexual urges, new vocational interests, or a changed social milieu, the interaction can trigger fresh growth. We come to respect anew how children vary in their resilience, strengths, charm, and ability to get affectionate care from those nearby. And we appreciate more deeply how unique is each person's struggle for competence, search for love, and making of a place for himself.

The psychiatric literature has placed great emphasis on what happened to the survivor before the Holocaust as predictive of post-Holocaust adjustment. The important questions seem to be not only what happened before, but what happened *during*—to ignore that *during* is to deny the Holocaust as a reality—and, most important, what happened after. Who was there after to love the child? Did they stay? Or were early losses compounded by later ones? What was the child's adapting style, to continue to try for love, or to withdraw and give up wanting in the face of unreliable supplies? The number of losses a growing child can cope with must vary with the individual, but surely there is some disastrous count which defeats even the most robust. In addition to resilience, it cannot hurt to have a little *mazal* or good fortune to be spared further losses, illnesses, and defeats.

The second idea to be reconsidered is the relatively minor place granted to date to the constancy provided by extended family or its facsimile in lifelong relationships. Because children's love and growth require long nurturance by people who do not leave, perhaps the focus of mother-child love, broadened so recently to include father-child, ought to be expanded further to embrace the extended family or its facsimile. The enduring commitment that Alice made was rare then, and is rarer still now, when long commitments are not popular either in employment or marriage. If anything is underscored by the devotion of Magda ("to be together for each other"), it is the value of the large family's protective ethos for humane survival. It would be disastrous if our current eagerness to focus on the conservation of material resources causes the drying up of crucial human resources, the networks of concerned relatives—aunts, uncles, cousins—who have been vital to our concepts of past, present, and future. If that happened, would there be many Alices? Would there be others who could, like she did, become so concerned about nonfamilial children that the emotional investment common in strong families could be duplicated in nonfamily groups? The evidence for that happening today is rare; on the contrary, the trend seems to be toward shorter, more fractioned commitments between adults to each other, to their children, and to the children they work with as teachers and counselors.

Having a person on the outside was of critical importance in the Lingfield lives. If that person was a relative, then the feeling of having "slight roots" was strengthened. If it was not a relative, and the relationship was nevertheless maintained, it was valuable and nourishing evidence of lasting concern and affection, and ultimately of one's human worth. Can substantial numbers of those people who are today making the decision not to have children of their own become the *lifelong* supportive outside people for a child somewhere "inside"? In this sense, the Lingfield lives present us with a major challenge.

The impressive evidence for the enormous importance of seemingly small acts of kindness must also be considered. In almost every interview, sounding a clear, countervailing high note against a heavy leitmotif of sorrow, these were the acts that stayed powerfully in memory: a peach placed on a plate for Magda by Sir Benjamin; Shana being taken by Sir Benjamin into the garden; the kiss from Tania's "aunt"; Lilliana and Andra welcomed at the hearth in the Fauds' home; the doll dress crocheted by Manna for Mirjam's doll; Gertrud taking Esther home overnight; Mr. White, Ervin's teacher, assuring him that he could learn. These and the infinite number of acts of kindness Alice performed in the daily flow of devotion, doing her work—as Julius understood—with all her heart, are treasures stored in memory. While other events have faded, these stay, bright despite time, lit by gratitude for hope kindled.

A last idea that bears attention is the relative neglect by scholars in human development and mental health workers of the role of religious community and religion in people's lives. Obviously, religious belief or its facsimile in some spiritually motivating life plan, such as kibbutz life, has played a major role in the development of more than the Lingfielders. It deserves serious study.

Religion was undoubtedly a stabilizing force in the Lingfielders' lives. They knew as children that their participation in the West London Synagogue was important to Alice, though like most children, they complained about having to go there—the long ride, the lessons, not enough time to play. Still, as adults, all who remained in England are involved in the same or other synagogues. Perhaps despite the fact that they did not perceive their experience as very rewarding at the time, there were some positive residues with which they could connect more deeply at a later age. So though as children they went to please Alice, later they found satisfaction for themselves —not, one suspects, an untypical pattern.

Given the historically antithetical relationship between psychoanalysis and religion, it is interesting to note that four of the six persons at Lingfield who had psychoanalysis are the most ardently involved in religion: two as Jews and two as Christians. Alice's thoughts on psychoanalysis are worth noting as well: the analysts who left in the middle, she maintains, caused great hardship. And having children leave Lingfield to go to town five days a week for analysis created a stigma. If it were possible to relive those years, she would have preferred one or more therapists to come to the house and help all the children, as a group, providing individual work from that base, as necessary. These thoughts are a radical departure for Alice from the thinking of Anna Freud, who maintained that each child was entitled to his own therapist. Such thoughts are proof of continued growth at any age.

Julius's observation that for Alice it was always children, children, remains true. Still uppermost in her thoughts as she approaches her eighty-fifth birthday are the lives of her children and their children. For the concern and affection she succeeded in weaving into their lives brought much joy into her own.

Notes

1. THE ARRIVAL: 1945

1. Edith and George Lauer, taped interviews, Pittsburgh, June 1979.
2. Joe Finkelstone, "They Find Refuge in the Lake District," *Carlisle Journal,* August 17, 1945.
3. Alice Goldberger, recollection in *Journal of the '45 Aid Society,* London 1977.
4. Margot Hicklin, "War Damaged Children: Some Aspects of Recovery," a pamphlet published by the Association of Psychiatric Social Workers, London 1946.
5. Goldberger, recollection in *Journal of the '45 Aid Society.*
6. Hicklin, "War-Damaged Children."
7. Ibid.
8. Anna Freud and Sophie Dann, "An Experiment in Group Upbringing," *Psychoanalytic Study of the Child* (New York: International Universities Press, 1951).

Additional references to Alice Goldberger on the Isle of Man: "Governor among the Aliens," *Isle of Man Examiner,* September 6, 1940; "Schools for Alien Children," *Isle of Man Evening Standard,* September 1940; "Von Theresienstadt nach Windermere," *Heute 4,* published by Amerikanishhe Informationstelle, undated; "Frauen im Internment Camp," *Die Zeitung,* p. 3, London, July 1, 1941.

2. TEREZIN

1. Jan Bilek, "Spa Guests from Theresienbad," *Canadian Jewish Outlook,* May/June 1971, Toronto.
2. Willie Groag, taped interview, Kibbutz Beit Ichud, Israel, July 1977.
3. Shlomo Schmiedt, "Hey Chalutz in Theriesenstadt," *Yad Vashem Studies* 7, Article 118, p. 12, ed. Livia Rotkirchen.
4. Renée Fodor, "Impact of Nazi Occupation on the Jewish Mother-Child Relationship," *YIVO Annual of Jewish Social Science* 11 (1956–57): 270–85.
5. Edith Lauer, taped interview in Pittsburgh, June 1979.
6. Raul Hilberg, "Confronting Moral Implications of the Holocaust," key-

note address at the Holocaust Conference, Jewish Federation Council, Los Angeles, Sunday, April 9, 1978.

7. H. G. Adler, *Theresienstadt, 1941–1945. Das Antlitz einer Zwangsgemeinschaft* (Tubingen: Verlag J. Mohr [Paul Siebeck], 1955).
8. O. Kraus and E. Kulka, *The Death Factory: Documents on Auschwitz 1966* (New York: Pergamon Press, 1966), pp. 116–17.
9. Martha Wenger in Anna Freud and Sophie Dann, "An Experiment in Group Upbringing," *Psychoanalytic Study of the Child* (New York: International Universities Press, 1951).
10. Martha Wenger, letter to Alice Goldberger from Deggendorf Camp, Germany, 1946.
11. Nellie Wolffheim, "Kinder aus Konzentrationslagern," *Praxis der Kinderpsychologie* 11 (December 1968): 123.

3. AT LINGFIELD

1. This entire chapter is based on Alice Goldberger's taped personal recollections, letters, and notes.
2. "The Lingfield Hostel, A Visitor's Impressions," *Synagogue Review* (London), 1946, p. 120.

4. THE SECOND GROUP ARRIVES: FROM AUSCHWITZ

1. Luigi Ferri, testimony before the Commission on Nazi Crimes in Auschwitz, excerpted in Inge Deutchkron, *Kinder in Ghettos und Lagern: ihrer war die Hölle* (Cologne: Mohn, 1965), pp. 82–83.
2. Erich Kulka, taped interview, Los Angeles, 1979.
3. Esther Wajs, eyewitness account #1354/1306, Yad Vashem Archives, Jerusalem.
4. Hanna Hoffman-Fischel in Deutchkron, *Kinder in Ghettos*, p. 54.
5. S. Smaglewská, Nuremberg testimony, 1946, in Kraus and Kulka, *The Death Factory*, pp. 112–14.
6. W. Poltawska, M.D., "On Examinations of the Auschwitz Children," in *Anthology* 2, part 3, Int. Auschwitz Committee, Warsaw, 1971.
7. Ibid.
8. Kraus and Kulka, op. cit., p. 107.
9. Erich Kulka, taped interview, Los Angeles, 1979.
10. Erich Kulka, *Auschwitz Hefte* [the records of transports and events kept by the SS in Auschwitz] 11, 12 (1944).

5. FROM ORPHANAGES

1. Raul Hilberg, *The Destruction of the European Jews* (Chicago: Quadrangle Books, 1961), p. 472.
2. Yitzhak Hertz, "The Dinslaken Orphanage," *Yad Vashem Studies* 11, ed. Livia Rotkirchen, Yad Vashem Archives, Jerusalem, 1976.

3. Hilberg, *The Destruction of the European Jews,* p. 418.

4. Adolf Berman, "The Fate of Children in the Warsaw Ghetto," in *The Catastrophe of European Jewry,* ed. Yisrael Gutman and Livia Rotkirchen (Jerusalem: Yad Vashem, 1976).

5. Janusz Korczak, *Ghetto Diary* (New York: Holocaust Library, 1978), p. 140.

6. Korczak, p. 166.

7. Adolf Berman, "The Fate of Children in the Warsaw Ghetto," p. 411.

8. Emmanuel Ringelblum, *Notes from the Warsaw Ghetto, The Journal of Emmanuel Ringelblum,* ed. and trans. by J. Sloan (New York: Schocken Books, 1978), pp. 233–34.

9. Hilberg, *The Destruction of the European Jews,* p. 315.

10. Nora Levin, *The Holocaust* (New York: Schocken Books, 1973), p. 622.

6. FROM HIDING

1. R. Lowrie, *The Hunted Children* (New York: W. W. Norton & Co., 1963).

2. Meyer Levin, "They Saved the Children," *Saturday Evening Post,* January 20, 1945.

3. Claude Levy and Paul Tillard, *Betrayal at the Vel D'Hiv* (New York: Hill and Wang, 1969), pp. 34–35.

4. Lowrie, *The Hunted Children,* p. 239.

5. Lowrie, *The Hunted Children,* pp. 232–35.

6. "About Jewish Children Who Survived WW II on the Aryan Side," *Yad Vashem Bulletin* 12 (1962), p. 49.

7. Dvorjetsky, "Psychological Problems of Jewish Children Hidden by Non-Jews during the Holocaust," *Dapuim Folia Medica,* undated document 3/7183, YIVO.

8. Claude Sjainman, cousin of the author, personal communication, Paris, 1977.

9. Dvorjetsky, "Psychological Problems."

10. Freyda Trajster, aunt of the author, mother of Claude Sjainman, personal communication, Paris, 1979.

11. Rabbi Abraham Hazelkorn, former chaplain with the liberation (American) army in France, taped interview, Salinas, California, January 1979, in which he described a scene in the orphanage he organized as an American Army chaplain in France, where crosses on all the children were removed one night in some cases by force.

7. THE LINGFIELD MILIEU

1. Judith Stern Sherman, as told to Alice Goldberger after her arrival at Lingfield, 1946.

2. Manna Friedman Weindling, taped interview, November 1977, London.

3. Ben Helfgot, taped interview, June 1978, London.

4. Sir Benjamin Drage, untitled appeal, *The Synagogue Review* (September 1946), p. 16.
5. The Lingfield House Committee consisted of Chairman Mrs. R. J. Pinto, Vice-chairman Mrs. Frances Rubens, Treasurer Alfred Rubens. Also Mrs. D. Balter, B. Bernard, C. Bernstein, Miss M. Blumenthal, Mrs. G. Fuerst, L. Hahn Warburg, J. Hart, C. Henry, L. Josephs, Lady Karminski, Mrs. M. Leaver, D. Levi, S. Levy, D. Mosely, K. Mosely, Rabbi Reinhart, Mrs. Reinhart, J. Shure, S. Speelman, E. Spier, C. Van Raalte, and K. Weiss (West London Synagogue, *Lingfield House Report,* 1952).
6. Anna Freud, in a letter to Alice Goldberger, December 3, 1954.
7. Edith Lauer interview in Pittsburgh, June 1979.

Additional taped interviews contributing to this chapter and others were the following. *Our Boys:* Rabbi Hugo Gryn (November 1977, London); Wolf Blomfeld (November 1977, London); Henry Green (June 1978, London); (Yezhek) Jerzy Herszberg (July 1979, London); Ben Helfgot (November 1977, London). *Big Girls:* Dora Teichner (July 1977, Kibbutz S'dot Yam Israel); Judith Stern Sherman (June 1979, New York). *Others:* Frances Rubens (November 1977); Lola Hahn-Warburg (November 1977); and Henny Spear (November 1977). My interviews with Anna Freud (July 4 and November 19, 1977) were not taped.

(ANDRA) ALESSANDRA BUCCI PEZZONI

1. The train ride took eight days. This was the train referred to by Luigi Ferri in his testimony before the Commission on Nazi Crimes in Auschwitz (April 21, 1945), quoted in Inge Deutchkron, *Kinder in Ghettos und Lagern,* pp. 82–83.

(JULIUS) URI HAMBURGER

1. This could, in fact, have been the inmate uprising of August 29, 1944, that forced open the gates of Sered Concentration Camp. See Livia Rotkirchen, "Vatican Policy and the Jewish Problem in 'Independent' Slovakia, 1939–1945" in *Yad Vashem Studies* 6 (1967), p. 50, ed. Nathan Eck and Arye Kubovy.
2. It is possible that Julius is referring here to one of the two following crematoria burnings by inmates: 1) "On the morning of September 6, the Greek Jews, with the help of two units of French Jews and one of Hungarian Jews, blew up two of the four crematoria at Auschwitz" (Nora Levin, *The Holocaust,* p. 526). 2) "On the afternoon of October 7, 1944, one of the crematoriums was blown up by the Sonderkommando. Four women in the 'Union' plant had furnished the men with explosives. The men were shot as they fled. The women were publicly hanged." (Raul Hilberg, *The Destruction of the European Jews,* p. 631).

(MAGDA) SARAH LIBERMAN KORNHAUSER

1. See Nora Levin, *The Holocaust,* p. 662.

REFLECTIONS

1. Terrence Des Pres, *The Survivors* (New York: Simon & Schuster, 1977).
2. See Bruno Bettelheim's discussion of Lina Wertmuller's conception of the survivor in the film *Seven Beauties,* in "Surviving," essay originally published in *The New Yorker,* August 2, 1976, pp. 31–52.
3. Robert Lifton, *Death in Life* (New York: Touchstone Books/Simon & Schuster, 1967), pp. 516–21.
4. Bruno Bettelheim, television interview with Helen Epstein, 1980; and Lifton, *Death in Life,* p. 519.
5. Nathan Epstein and Louis Vlok, "Research on the Results of Psychotherapy: A Summary of Evidence," *American Journal of Psychiatry* 138 (1981): 1027–35.
6. Henry Maas, "The Young Adult Adjustment of Twenty Wartime Residential Nursery Children" in *Successful Group Care,* ed. M. Wolins (Chicago: Aldine Press, 1974), pp. 157–81; Hans Keilson, "Sequentielle Traumatisierung bei Kindern" in *Forum der Psychiatrie* (Stuttgart: Enke Verlag, 1979).
7. Paul Chodoff, "Psychiatric Aspects of Nazi Persecution," chap. 41 in *New Psychiatric Frontiers* 6, ed. Hamburg D. Arieti and K. Brodie (New York: Basic Books, 1974–75), 940–42; Joel Dimsdale, "The Coping Behavior of Nazi Concentration Camp Survivors," *American Journal of Psychiatry* 131 (1974): 793.